The rear tyre tread pattern of the Porsche 917, which won at Le Mans in 1970. (Goodyear Tyre & Rubber Co (GB) Ltd)

With illustrations by Gordon Davies
Terry Hadler
James Leech
Martin Lee
David Warner

Cars in Profile

Profile 1

Collection

General Editor Anthony Harding

Profile Publications Ltd Windsor Berkshire England
Doubleday & Company Inc Garden City New York

© Profile Publications Limited 1973
Doubleday & Company Inc edition 1974

First published in England 1973
by Profile Publications Limited
Coburg House Sheet Street Windsor
Berkshire England

ISBN 0 85383 040 1
ISBN (USA) 0 385 09672 0
Library of Congress Number 73–14048

Acknowledgements

The authors, artists and publishers wish
to acknowledge the kind assistance
given by many learned bodies, societies,
Government departments, car
manufacturers and individuals during the
course of preparation of the various
Profiles. Without their help this book
could not have been produced.

Publisher's Note

Whilst we appreciate that convention has
always been to place the Index at the
back of the book, we have deliberately
removed it to the front section to
maintain the high quality and strength of
the binding that we believe our readers
require. Placing small sections at the
front or back of the main text has a
tendency to weaken both the joint and
hinge between case and text.

Uniform with this volume

Cars in Profile Collection 2

Warships in Profile

Aircraft in Profile Series

History of the AFVs of the World Series (1st Edition)

Locomotives in Profile Series

Small Arms in Profile

Printed in England by Edwin Snell printers Yeovil Somerset

Foreword

By the Right Honourable The Lord Montagu of Beaulieu

Seven years ago the first Classic Car Profile — on the Grand Prix Mercedes of 1908 and 1914 — was published.

One of the problems of a subject as fashionable as motoring history is that there aren't enough ideas. Write a book on some aspect of the game, and in theory it should spur someone else either to produce a better one, or to explore different cars, different people, or a different era.

Unfortunately, this seldom happens. A bandwagon is set rolling, and everybody jumps aboard. In the wake of the 'definitive' works come the potboilers, and the essence of a potboiler is that its gestation should be brief, and its cost low. Thus the only thing the unhappy reader hasn't seen before are the words, and we have enough of these converging on us from far too many media.

Profiles, however, broke new ground. Their content was specialised, dealing with individual models rather than individual makes. Authors were carefully chosen, ensuring the highest standards of accuracy. They were short, so that scholarship never became a bore. They were well produced on high-quality art paper, with illustrations that few of us had seen before. Above all, they were inexpensive — probably *too* inexpensive — which is why they disappeared just when they were becoming an essential adjunct to every enthusiast's bookshelf. The last of the original series dealt (ironically) with that gallant failure, the V-16 B.R.M; in spite of which we all hoped that it would be *au revoir,* and not goodbye.

Fortunately, this has proved to be the case. The Mark II Profile can't, of course, retail for tenpence. As yet the accent is on modern competition machinery rather than on the Veteran and Vintage cars some of us would like to see, though curiously this fulfils an even greater need; it is very hard to discover anything definitive on an important Group 6 car without delving through volume after volume of contemporary magazines. Further, there are more words and more pictures for the extra outlay, the layout has been subtly improved, and the list of contributors retains its 'Who's Who' attributes. It is also good to see Tony Harding back at the helm.

I wish the new Profiles every success — and with it, perhaps, something more on older, road-going cars.

Palace House, Beaulieu.   *Montagu of Beaulieu*
January, 1973.

Contents

Index

Rear-engined Ferrari Prototypes 1961/67

by PAUL FRÈRE

With a grand total of nine successes, six of which were consecutive, Ferrari is, by a handsome margin, the absolute record holder of Le Mans victories. His nearest rivals are Bentley and Jaguar, each with five non-consecutive victories to their credit. In addition to this, the Maranello-made cars have probably won more major races than any other marque in the history of motor racing and have dominated the scene in all the fields that matter: Grand Prix, Sports Car Racing (including, of course, Prototypes) and GT Racing. In all these specialist fields, success has alternated with failure, but in contrast to most others, Enzo Ferrari has never either given up the struggle or rested on his laurels. Having been a racing driver of some repute himself in the 'twenties, he became the head of the Alfa Romeo racing department, then set up his own business to run Alfa Romeos on behalf of the manufacturer, just as John Wyer did for Ford in 1968–69 and for Porsche in 1970–71. His first personal project was the "Bimotore" (twin-engined) Alfa, devised in 1936 to try and break the German supremacy at least in Formule Libre races (with no maximum weight limit), a task in which it failed. During the war, Ferrari's workshops were converted to the manufacture of machine tools and, shortly after the war, he began to produce high-grade sports-cars for sale to the public and racing cars directly derived from them. Thus ever since he left school, motor racing has been his very life and soul whilst his persistence in continuing to race re-

gardless of commercial considerations, has been helped by the fact that, up to 1969, he remained the sole owner of his company, and even since the 50% takeover by Fiat, he has, by mutual agreement, retained for life his complete right to rule the racing department and the racing policy of the firm.

Though Ferrari's degree in engineering is an honorary one, it is certainly well deserved, for the evolution of the design of Ferrari cars displays a remarkable continuity which bears the stamp of one man, even though several others have been responsible for the design of the cars in the 25 years of Ferrari production.

Background to the Period

Even when he started to produce his own cars, back in 1947, Ferrari, who was born in 1898, was not a very young man any more and he had a long racing tradition behind him. It is thus not surprising that his approach to design has always been rather conservative: after the Mercedes-Benz racing cars had swept the board with their fuel-injected engines in 1955, and at a time when the fuel-injected Vanwalls were making Ferraris eat their dust in 1958, I remember him telling me, in one of the many conversations I had with him, that "if all cars had had fuel injection up to then and someone suddenly came up with a carburettor, everyone would marvel at its simplicity and efficiency". It also took him a long time to realize that in a racing car, the more logical place for the engine

1

is behind the driver, just as for a long while he dismissed proper aerodynamics as "something he would leave to those people who were unable to muster adequate horsepower". There is probably no better example of this attitude of mind than the 3-litre "Testa Rossa" which I drove to victory at Le Mans, with Olivier Gendebien, in 1960. With some 290 real horsepower, our V-12 did not exceed 160 m.p.h. down the straight, some 20 m.p.h. less than the Jaguars had reached on about the same horsepower three years before (albeit with a larger engine) and 12 m.p.h. slower than Masten Gregory's special-bodied, but certainly less powerful, 4-cylinder "Bird Cage" Maserati in the same race, to which the Ferrari just could not hold a candle for the short while it ran — but it did not run for long. Ferraris were supreme at the time and the *Commendatore* (he was not yet *Ingegnere* [Engineer] at the time) just could not be bothered by such a trivial matter as aerodynamics. In fact, in those days, the "Testa Rossa" was very little faster than the better-shaped "Berlinetta" GT car with 30 h.p. less and, except for the 5-speed gearbox and the de Dion rear suspension (later to become independent), differed very little from it in its general technical specification.

The period under review, 1961 to 1967, is the more interesting because it covers the years when Ferrari, who had regained his dominance of Formula One as soon as he swopped over to the rear engine layout (a supremacy aided by a change of Formula for which he had a better engine in stock than the opposition), realized that even for two-seater prototypes, it would be beneficial to have the engine behind the driver, and when, beginning with 1964, he had to combat the most formidable opponent he had faced in sports-prototype racing since the Daimler-Benz days: the Ford Motor Company.

The 246 SP, 1961
The first rear-engined Ferrari dates back to 1960. On a few occasions before this, Ferrari had entered a single front-engined car in the odd 1500cc. Formula Two race with the object of developing a small V-6 with an eye to future

Formula One races, which were to be limited to 1500cc. by 1961. This V-6 was the first of the "Dino" range of engines designed by Vittorio Jano after he joined Ferrari as a consultant, together with the Grand Prix cars he had originally designed for Lancia. Ferrari's Formula Two appearances had been moderately successful, but he really shook everyone when a brand new rear-engined model was driven by Wolfgang von Trips straight from the racing shop to victory in its first race, the Solitude Grand Prix for Formula Two cars, held near Stuttgart, beating most redoubtable opposition from Porsche, Lotus, Cooper and lesser contenders. This car was to all intents and purposes the prototype for the 1961 Formula One cars and Ferrari realized that the advantages of a lower frontal area, lower centre of gravity, lower polar moment of inertia and smaller change in weight distribution as the fuel was used up, would apply to a sports car as well as to a single-seater. But he seemed to be apprehensive that accommodating the relatively long and heavy V-12 engine of the "Testa Rossa" behind the driver compartment would bring up insurmountable problems of handling, weight distribution and also of general "architecture", the belief then being still quite strong that too far forward a driving position was detrimental to the driver's ability properly to control his car. Consequently Ferrari's first rear-engined prototype was built around the 2417cc. V-6 engine which had been used in the front-engined Formula One cars of the previous three years. Apart from the fact that it had the compulsory two-seater, all-enveloping body, built up on an appropriately widened tubular girder chassis frame, and featured the larger version of the 60 degree V-6 "Dino" engine, the 246 SP was very similar to the Formula One car of 1961 (of which, incidentally, the later examples had a 120 degree V-6 engine). Its wheelbase of 2,32 m. (7ft. 6.5in.) was 2 centimetres (about .8in.) longer than the single-seaters and it had the same narrow track of 1,20 m. (3ft. 11.2in.) Suspension was by transverse wishbones all-round and Koni damper-spring units, while the rack-and-pinion steering was completed by an hydraulic Koni steering damper. Dunlop disc brakes — another technical advance which Ferrari treated with diffidence until as late as 1958 — were fitted all-round. They were ventilated and the rear ones were inboard. The alloy-rimmed wire wheels were fitted with 5.50–15 Dunlop tyres at the front and 6.50–15 at the rear, the rims being 5 and 6in. wide respectively. The transmission incorporated an over-hung five-speed dog-clutch (but not synchromesh) gearbox, the drive from the engine being by a long shaft going through the hollow gearbox primary shaft to a small multi-disc clutch at the rear of the gearbox. This transmission layout was used on all the works cars up to and including 1965 and it had the advantage of making the clutch plate renewal a comparatively quick and easy job, while from a manufacturing point of view, it made it easy to adapt the clutch to any torque increase by just adding a plate or two without having to contend with problems of space. The car had the characteristic "twin-nostril" nose cherished by Carlo Chiti who was then responsible for the design of the racing cars, and it had a quite small frontal area, being only 1,48 m. (4ft. 10.5in.) wide and 1,05 m. (3ft. 5.3in.) high to the top of the screen. It was this car which pioneered the rear "spoiler" which was "invented" in the course of a practice session at Monza when Richie Ginther found that the lift on the rear deck, combined with the rear weight bias, made handling im-

possible in the "Curva Grande". The suspension geometry was designed to produce considerable camber variations, the already considerable static negative camber increasing strongly with bump, as was current practice at the time, but this was more marked than usual.

The V-6 engine was to all intents and purposes a straight copy from the previous year's Formula One car. Its bore and stroke dimensions of 85 × 71 mm. gave it a capacity of 2417cc. and the four overhead camshafts were driven by a gear train. Lubrication was of the dry sump type and the engine breathed through three twin-choke down-draught Weber carburettors across the V. With a 9.8 : 1 compression ratio, Ferrari claimed an output of 270 h.p. at 8000 r.p.m. on 98–100 octane fuel. To make more room for the intake system, the V-angle was increased from 60° to 65° and the crankpins were offset accordingly. The following year, 1962, 275 h.p. were claimed at 7500 r.p.m. on a 9.5 : 1 compression ratio. Several years later, this engine again went into a single-seater and was developed to produce some 320 h.p. with Lucas fuel injection. In this form it took the Tasman Championship twice in succesion, in 1969 and 1970.

The 246 SP's first outing was the Sebring 12 hours race in which it retired with steering trouble, but it scored a dramatic win in the Targa Florio of 1961, its second race, when it was driven by von Trips and Gendebien, the former setting up a new circuit record on the very last lap in an effort to catch Moss' Porsche which broke up its suspension five miles from the finish. Admittedly, the tortuous Sicilian course admirably suited the compact rear-engined car weighing only about 700 kg. without fuel, but only a month later it really shook everyone when it ran a consistent third at Le Mans, headed only by the V-12 front-engined 3-litre "Testa Rossa" models. It was put out of the race by running out of fuel after its Grand Prix engine had run for 16 hours without ever missing a beat.

In 1962, now with 7.00 × 15 rear tyres, the 246 SP again won the Targa Florio (Mairesse, R. Rodriguez, Gendebien), then proceeded to win the Nürburgring 1000 Kilometer race, Gendebien-Phil Hill beating a special version of the famous Ferrari GTO "Berlinetta", fitted

Olivier Gendebien near Collesano on his way to winning the 1961 Targa Florio on a 246 SP (A. Giuliano, Palermo)

3

with a V-12 4-litre engine (in place of the stan-dard 3-litre) into 2nd place. The same chassis was also adapted to take the existing 2-litre, single cam-per-bank 60 degree V-6 developing 210 h.p., and also a 90 degree V-8 engine. The former took second place overall in the Targa Florio (winning its class, of course) with Bandini-Baghetti, and served Scarfiotti well enough for him to win the European Mountain Championship. To all intents and purposes, its engine amounted to half the 4-litre V-12 which won at Le Mans in a "Testa Rossa" chassis the same year, and it had bore and stroke dimen-sions of 77×71 mm. The 8-cylinder version – the only V-8 ever designed by Ferrari if we con-sider that the 1956–57 Grand Prix engine was a takeover from Lancia – never made any news. It appeared in 2458cc. form (77×66 mm.) at the Nürburgring 1000 Km. Race, where Pedro Rodriguez crashed it and in 2645cc. form (77×71 mm. again) at Le Mans where it retired after 16 hours' racing, while running as high as second. As this single cam-per-bank engine produced 10 h.p. less than the 275 h.p. claimed for the 2.4-litre "Six" and was also slightly longer and heavier, it seemed rather pointless and its development was not pursued.

However, the handling of the V-8 car was just as good as that of the V-6, and it possibly had the merit of convincing Enzo Ferrari that putting the even longer V-12 engine behind the driver might not be an impossible proposi-tion, and this is just what was done for the 1963 season.

The Ferrari V-12 Engine

The career of the Ferrari V-12 engine is one of the most remarkable success stories of motor racing. The original design, intended for use both in production and in racing cars, was the work of Gioacchino Colombo who already had the design of the famous "Alfetta" (Alfa Romeo Type 158/159) to his credit. The first version had a capacity of 1497cc., but had been con-ceived from the start for a capacity increase to 2 litres. The task of increasing the capacity was left to a young draughtsman with an engineer-ing degree, Aurelio Lampredi, who brought the engine up to its intended limit and provided the winner of the first post-war Le Mans in 1949. He then proceeded to design a scaled-up ver-sion of, originally, 3.3 litres, but this was in-creased, step by step, to 3.5, 4.1, 4.5 and finally to 4.9 litres. Put in a Grand Prix chassis, the 4.5-litre finally stopped the all-conquering career of the supercharged 1500cc. Alfas in 1951 and it won the 1954 Le Mans in 4.9-litre form. In the meantime however, the casting and bearing techniques had further progressed and it became possible further to stretch the original 1500cc. engine within its original frame: from two litres it went up by steps to 2.3, 2.7 and finally to 3-litres with the famous bore and stroke dimensions of 73×58.8 mm., in which form it went into the 250 GT "Berlinetta" in 1956 and into the sports/racing "Testa Rossa" which appeared in 1957, of which the chassis featuring a live rear axle and coil springs all-round was derived from the previous year's 2-litre, 4-cylinder car bearing the same name (literally "Red Head", the racing cylinder heads

being painted red). In 1958, coil valve springs replaced the hairpin springs, the 5-speed gear-box was combined with the differential housing and a de Dion axle was used for the rear sus-pension. In this form the "Testa Rossa" won Le Mans with Gendebien and Phil Hill. One year later, it at last acquired disc brakes, but lost Le Mans to Aston Martin mainly because of rivalry within the team. In 1960, a variant with inde-pendent rear suspension by wishbones was introduced, two independent and two de Dion cars being entered for Le Mans, which was won by a de Dion version, driven by Gendebien and the writer, after two of the team cars had run out of fuel after one hour's racing, the fourth retiring with a broken universal in the 14th hour. Appal-ling weather conditions did not favour any record speeds, but the winning car probably set up a record of domination by leading the race from the second hour for nearly 23 hours out of 24. A much better-streamlined version with an independent rear end won again in 1961 (Gendebien-Phil Hill once more) and in 1962 Gendebien broke the absolute record of Le Mans victories, both for himself (four) and for Ferrari (six), again partnered by Phil Hill. On this occasion, the car was a combination of the independently-sprung "Testa Rossa" chassis with a new 4-litre engine and 16 in. diameter wheels. This car had been built specially for Le Mans in view of a strong challenge from Aston Martin (the Project 212) and Maserati, all 4-litre cars which looked like quite formidable opposition for the old 3-litre and the new 2.4- and 2.6-litre rear-engined models. It was to be the last of the front-engined full-blood sports/racing Ferraris and only one was built (see page 9), but it was interesting because its 4-litre engine was a further development of the 3-litre "Testa Rossa", still within the conception of the original 1500cc. unit, rather than the Lampredi-designed scaled-up version. This engine had been tried out in a special GTO "Berlinetta" which had finished second to the 2.4 V-6 in the Nürburgring 1000 Km. Race, driven by Mair-esse and Parkes. At Le Mans, the same car was irretrievably buried in the sand by Parkes, on the first lap, at Mulsanne Corner. The 4-litre engine had bore and stroke dimensions of 77×71 mm., giving a swept volume of 3968cc. and, though it breathed through six twin-choke Webers, it seems to have been a lightly stressed engine having, amongst others, the compara-tively low compression ratio of 8.7 : 1. 390 h.p. at 7500 r.p.m. were announced by Ferrari in his press release, but this should be treated with some scepticism, since even two years later only 370 h.p. were claimed for this type of en-gine. Ferrari certainly knew what he was doing when he entrusted this one-off car to the ack-nowledged long-distance experts Gendebien and Phil Hill as, but for a reinforced (but still rather weak) clutch, the transmission was standard "Testa Rossa". The drivers knew what they were about and drove it from start to finish with velvet gloves – and even then a snap gear change would slip the clutch towards the end of the race. Although the car was driven only just as fast as was necessary to win, it beat the official lap record which had stood to the credit of Mike Hawthorn's 4.5-litre Ferrari for the last

The sleek lines of the 1962 rear-engined Ferrari: there was no external visible difference to show if a V-6 engine of 2.0, 2.4 or 2.8 litres, or a V-8 of 2.4 or 2.6 litres, was fitted (SEFAC Ferrari)

Willy Mairesse on his way to second place in the 1963 Targa Florio, driving a 2-litre V-6 (Geoffrey Goddard)

The 246 SP, driven here by Pedro Rodriguez, winning the 1962 Targa Florio at 63.47 m.p.h. His co-drivers were Olivier Gendebien and Willy Mairesse (Bernard Cahier)

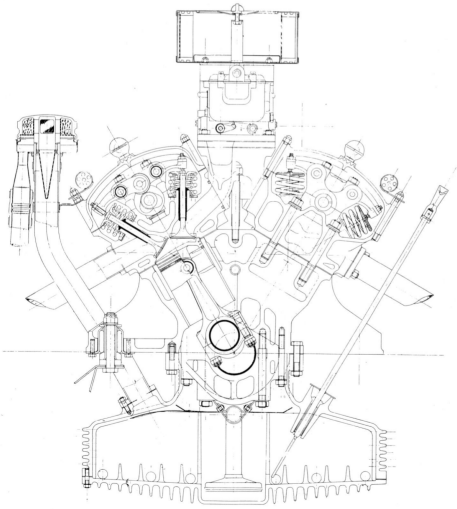

All the atmosphere and excitement of narrow streets and torrid sun are captured in this shot of car 198, winner of the 1965 Targa Florio. The drivers were Vaccarella and Bandini in a 275 P2 (Geoffery Goddard)

Section drawing of the 250 GT engine. This V-12 unit is typical of all Ferrari V-12 engines of the 1958 to 1964 period, the racing units differing from the GT engine mainly in that the latter had a wet sump and 3 twin-choke carbs. whilst the ''Testa Rossa'' unit had a dry sump lubrication system and six twin-choke carburettors. The GTO engine was to ''Testa Rossa'' specification. (SEFAC Ferrari)

5 years and which had been preserved, until then, by the enforcement of the 3-litre capacity limit. But even the new record of 3' 57''3 was well below the car's true potential, as this time was more than two seconds slower than its fastest practice lap.

The 250 P and 330 P

Two years' experience with rear-engined sports cars had apparently convinced Ferrari that putting the 3-litre V-12 engine, which was both more reliable and more powerful than the 2.4-litre V-6 and the makeshift 2.6-litre V-8, into the chassis behind the driver was not an insurmountable problem, and this is what he did for 1963. By that time, the output of the V-12 had been raised to 310 h.p. at 7500 r.p.m. on a 9.5 : 1 compression ratio, the general specification remaining much as in previous years, and to accommodate it, the chassis was slightly enlarged, both in wheelbase and track dimensions, and the officially quoted weight of 760 kg. dry was 100 kg. higher than for the previous year's 2.4 V-6.

The notably wider track, wider wheels and a less exotic suspension geometry endowed the 250 P, as it was called, with much improved handling and road holding. It was unrivalled among its contemporaries and won three of the four major events counting towards the Manufacturer's World Championship: the Sebring 12 Hours (Surtees-Scarfiotti), the Nürburgring 1000 Km. (Surtees-Mairesse) and the Le Mans 24 Hours (Scarfiotti-Bandini). It only lost the Targa Florio to Porsche because the Ferrari of Surtees-Parkes was driven off the road, and even then Maranello's honour would probably have been saved by a 2-litre V-6, had not Willy Mairesse, who was still leading by a fractional margin, put his car off the road some eight miles before the finish, when a rain shower made the roads appallingly slippery.

Apparently even before the 250 P had proved itself, Ferrari had built yet another one-off front-engined "Le Mans Special" which, curiously, was based on the production model "Berlinetta Lusso" rather than on the more race-orientated GTO, but although it looked like a "Berlinetta

Lusso" with fatter tyres, it was aluminium panelled and had a 4-litre engine, identical with that of the 1962 winner, under its bonnet. In accordance with the standard model, it had a rigid rear axle and only a 4-speed gearbox, but the wheelbase was lengthened 10 cm. (3.9in.) to 2.50 metres (8ft 2.5in.). The 250 P having proved very reliable, this special 330 LMB was not included in the works team and, driven by Jack Sears and Mike Salmon, it finished 5th overall, but was headed by two 3-litre GTOs.

The 250 P was by far the neatest-looking of the rear-engined sports Ferraris so far and was remarkable for its integral roll-bar also acting as an air slot in an effort to steady the air flow over the rear deck. In view of its success, no one was surprised when it remained substantially unaltered for the following (1964) season, except that the capacity of its V-12 engine was further increased to 3285cc. by using the same wet cylinder liners of 77 mm. bore as those in the 4-litre engine, while retaining the 58.8 mm. stroke. This increased the unit capacity to 275cc. and the car became the 275 P, all the major dimensions, including the dry weight of 755 kg. (as released by Ferrari), remaining unaltered. According to the official documents, the power increase was only a modest one, from 310 h.p. to 320 h.p. (at 7700 r.p.m.) with a compression ratio of 9.8 : 1. By this time, however, Ferrari

The 250 P of 1963 had no rivals. Willy Mairesse drove this one to victory (with John Surtees) in the Nürburgring 1000 Kilometres race at 82.72 m.p.h. The second team car (No. 111) of Scarfiotti and Parkes was crashed by the latter when lying a comfortable second
(Motor & Geoffrey Goddard)

Start of the 1963 Nürburgring 1000 Kilometres race
(Geoffrey Goddard)

Cockpit of a 275 P ready for Le Mans, with torch, tool bag and wire mesh in case the car should get stuck in one of the safety sand banks
(Phipps Photographic)

0 2ft

Car No. 6

1962 front-engined 4-litre V12 which won the Le Mans 24-hours race of that year driven by Phil Hill and Olivier Gendebien, at an average speed of 115.24 m.p.h. (184.38 k.p.h.) for 2766.0 miles (4425.6 kms.)

Martin Lee © Profile Publications Ltd.

Car No. 21

1967 330 P4. In the 1967 Le Mans 24-hours race, the 330 P4 of Mike Parkes and Ludovico Scarfiotti came an honourable second (four laps behind) to the winning Ford GT40 Mk 4 of Dan Gurney and A. J. Foyt, the latter car averaging 135.4 m.p.h. (216.6 k.p.h.) for 3249.6 miles (5199.3 kms.). Both cars covered a record distance for the event.

seemed to have become more realistic in his claims of power output, as that year only 370 h.p. at 7200 r.p.m. were claimed for the 4-litre engine which was also dropped into the same chassis to make the 330 P. Compared with the previous year's 250 SP and 275, the 330 Ps mainly differed externally by their wider wheel rims: 6 in. instead of 5 in. at the front and 7.5 in. instead of 6.5 in. at the rear. It was the smaller-engined car which clinched the Manufacturers' Championship for Ferrari again, with a 1-2-3 victory at Sebring (the winners being Parkes-Maglioli), a win at the Nürburging 1000 Km. (Scarfiotti-Vaccarella) and a win for Guichet-Vaccarella at Le Mans with two 330 Ps second and third. Ferrari did not enter for the Targa Florio in 1964. The smaller car was not much slower than the 4-litre and its main asset was its greater reliability, but the 330 P was progressively developed, specially in its transmission department which had not been designed with the torque of the 4-litre engine in mind. The redesigned gearbox had individually interchangeable gears, instead of the complete gear cluster of the former types, of which a wide choice was available to the factory team. In the second half of the season, the 330 P won three non-championship events: the Tourist Trophy, the Canadian Grand Prix and the Paris 1000 Km. race.

The 250 LM

Before we proceed to the developments of 1965 and the increased threat from Ford, let us go back to the end of 1963 and the introduction of an important new model. At this time, with his rear-engined 250 P sweeping the board, Ferrari considered that, as a competition car, his GTO had become obsolete. The Ford-subsidised Cobras were putting the pressure on

An old 275 LM suitably modified to take more modern tyres, was still driven very successfully in non-championship events by David Piper (mostly co-driven by Dickie Attwood) as late as 1968. Here he is seen running at Le Mans that year when the four-year-old car finished seventh
(Geoffrey Goddard)

1964 Tourist Trophy at Goodwood: Graham Hill, in the Maranello Concessionaires 330 P won the 312 mile race from the 250 LM of David Piper
(Michael Cooper)

10

and Ferrari's position in GT racing where he had reigned supreme for eight years, looked like being threatened. His answer to the problem was the 250 LM which was revealed to the startled visitors to the Paris Motor Show of 1963. This was to all intents and purposes a full-blood 250 P with a roof linking the top of the windscreen to the roll bar. The only significant departure from the racing model, as raced by the factory, was that it had a better freeing single dry-plate clutch located between the engine and the overhung gearbox, the latter being obviously a different design, but still with 5-speeds selected by dog-clutches, without synchronizing mechanism. The five ratios could not be chosen and changed individually, but there was a choice of several final drive ratios. It was announced that a batch of 100 cars would be manufactured in order that the model could be homologated as a Grand Touring car, but the C.S.I. was never satisfied that the required number had, in fact, been produced and it never actually became eligible as a GT model. In fact, the 250 LM never lived up to its type number, as by the time it went into production, its engine size had been increased to 3.3 litres (exactly 3285cc.) and was in every detail identical with the engine of the 275 P; but officially, it continued to be called a 250 LM, though motoring writers frequently refer to it as a 275 LM which seems more logical.

As a consequence of the 250 LM not being homologated, a Cobra won the GT class at Le Mans in 1964, beating the GTOs, but the LM was nevertheless bought by many private owners and scored many victories in the Prototype class against all-comers. Its most clamorous victory came at Le Mans in 1965 when a by-then outdated model, entered by the North American Racing Team and driven by Jochen Rindt and Masten Gregory, followed by a Belgian-entered similar model, saved the day for Ferrari who had lost all his more modern team cars following the battle they fought to stave off the Ford onslaught. It was a most extraordinary win, the car having moved up from 18th place in the fourth hour, after some delay due to ignition trouble, to first in the 21st hour after an epic drive, the rev-counter "spy" showing 9000 (instead of the maximum permitted 7700) almost every time the car came in for refuelling, so Luigi Chinetti, the N.A.R.T. boss and triple Le Mans winner, told me. Incidentally, the same old car still managed to finish 8th at Le Mans in 1969, five years after it was built.

The 275 P2 and 330 P2

For two years now, Ferrari had been able to counter the large-scale attack mounted by Ford who, in 1963, had very nearly succeeded in buying the Maranello factory. Up to then, Ferrari had been able to meet the challenge, but it was obvious that the Ford GT40 and its derivatives were becoming more and more competitive. For 1965 Ferrari needed something better than the 275 and 330 P, incorporating the latest developments in suspension design to take advantage of the rapidly progressing tyre techniques, a car featuring lower drag and developing more power. His answer to the challenge was a completely new car. The chas-

Low flying by the Graham Hill-Innes Ireland Ferrari 330 P at Nürburgring, 1964
(Geoffrey Goddard)

How rear spoilers were born, when Richie Ginther, then test driver for Ferrari, found the 246 SP unstable at speed. This picture was taken at Le Mans several years later, and shows a supplementary makeshift spoiler on a 275 P2
(Geoffrey Goddard)

sis was again a tubular structure, and the body was still made entirely of aluminium, but aluminium panels were now riveted to some of the chassis tubes for increased rigidity, a technique inspired by the works' Formula One cars. The rear suspension followed Grand Prix practice in having forward facing radius arms to provide a very large base of triangulation, and less camber variation to suit the wider tyres. The wire wheels were discarded in favour of cast magnesium, with 8 in. wide rims at the front and 9 in. at the rear, to permit the use of the latest tubeless racing tyres, and for the first time in the history of the V-12 engine (except for a short-lived supercharged Grand Prix version in 1949), the single camshaft cylinder heads were discarded in favour of twin cam heads, with a twin ignition system.

The "P2", as it was called, was essentially the brainchild of Mauro Forghieri, a then very young engineer, who had taken over from Carlo Chiti who, following a disagreement, had left Ferrari in 1961 together with several other key-men, including Giotto Bizzarini who had been responsible for the GT car development. It was produced in 3.3-litre (275 P2) and 4-litre (330 P2) forms developing 350 and 410 h.p.

Car No. 198

1965 275 P2, winner of the Targa Florio. Nino Vaccarella and Lorenzo Bandini averaged
63.73 m.p.h. (102.56 k.p.h.) for the 450 miles (720 kms.), taking 7 hours 01 min. 12.4 sec. to
complete the course, and setting a new record lap in 39 min. 21.0 sec., 68.61 m.p.h. (109.784 k.p.h.)

Martin Lee © Profile Publications Ltd.

O   2ft

respectively, with open or closed body. The smaller version won the Targa Florio in the capable hands of Bandini and Vaccarella, while the 330 won the Nürburgring 1000 Kilometres (Surtees-Scarfiotti), followed by a 275. Earlier in the season, the Surtees-Rodriguez 330 P2 had been defeated by Ford (scoring their first major victory) in the Daytona Intercontinental, partly due to the failure of the tyres to stand up to the strain imposed by the banking, and the works cars were not entered for the Sebring 12 Hours. At Le Mans, the Fords succumbed first, but the surviving Ferrari works' cars all fell by the wayside too, after having been plagued by cracked brake discs. It was the first time Ferrari had used ventilated discs at Le Mans and the stress concentration along the ventilating channels when the brakes were applied firmly at Mulsanne, after they had cooled down completely along the long Hunaudières straight, caused their failure. But clutch and engine troubles were other causes of the retirement of the works' cars which left victory to the old 250 LM of Rindt and Gregory.

The 365 P2 and 166 P

No four-cam engines were entrusted to private customers or non-works teams, but a limited number of P2 cars were delivered with an even larger version of the single camshaft head engine in which the bore was increased to 81 mm. giving a total capacity of 4390cc. and a power almost equal to that of the works 4-cam engine. These cars were called 365 P2 and two were entered for Le Mans. Only one finished however, struggling home in 7th place after having run 3rd early in the race. Nevertheless, P. Rodriguez-Guichet and Surtees-Parkes were first and second in the Rheims 12 Hours Race that year (1965), and David Piper was quite successful with one of these cars in 1966 and 1967, his score including winning the Kyalami 9 Hours Race of 1965 and 1966 as well as a second place in the Rheims 12 Hours Race of 1967.

Apart from its 10% larger engine capacity, the 275 P of 1964 was identical to the 250 P of 1963. The Scarfiotti-Vaccarella car is shown winning the 1964 Nürburgring 1000 Kilometres at 87.30 m.p.h.
(Geoffrey Goddard)

The Nürburgring 1000 Kilometres of 1965 was dominated by Ferrari. It was won by the 330 P2 of Surtees-Scarfiotti and second was the 275 P2 seen here which was driven by Parkes and Guichet
(Michael Cooper)

Brake, clutch and engine troubles eliminated all the works Ferraris from Le Mans in 1965, including Mike Parkes and Jean Guichet's 275 P2
(Michael Cooper)

When the 250 LM failed to be homologated as a GT car, Ferrari produced a 250 GTO with a body similar to that of the LM. Here, in the 1965 Targa Florio, both cars are seen together, with the GTO preceding the LM (Geoffrey Goddard)

The N.A.R.T.-entered 250 LM of Rindt-Gregory saved the day for Ferrari at Le Mans in 1965 when all the works cars retired following their battle against the Fords. Their average speed was 121.09 m.p.h. (Geoffrey Goddard)

Externally the 365 P delivered to selected private entrants was identical with the 330 P2 works cars, but they had a larger (4.4-litre) engine with two instead of four camshafts. Graham Hill taking stock of the Maranello Concessionaries' car at the start of the 1965 Nürburgring 1000 Kilometres (Michael Cooper)

Car No. 198

1965 275 P2, winner of the Targa Florio. Nino Vaccarella
and Lorenzo Bandini averaged 63.73 m.p.h. (102.56 k.p.h.)
for the 450 miles (720 kms.), taking 7 hours 01 min.
12.4 sec. to complete the course, and setting a new
record lap in 39 min. 21.0 sec., 68.61 m.p.h.
(109.784 k.p.h.)

Martin Lee © Profile Publications Ltd.

During 1965, a significant new car also appeared. Until then the name of "Dino", after Enzo Ferrari's prematurely deceased son, had been given only to the V-6 series of Ferrari engines which had allegedly been laid down by young Dino Ferrari. Now it was given to a complete car and it has since become the trade name of all the V-6-engined cars, made by Ferrari. The first model, called 166 P was practically a scaled-down version of the P2, except for the fact that it was fitted with a roof. Its 65 degree V-6 engine was the smallest Ferrari had built for a sports-racing car since his very early days: with bore and stroke dimensions of 77 × 57 mm. it had a capacity of 1592cc. and was fitted with twin-camshaft, twin ignition heads.

In its very first major race, the car which Bandini had already driven to victory at Vallelunga went so fast in the Nürburgring 1000 Kilometres that it completely ran away from the 2-litre Porsches, including the flat-8-engined model of Bonnier-Rindt which beat it into 3rd place (behind the two P2s) only because a jet of one of the Dino's three twin-choke Weber carburettors became choked, causing a power loss towards the end of the race. In fact the Stewards were so incredulous that they ordered a check on the engine size to make sure it really belonged in the 1600cc. class! A 2-litre version, with the bore increased to 86 mm. came soon after, and with this car, Scarfiotti managed to beat the Porsche works cars in the European Mountain Championship, in spite of having to miss out the first two events. For this purpose, he used an open version, as were most of the 2-litre Dinos, and he repeated his victory in 1966 with a car that was generally similar, except that wider wheels gave it a wider track. The works Dino 206 SP had Lucas fuel injection and an output of 220 h.p. was claimed for it at 9000 r.p.m., but the batch of cars that was built for private customers had Weber carburettors and single ignition heads which, rather surprisingly, were supposed to drop only 2 h.p. compared with the "works" cars!

Due to hasty preparation in strike-stricken Italy, the Dinos failed dismally at Le Mans, but the works cars took 2nd place in the Targa Florio and 2nd and 3rd overall in the Nürburgring 1000 Km. in 1966. The Dino's last stage of development was a very lightweight version with three-valve-per-cylinder heads. It was seen in the Targa Florio of 1967 and went very fast until Günther Klass put it off the road in the second lap. He was killed in the same car, two months later, practising for the Mugello race and that was the last time Ferrari ran a Dino 206 as a works entry. The Dino series is nevertheless an important one in the range of racing Ferraris, for it is from the "customer" version of its engine that the power unit of the Ferrari Dino 206 and 246 GT, and of the 2-litre and 2.4-litre Fiat Dinos, was developed.

The P3

In fact Ferrari only took a real interest in the Dino when it had a chance of winning a race outright—class wins just don't interest him, so his main effort for 1966—apart from Formula One—went into the big Prototype which was developed from P2 to P3 stage. The general

The Gosselin-Dumay 275 LM in a typical Nürburgring jump (1965) (Michael Cooper)

They have very brave policemen in Sicily . . . and brave drivers too. Jackie Stewart would not approve of this sort of safety! Vaccarella leading the 1966 Targa Florio with a 330 P3. Later Bandini crashed when trying to overtake another competitor (Geoffrey Goddard)

The 330 P3 of Scarfiotti-Parkes won the Spa 1000 Kilometres race at 126.43 m.p.h. (Geoffrey Goddard)

Biscaldi-Casoni, Dino 206, in the 1966 Targa Florio where they finished well down after a chequered run. A similar car was driven into second place by Guichet and Baghetti (Geoffrey Goddard)

chassis layout remained substantially unaltered, but still wider wheels were fitted (8.5 and 9.5 in. front and rear respectively) and the track was increased by about 6 cm. (2.3 in.) front and rear while the suspension geometry was altered to suit the wider tyres. The carburettors were replaced by a Lucas fuel injection system. 420 h.p. were now claimed at 8000 r.p.m. The transmission was completely redesigned to put the multi-disc clutch between the engine and gearbox, the overhung small multi-disc clutch having become marginal with the power available. A 5-speed ZF box was used as a Ferrari box could not be made in time. Considerable development had gone into the brake discs to obviate the cracks which had plagued the cars at Le Mans the previous year, and the body, in both open and closed forms, between which the only difference was the diminutive roof joining the windscreen to the rear deck, was much more carefully streamlined. For the first time too, it incorporated some fiberglass panels, though the main body structure was still of aluminium.

Unfortunately, 1966 was a year of austerity for Ferrari, who decided to enter only one P3 for any one race, and he had, in addition, to

Dino 206 S: in the 1966 Nürburgring 1000 Kilometres these cars came second (Scarfiotti-Bandini) and third (Rodriguez-Ginther, seen here) to a Chaparral 2D
(Geoffrey Goddard)

The 1966 330 P3 V-12 engine
(Geoffrey Goddard)

Ferrari sent but one car to the 1967 Targa Florio —a 330 P4 for Vaccarella-Scarfiotti, which the former crashed when in the lead (Geoffrey Goddard)

Daytona hat trick: the 1967 24 hours race was won by the 330 P4 of Bandini-Amon at 105.70 m.p.h. Scarfiotti-Parkes were second in another 330 P4 and third came the 412 P of Rodriguez-Guichet (London Art Tech.)

The complexities of the 330 P4—the most advanced of the sports-racing Ferrari Prototypes (Courtesy of Shell Oil Company Limited)

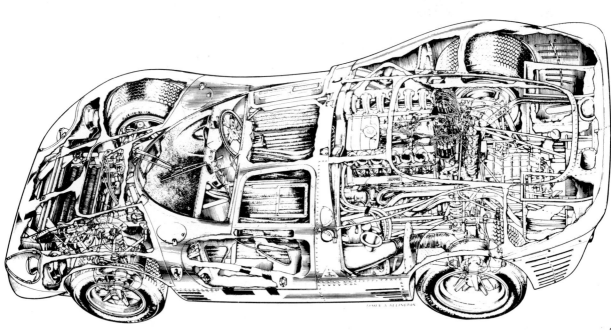

cope with a wave of strikes that had broken out in Italy. No factory cars were entered for the Daytona 24 Hours; at Sebring, the lone P3 led the race, but was later overtaken by two 7-litre Fords and it finally went out with gearbox trouble. In the Targa Florio, Bandini was pushed off the road while overtaking another car, when firmly in the lead, during the last third of the race. A P3 won both the Monza 1000 Kilometre and the Spa 1000 Kilometre races (Parkes-Surtees and Parkes-Scarfiotti), which in that year did not yet count for the Manufacturers' World Championship, but it retired at Nürburgring after having broken a damper bracket. An exception was made for Le Mans, where two cars were entered by the factory and a third P3 was entrusted to the North American Racing Team. After 8 hours' racing. Ferrari P3s were 1st and 2nd, but they had a rather hard time keeping up with the 7-litre Ford Mk IIs and they all eventually retired, unfortunately in Scarfiotti's case as the result of a compound accident provoked by the inexperienced driver of a small car, when his P3 was still fully efficient. The previous year's privately-owned 365 P2s, with the single cam 4.4-litre engine, which had been partially brought up to P3 specification as far as their chassis was concerned, were completely out-classed and also all retired.

The 330 P4

The complete defeat he suffered at Le Mans in 1966 seemed to sting Ferrari's pride and his effort for 1967 was much more convincing. The P3s were sold to private customers after their chassis had been modified to take even wider wheels at the rear (now 11.5 ins in width), while for its own use, the factory built the 330 P4 with slightly wider tracks, and cylinder heads incorporating 3 valves per cylinder (two inlet and one exhaust) and with the inlet tracts between the camshafts of each bank, as developed for the Formula One cars. As before there were two plugs per cylinder, fired by the normal battery and coil system, four separate coils being used, and the plug size was reduced from 12 to 10 millimetres. This engine raised the power output from 420 to 450 h.p. at 8000 r.p.m. with an 11:1 compression ratio. On the team cars, Firestone tyres were used fo the first time instead of Dunlops, their size being 10.15 × 15 at the front and 12.15 × 15 at the rear, on 9.5 and 11.5 in. wide rims respectively and a Ferrari-designed-and-made gearbox replaced the ZF unit.

At its first outing in the Daytona 24 Hours race, the new model scored a resounding success, leading the race from the fourth hour and taking the first two places, followed by a modified P3 (officially called a 412 P, but more often referred to as a P3/4), after all the 7-litre Fords had retired or been seriously delayed. The cars were not entered at Sebring, but Bandini and Amon won again at Monza with Scarfiotti and Parkes second on the same lap, the order being as at Daytona, but this time, the official works Fords were absent. In the Spa 1000 Km. Race, Ickx's mastery in the rain prevailed and made it a victory for John Wyer's 5.7-litre Mirage-Ford, L. Bianchi-Attwood finishing 3rd in

the British-owned P3/4 of Maranello Concessionaires, while Scarfiotti-Parkes could do no better than 5th in the factory's P4. In the Targa Florio, Vaccarella crashed his P4 when in the lead and, then came Le Mans. . . .

This was to be the last Le Mans run under the unlimited capacity formula—the last major confrontation between Ford and Ferrari. The previous year, Fords had scored an overwhelming victory, but in the first big race of 1967, the Daytona 24 Hours, they had been well and truly beaten by the P4s. In order the better to prepare his cars for the great day, Ferrari had even forsaken the Nürburgring 1000 Kilometres. Three P4s comprised the official factory team and a fourth one was entrusted to the Belgian Ecurie Francorchamps, with Mairesse-Beurlys as drivers.

Practice revealed that 7-litres of push-rod Ford engine just had the edge on 4-litres of high-revving racing machinery, and this was

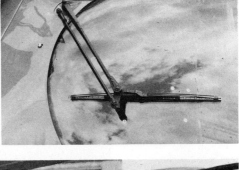

Some details of the 1967 330 P4.

(far left) Ferrari bodies of 1967 were still made entirely of aluminium sheet. Note the twin regulation "luggage boots".

In contrast to earlier models, the 330 P4 had outboard rear brakes. They were first introduced on the previous year's P3.

Parallel action screen wipers on a 330 P4— the only type that will not lift on a sharply raked screen at high speed

The final stage of the development of V-12, 4-litre engine was the P4 with 3 valves per cylinder. It is easily identified by its induction pipes which run between the camshafts. 1967 was the first year in which Ferrari used fuel injection for the Prototypes.

When most of his competitors had switched over to electronic ignition, Ferrari stuck with the established coil and breaker system. To get sufficient tension build-up in a fast revving 12-cylinder twin ignition engine, four coils were used.

(All Spencer Smith Photography)

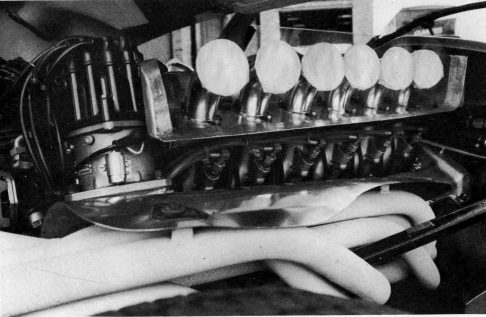

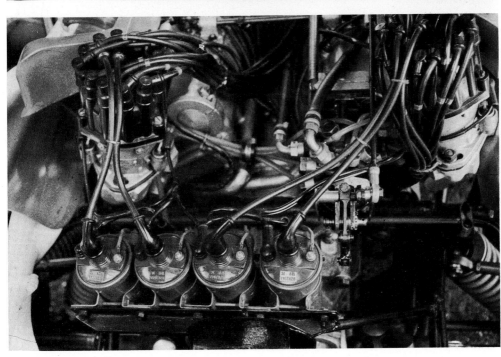

confirmed in the actual race. The Scarfiotti-Parkes P4 was never far behind however. Following a multiple crash involving three Fords before half distance, the Mairesse-Beurlys P4 had moved into 3rd place, and the works car really went after the leaders Gurney and Foyt, who never put a wheel wrong, however, and who clinched Ford's second win at Le Mans. The works Ferrari finished just four laps behind, and the first three cars—one Ford and two Ferraris—covered a distance unprecedented in the history of Le Mans. Ferrari had lost the unequal battle, but this time he had lost it with full honours. There were no sad faces in the Italian pit, for everyone felt he had done his very best and had earned the respect of all followers of motor sport. "Never in my life have I driven a car so hard for so long," Mike Parkes told me after the race, tired, but satisfied that he had done his utmost.

Later in the season, another 7-litre car, this time the Chevrolet-engined Chaparral, defeated the P4 driven by Chris Amon and guest driver Jackie Stewart in the Brands Hatch 500, but their second place clinched the Prototype World Championship for Ferrari for the sixth time in the seven years 1961 to 1967.

The P4 was certainly not the most successful of all the sports-racing Ferraris, but it was probably one of the most advanced ones in the context of contemporary automotive technology, as it was the end result of Ferrari's direct competition with the world's second largest company in the automobile industry.

The Guichet-Baghetti 330 P2 sweeping through Collesano in the 1965 Targa Florio, won by Bandini and Vaccarella's similar car. (Geoffrey Goddard)

Easy does it! Ferrari mechanics install a 330 P4 engine, Le Mans, 1967 (Geoffrey Goddard)

The modified 330 P3 models entered by private teams in 1967 races were virtually indistinguishable from the works P4 cars, but they still had the earlier 24 valve engine fed by carburettors. This is the Maranello Concessionaires car driven by Piper-Attwood at Brands Hatch (Geoffrey Goddard)

DETAILED SPECIFICATIONS OF FERRARI MODELS, 1961–67.

Year	1961	1962			1963	1964			1965
Model	246 SP	196 SP	246 SP	268 SP	250 P	275 P	330 P	250 LM	275 P2
Body	Open	Open	Open	Open	Open	Open	Open	Coupé	Open
ENGINE									
Number of cyl.	6	6	6	8	12	12	12	12	12
V angle	60°	60°	65°	90°	60°	60°	60°	60°	60°
Bore × Stroke (mm.)	85 × 71	77 × 71	85 × 71	77 × 71	73 × 58.8	77 × 58.8	77 × 71	77 × 58.8	77 × 58.8
Capacity (cm³)	2417	1983	2417	2645	2953	3285	3967	3285	3285
Compr. ratio	9.8	9.8	9.5	9.6	9.5	9.8	8.8	9.8	9.5
Max. power (h.p.)	270	210	275	265	310	320	370	320	350(*)
at r.p.m.	8000	7500	7500	7000	7500	7700	7200	7700	8500
Fuel system	Carb.	Carb.	Carb.	Carb.	Carb.	Carb.	Carb.	Carb.	Carb.
Number of camshafts	4	2	4	2	2	2	2	2	4
Ignition	Single	Single	Single	Single	Single	Single	Single	Single	Twin
CHASSIS									
Type	Tubes	Tubes	Tubes	Tubes	Tubes	Tubes	Tubes	Tubes	Tubes
Wheelbase (mm.)	2320	2320	2320	2320	2400	2400	2400	2400	2400
(ins.)	91.54	91.54	91.54	91.54	94.5	94.5	94.5	94.5	94.5
Track front (mm.)	1200	1200	1200	1200	1350	1350	1350	1350	1400
(ins.)	47.24	47.24	47.24	47.24	53.14	53.14	53.14	53.14	55.11
Track rear (mm.)	1200	1200	1200	1200	1340	1340	1340	1340	1370
(ins.)	47.24	47.24	47.24	47.24	52.75	52.75	52.75	52.75	53.93
Tyres front	5.50–15	5.25–15	5.50–15	5.50–15	5.50–15	5.50–15	6.00–15	5.50–15	5.50–15
Tyres rear	6.50–15	6.50–15	7.00–15	7.00–15	7.00–15	7.00–15	7.25–15	7.00–15	6.50–15
Rim width front (ins.)	5	5	5	5	5	7.5	7.5	7.5	8
Rim width rear (ins.)	6	6	6	6	6.5	7.5	7.5	7.5	9
Weight (kg.)**	730	690	755	770	840	925	940	950	980
(lbs)	1609	1521	1664	1698	1852	2050	2070	2100	2160

(*) Estimated
(**) Most weights based on Le Mans weighing and thus for cars with full 24 hours equipment, less fuel but with other liquids

DETAILED SPECIFICATIONS OF FERRARI MODELS, 1961–67.   DINO MODELS

Year	1965		1966	1967			1965		1966	
Model	330 P2	365 P	330 P3	330 P4	412 P (***)	166 P	206 SP	206 S	206 SP	
Body	Open	Open	Open or Coupé	Open or Coupé	Coupé	Coupé	Open	Open	Open or Coupé
ENGINE									
Number of cyl.	12	12	12	12	12	6	6	6	6
V angle	60°	60°	60°	60°	60°	65°	65°	65°	65°
Bore × Stroke (mm.)	77 × 71	81 × 71	77 × 71	77 × 71	77 × 71	77 × 57	86 × 57	86 × 57	86 × 57
Capacity (cm³)	3967	4390	3967	3967	3967	1592	1986	1986	1986
Compr. ratio	9.8	9.5	11.4	11	11	9.8	12.5	10.8	11
Max. power (h.p.)	400(*)	390(*)	420	450	420	185(*)	218	218	220
at r.p.m.	8000	7200	8000	8000	8000	9000	9000	9000	9000
Fuel system	Carb.	Carb.	Lucas inj.	Lucas inj.	Carb.	Carb.	Carb.	Carb.	Lucas inj.
Number of camshafts	4	2	4	4 (36 valves)	4	4	4	4	4
Ignition	Twin	Single	Twin	Twin	Twin	Single	Twin	Single	Twin
CHASSIS									
Type	Tubes	Tubes	Tubes + alu. sheet	Tubes + alu. sheet	Tubes + alu. sheet	Tubes	Tubes	Tubes + alu. sheet	Tubes + alu. sheet
Wheelbase (mm.)	2400	2400	2400	2400	2400	2280	2280	2280	2280
(ins.)	94.5	94.5	94.5	94.5	94.5	89.76	89 76	89.76	89.76
Track front (mm.)	1400	1400	1462	1488	1466	1335	1377	1360	1392
(ins.)	55.11	55.11	57.54	58.57	57.70	52·55	54·21	53.54	54.79
Track rear (mm.)	1370	1370	1431	1450	1484	1335	1412	1355	1414
(ins.)	53.93	53.93	56.32	57.07	58.40	52·55	55·59	53.33	55.66
Tyres front	5.50–15	5.50–15	5.50–15	10.15–15	7.00–15	6.50–13	5.50–13	5.50–13	5.50–13
Tyres rear	6.50–15	6.50–15	7.00–15	12.15–15	7.00–15	7.00–13	7.00–13	7.00–13	7.00–13
Rim width front (ins.)	8	8	8.5	9.5	9.5	7·5	9·0	8.5	8.5
Rim width rear (ins.)	9	9	9.5	11.5	11.5	8·5	10.5	10.5	10.5
Weight (kg.)**	1000	990	970	965	965	800	800	800	800
(lbs)	2205	2185	2140	2130	2130	1770	1770	1770	1770

(***) Better known as 330 P3/4

GENERAL SPECIFICATIONS APPLYING TO ALL REAR-ENGINED MODELS, 1961–67.

Engine. Location in front of the rear axle; gearbox overhung. 6-cylinder V-engines have four, V-8 engines five, and V-12 engines seven, main bearings. Main bearings, connecting rod bearings and camshaft bearings are plain. Dry sump lubrication. Aluminium alloy cylinder block and heads. If carburettors, they are Weber 2 bbl., each choke feeding one cylinder.

Gearbox. 5-speed constant mesh. No synchromesh.

Clutch. Multiple disc, dry. Location behind the gearbox, except 250/275 LM and P3 and P4 models where it is in unit with engine.

Suspension. Front by transverse wishbones, coil spring and damper units and anti-roll bar. Rear by transverse wishbones, coil spring and damper units and anti-roll bar for all models up to 1964 inclusive. From 1965 (Ferrari P2, P3 and P4 and all Dino models) parallel radius rods were used for fore-and-aft location.

Steering. Rack and pinion with hydraulic damper. Right-hand steering.

Brakes. Disc front and rear. No servo assistance.

Wheels. Centre lock wire wheels with aluminium alloy rim on all models up to 1964 inclusive. From 1965 (Ferrari P2, P3 and P4 models and all Dino models) centre lock cast magnesium wheels.

Tyres. (Works cars.) Dunlop up to 1966 inclusive. Firestone in later years.

Body. Light alloy panels on light alloy frame.

FERRARI TYPE NUMBERS

Since the start of Ferrari production, the 12-cylinder-engined models have usually been named by the unit capacity of their cylinders. The first production car, that had a total capacity of 1500cc. was called "Tipo 125" and when this was increased to 2 litres, it became the "Tipo 166" (*Tipo* being, of course, the Italian word for "type").

A different system was used when the "Dino" series of V-6 engines was introduced and was also adhered to for the few V-8 models made in Maranello. In this case the first two figures indicated the total capacity and the last figure the number of cylinders. For example "246" stands for 2.4 litres, 6-cylinders. From 1968 on, the same system was applied to 12-cylinder racing cars, the 312 series being 3 litre, 12-cylinder models.

The suffixes are easily understood; S = Sport; P = Prototipo (prototype); SP = Sport Prototipo; LM = Le Mans, LMB = Le Mans "Berlinetta"; GT = Gran Turismo (Grand Touring). The story of the initials "GTO" is rather funny. For several years, Ferrari had built a model called 250 GT—a very successful 2-seater sports coupé. In 1961, when competition became fiercer, a special lightweight racing version was made, using the racing "Testa Rossa" 3-litre engine, and this was simply going to be the 1961 version of the 250 G.T. However when a sufficient number of parts were ready to assemble a first batch of 100 cars, Ferrari applied to the Automobile Club of Italy for homologation of the new 250 GT as a production car, as the rules allowed at that time. This was promptly granted and someone added a letter "O" with a pencil or pen behind the type name 250 GT to indicate that the model had been "omologato" (homologated). And so the car became generally known as the "250 GTO", Ferrari himself finding it very convenient to use that type name to distinguish between this model and its predecessors.

RACING SUCCESSES IN WORLD CHAMPIONSHIP EVENTS

246 P or SP:	1st Targa Florio, 1961 (von Trips-Gendebien, 64.27 m.p.h.) and 1962 (Mairesse-R. Rodriguez-Gendebien, 63.47 m.p.h.) 1st Nürburgring 1000 Km., 1962 (Phil Hill-Gendebien, 82.39 m.p.h.)
196 SP:	2nd Targa Florio, 1962 (Baghetti-Bandini) and 1963 (Bandini-Scarfiotti-Mairesse)
250 P:	1st Sebring 12 Hours, 1963 (Surtees-Scarfiotti, 90.39 m.p.h.); 2nd (Mairesse-Vaccarella) 1st Nürburgring 1000 Km., 1963 (Surtees-Mairesse, 82.72 m.p.h.) 1st Le Mans 24 Hours, 1963 (Scarfiotti-Bandini, 118.10 m.p.h.); 3rd (Parkes-Maglioli)
275 P:	1st Sebring 12 Hours, 1964 (Parkes-Maglioli, 92.36 m.p.h.); 2nd (Scarfiotti-Vaccarella) 1st Nürburgring 1000 Km., 1964 (Scarfiotti-Vaccarella, 87.30 m.p.h.) 1st Le Mans 24 Hours, 1964 (Guichet-Vaccarella, 121.55 m.p.h.)
330 P:	3rd Sebring 12 Hours, 1964 (Surtees-Bandini) 2nd Le Mans 24 Hours, 1964 (Bonnier-G. Hill); 3rd (Bandini-Surtees)
250 LM:	1st Le Mans 24 Hours, 1965 (Gregory-Rindt, 121.09 m.p.h.); 2nd (Dumay-Gosselin)
275 P2:	1st Targa Florio, 1965 (Vaccarella-Bandini, 63.70 m.p.h.)
330 P2:	1st Monza 1000 Km., 1965 (Parkes-Guichet, 125.90 m.p.h.) 2nd Nürburgring 1000 Km., 1965 (Parkes-Guichet)
330 P3:	1st Monza 1000 Km., 1966 (Surtees-Parkes, 110.45 m.p.h.) 1st Spa 1000 Km., 1966 (Parkes-Scarfiotti, 126.43 m.p.h.)
330 P4:	1st Daytona 24 Hours, 1967 (Bandini-Amon, 105.70 m.p.h.); 2nd (Scarfiotti-Parkes) 1st Monza 1000 Km., 1967 (Bandini-Amon, 126.10 m.p.h.); 2nd (Scarfiotti-Parkes) 2nd Le Mans 24 Hours, 1967 (Parkes-Scarfiotti); 3rd (Mairesse-'Beurlys') 2nd BOAC Brands Hatch 500, 1967 (Stewart-Amon)
412 P:	3rd Daytona 24 Hours, 1967 (Rodriguez-Guichet) 3rd Spa 1000 Km., 1967 (Attwood-Bianchi)
Dino 166 P:	4th Nürburgring 1000 Km., 1965 (Bandini-Vaccarella)
Dino 206 SP:	2nd Targa Florio, 1966 (Guichet-Baghetti) 2nd Nürburgring 1000 Km., 1966 (Scarfiotti-Bandini); 3rd (Rodriguez-Ginther)

Lago forebear 1: the 4-litre six-cylinder Talbot sports-racing car as first introduced in 1936.

The 4½-litre LAGO-TALBOT

by Cyril Posthumus

After 27 years of confusion between Talbot, Talbot-Darracq and Darracq racing cars, which frequently changed their name and sometimes even their nationality to suit the country in which they were racing, it was a relief to learn, late in 1947, that the S.A. Automobiles Talbot of 33 Quai du Général Galliéni, Suresnes, Paris, were to build a batch of 20 single-seater racing cars specifically bearing the name Talbot-Lago for the 1948 season. When the cars materialised that was the nomenclature firmly cast in their valve covers, yet colloquially the order was more often reversed to Lago-Talbot. Not that it mattered; the chief progenitor, "Tony" Lago, was happy either way, so long as his cars won races.

They obliged more often than many people expected, and but for changes both of GP Formula and company fortune might have enjoyed a longer racing career. The Talbot-Lago story extends over six years, no more, yet in that time the marque contributed greatly to the interest of International motor racing, and did a vast amount for French racing prestige.

The man behind them

Like the illustrious Ettore Bugatti, the man who allied his name with Talbot, variously called Antonio, Antoine, Anthony and Tony Lago, was Italian by birth (Venice 1893) but a French resident by preference. Before the Great War he had studied at the same Milan technical polytechnic where Paul Zuccarelli of Hispano-Suiza and Peugeot fame was a pupil. During the war

Lago rose to the rank of Major in the Italian forces, and early in the '20s he came to England, first to join Isotta-Fraschini in London, and then becoming technical director of LAP Engineering, who attempted to launch the Restelli car, designed by Enrico Restelli of Milan, in Britain, and also marketed Silvani overhead valve cylinder head conversions for Fiats. Next he joined the Wilson Self-Changing Gear Co., rising to become general manager, and devising a one-pedal operational system for the Wilson epicyclic gearbox by means of a friction clutch actuated by the accelerator pedal.

In 1933 Lago joined Sunbeam-Talbot-Darracq, albeit at a time when group fortunes were at an ebb. After a short spell as assistant director at Sunbeams in Wolverhampton, the S-T-D Board asked him to take over management of the Talbot-Darracq works at Suresnes. These were operating very dispiritedly, though Lago did his enthusiastic best with virtually no capital to instil some life into the old "Usines Perfecta" where once had poured forth a stream of fast-selling Darracqs and many successful racing cars.

By 1935 the inevitable happened, S-T-D collapsed and was taken over by the Rootes Group, and the fate of Suresnes hung in the balance. Lago scrambled around for financial support to set up Automobiles Talbot independently and, surprisingly in the then depressed French economy, contrived somehow to find it, and the French Talbot was saved.

25

The heritage

Major Lago inherited a rather stodgy range of cars in the French idiom of the day—Weymann close-coupled and claustrophobic bodies, separate luggage boots and artillery wheels—but underneath was independent front suspension by a transverse leaf spring, and an engine potential in the 23CV six-cylinder model which Lago lost no time in exploiting. In July 1934 Automobiles Talbot had taken out patents for an overhead-valve engine with cross pushrods in a pent-roof head, and once in command of the firm, Lago set his chief designer, the Italian Walter Becchia who had been with Fiat in their great racing days, to work applying this head to the rugged 23CV unit with its seven-bearing crankshaft. The result was a 160 b.h.p., 4-litre engine ideal for a new sporting range of models, but also just asking to be raced.

In that summer of 1935 the French were much disgruntled at the repeated German victories in Grand Prix racing, and the eclipse of their own cars. Their very own Grand Prix at Montlhéry had seen the Mercedes-Benz team romp home to a galling 1-2-4 victory, Auto Union rubbing German salt into the wound by taking 5th place, with Italian cars filling in the spaces, the French cars nowhere. This, the French resolved, must not happen again, and in due course announced that the 1936 French Grand Prix, and sundry other French races, would be open to sports-cars only!

This was the encouragement Lago needed. His backers agreed on a sports-car racing programme, and the elated Major went to Nice to persuade Réné Dreyfus, then a member of the Scuderia Ferrari, to join the venture both as No.1 driver and team manager. With new Talbots, a team of Delahayes also under development, and Bugatti tired of placing 'also ran' in Grand Prix racing, the switch to the sports-car class was highly convenient all round; as eminent reporter /organiser Charles Faroux said—*les constructeurs* had new objectives, *le publique Francais* could look forward to some French victories for a change, and the prize money would stay at home instead of going to swell Nazi Germany's or Fascist Italy's coffers.

Thus the name Talbot returned to racing after nine years' absence, and the beautiful pale blue newcomers from Suresnes fought doughtily in their first race, the Marseilles 3 Hours at Miramas in May 1936. Two Talbots against ten Delahayes, one retired early, the other after leading for $2\frac{1}{2}$ hours, both with broken rockers. As they raced further they moved up the scoreboard—9th and 10th in the French GP, 3rd and 4th at Rheims, 2nd and 3rd at Comminges, beaten each time by Bugatti. Persistence paid off in 1937, when out of seven races they won four, including the 2nd French GP for sports-cars, where they finished 1st, 2nd and 3rd, and the TT in Britain, where they placed 1st and 2nd. And, reflecting in the glow of these successes, Talbot road sports-cars sold well too.

1938 brought a new GP Formula allowing up to $4\frac{1}{2}$-litre unsupercharged cars and up to 3-litres supercharged, and with Talbot, Delahaye, Bugatti and SEFAC all rashly undertaking to compete, the French GP reverted to real Grand Prix status. When the smoke from

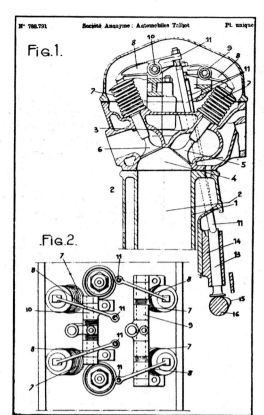

Becchia's original Talbot inclined valve conversion, achieved with a single camshaft in the crankcase, cross pushrods and rockers—from the Patent Specification, July 19th, 1934. (Automobiles Talbot)

Joint artificers of the Talbot-Lago, Antonio Lago and his chief engineer Carlo Marchetti, in the drawing office at Suresnes.

the Mercedes-Benz 1-2-3 triumph had cleared, however, a single Talbot was the only other finisher, 48 miles behind! It was merely a sports-car stripped of wings and lights, with full $4\frac{1}{2}$-litre engine and raised compression.

Back in sports-car trim, a similar car won the Paris 12 Hours race that year, but Tony Lago shared that love for out-and-out racing which distinguished his predecessor at Sunbeams, Louis Coatalen, and having tasted success, now

Lago forebear 2: the 4.5-litre offset GP car of 1939, showing cockpit set to the right, and the engine and transmission to the left.

Lago forebear 3: the first central single-seater, the monoplace of 1939, being driven in the French GP at Rheims by Raymond Mays, who kindly loaned this photograph.
(Louis Klemantaski)

wanted to build real Grand Prix cars for 1939. Three new machines were laid down at Suresnes, two of them offset single-seaters to take unblown 4½-litre six-cylinder engines, and one a central-seated *monoplace* to take a supercharged 3-litre V-16 cylinder engine designed by Becchia. This exciting unit, alas, was but a paper dream which never materialised, but the car was fitted instead with one of the 4½-litre unblown sixes, coupled up to a special 5-speed Wilson preselector gearbox developed by Talbot for the V-16.

The *monoplace* was not ready in time for the Pau GP, where one offset car finished 3rd, nor for the Eifelrennen where they were outclassed, one placing 11th. For the French GP at Rheims, Lago invited Britain's Raymond Mays to drive the new single-seater, but in pre-race tests at Montlhéry the special aluminium fuel tank split, and Mays lost a day's practice while a replacement was made. He found the car could manage 155 m.p.h. down the straight and was pleased with its handling. Unfortunately, while the two-seaters took excellent 3rd and 4th places in the Grand Prix, Mays' run lasted less than quarter-distance when the fuel tank split again, losing about 20 gallons in one lap, and Lago's beautiful new car had to retire, fortunately without catching fire. Mays was much taken by the car and its excellent brakes and suspension, although the latter was inclined to hop. This car was the true precursor to the post-war Talbot-Lago, and as such merits closer examination.

The first monoplace
Despite its sleek appearance, enhanced by the pale blue and silver finish, there was much that was old-fashioned about this car, even in 1939. This was not decadence on Lago's or Becchia's part, but simply expedience. Automobiles Talbot had no big resources for development as had Mercedes-Benz and Auto Union under the Nazi spur for International prestige, and thus had to make the best of available materials. In this car the old tenet that "the racing-car of today is the sports-car of tomorrow" was completely reversed; it was almost a sports-car converted to a racing-car, only the narrow frame being built for a specific purpose.

Even then, this had chassis rails derived directly from Talbot sports-car pattern, being of pressed steel channel section, boxed and cross-braced by large-diameter tubes, underslung at the rear, and carrying semi-elliptic leaf springs on which the rigid rear axle was suspended. At the front, independent suspension utilised Suresnes' long-established transverse leaf spring, this also serving as the lower wishbone, being attached direct to the king-pin posts or hub carriers as we term them now. The upper wishbones or 'A-arms' were solid-looking pressed and welded fabrications in chromed steel plate, pivoted to the top of the chassis rail on the inside, and to the hub carriers on the outside. Both friction and Newton-Bennett hydraulic shock absorbers were fitted, and Bendix cable-operated mechanical brakes were employed, the big-diameter alloy drums having large air scoops.

The engine, as in the two 1939 offset cars, was a six-cylinder with hemispherical head and overhead valves operated by crossed pushrods and a single camshaft in the crankcase, all very much as in the successful sports-cars of 1936–38. The block and head were of light alloy, with Nitralloy steel cylinder liners and bronze valve seats. Bore and stroke were 93 × 110 mm., giving 4,482cc., the power output on a 10½ : 1 compression ratio being approx. 210 b.h.p. at 4500 r.p.m. The sparking plugs, one per cylinder, were sunk deep in tubes to protect them from any oil straying from the valve rockers; three Zenith-Stromberg horizontal carburettors were fitted on the nearside of the engine, ignition was by a single magneto driven off the front timing gears, the seven-bearing crankshaft ran in plain mains, and lubrication was of dry-sump type, the tank in the scuttle having two neat finned oil coolers set in the air stream.

This engine of frankly sports type, substituting for the hypothetical 3-litre 16-cylinder, was set centrally in the *monoplace,* and despite the Wilson gearbox looming into the cockpit, the driver was still seated fairly low as the propeller shaft was set to the offside through an enclosed gear-train, and driving an offset rear axle. The drive was of the 'Hotchkiss' type wherein the semi-elliptic springs take the torque; dry weight was given as 850 kg. or 16.8 cwt., and speed was reckoned at 156 m.p.h.

A shapely radiator grille, recalling the old GP Talbot-Darracqs of 1926–27, graced the nose of the car, a single low-mounted exhaust pipe protruded from the offside of the bonnet, and in general the body was very *à la mode* for 1939, spoiled only by the semi-elliptic rear springs projecting naked and unashamed outside the sleek blue-painted flanks. For all its elegance, however, this unsupercharged six-cylinder car hadn't a chance against such fire-eating GP cars as the contemporary 2-stage blown 3-litre V-12 Mercedes-Benz W163s with their 470 raucous b.h.p. and *circa* 190 m.p.h. maximum. Only on fuel consumption, reckoned at about 10 m.p.g. to the wolfish German cars' 2½ m.p.g., could it save time, but in 1939 it and its offset brothers lost more on lap speeds than could be saved by a pit stop or two less.

The mooted 3-litre 16-cylinder engine was to have had one overhead camshaft per block, roller bearings throughout, and twin Roots-type superchargers giving two-stage blowing. Its manufacture and development would have cost Talbot a large sum of money not readily forthcoming. In any case, the second World War intervened, consigning this exciting project to the limbo of the "might-have-beens" in motor racing. Thanks to changing circumstances, however, Talbot's sports-based unblown six-cylinder unit had an unexpectedly bright future ahead of it.

Getting going
When the war was over, the French showed their innate love for motor racing, and their remarkable ability to overcome seemingly insuperable organisational problems when they really want to, by staging their first post-war race meeting on September 9th, 1945, a mere 3 weeks after the end of hostilities with Japan. Nor did they resort to some redundant airfield

for their race, but chose the Bois du Boulogne itself—Paris's Hyde Park!

The big event was the Coupe des Prisonniers for over-3-litre racing cars, and there amongst the runners was the Talbot *monoplace,* as handsome and impeccable as ever it was in 1939, indicating that regardless of Nazi occupation Lago had somehow contrived to preserve it unspoiled. This time it was driven by the gay and dashing Raymond Sommer. In view of tyre and fuel shortages the race was a short one—43 laps, 75 miles—and even Sommer the *Coeur de Lion* could not get the better of Wimille driving a supercharged 4.7-litre Bugatti. But the *monoplace* finished 2nd in only its 2nd race, after a six-year sleep.

Two remarkably busy seasons ensued for this Talbot. International racing resumed in 1946 under somewhat free and easy rulings that admitted almost any racing car that would run. Like the Alfa Romeos that in prewar days were raced for the company by the Scuderia Ferrari, so, now, the *monoplace* was raced by the Ecurie

France run by Paul Vallée, preparation of the car being at Suresnes. Talbot representation was also augmented by one of the 1939 offset GP cars and various pre-war sports 4- and 4½-litre models converted to racing trim.

The third race for the *monoplace* was the 1946 Nice GP, where the great Louis Chiron drove it to 6th place, dogged throughout by plug trouble. Then he scored two 2nd places, one on the Bois du Boulogne, the other in the GP de St Cloud. Back in the Bois yet again at end of season, Chiron smote a dog at 120 m.p.h. or so when lying 2nd, doing neither the dog nor the Talbot's handsome grille any good. During the winter spell Lago and his new chief engineer Carlo Marchetti put in some hard work on the car, squeezing perhaps another 10 b.h.p. from the engine, converting the brakes to hydraulic operation, and improving the suspension.

Its 1947 season began somewhat unexpectedly (and uncomfortably) on frozen Lake Vallentuna in Sweden, but the February cold did

Louis Chiron winning the 1947 French GP at Lyons in the Talbot "monoplace".
(The Motor)

Nose to tail at Montlhéry—Louis Rosier, winner of the 1948 Coupe du Salon, and second man Pierre Levegh in battle with their Talbot-Lagos.
(Louis Klemantaski)

not agree with it and Chiron retired. Another Ecurie France driver, Eugene Chaboud, drove at Pau, only to break a pushrod when lying second, but at Perpignan he won the GP de Roussillon—the first outright victory for the *monoplace*—and three weeks later won again, this time in the Marseilles GP over the truly tortuous 2.7 mile Prado circuit.

The significance of these successes was brought home by the sudden demand for new Talbots by drivers plodding along with their modified prewar sports models, and Lago and Marchetti took action, laying down a new design based very much on the old, but with an improved engine and sundry refinements. While this was gestating it was Chiron's turn to drive the *monoplace* again, and he placed 2nd in the Nimes GP, 2nd in the Marne GP, then won the Comminges GP at St. Gaudens, chased home hard by two sports-based Talbots in a fine 1-2-3 success.

Then came the first post-war French GP at Lyons, and, joy of joys for Talbot, Ecurie France and for France as a whole, Chiron and the gallant old *monoplace* won again, the "Wily Fox" nursing his car home with a blown gasket for the last few laps yet staving off the Maserati opposition to the finish. Now the news leaked from Suresnes that the new cars, to be called Talbot-Lagos, were actually under construction, and that 20 of them would be available for sale to private owners as well as the Ecurie France. Lago's order book filled long before the cars were ready, and one would-be customer at least, the English driver Leslie Brooke, grew tired of waiting and obtained a Maserati instead. For those more patient, the waiting generally proved worth while.

Enter the Talbot-Lago

Until 1948, the "ultimate" class in motor racing had been governed by what was called simply the Grand Prix Formula, but that year marked the introduction of the first Formula One, supplemented by Formula Two, formerly the voiturette class, and, later, Formula Three. The new Formula One permitted supercharged cars of up to 1½-litres, and unsupercharged up to 4½-litres capacity—the Formula, indeed, which would have been adopted in 1940 had not war intervened. It guaranteed the continued appearance of 1500cc. supercharged cars such as the famous Type 158 Alfa Romeos, the Maseratis, the British ERA, Alta etc., and of unsupercharged cars such as the new Talbot-Lagos, diverse old ones still in circulation, Delahayes and Delages.

As with most new Formulae, new cars took their time in appearing, and in Talbot's case the strikes which at that time plagued the French industry had a serious effect on production. The first Formula One race of all, the Pau GP on March 29th 1948, fell to a 1947 Maserati with sports-based Talbots 2-3-4 after Chiron's *monoplace* engine failed him. The GP of the Nations at Geneva was another Maserati success, Chiron's car again defecting. But the historic Monaco GP, revived for the first time since 1937, marked the debut of the new Talbot-Lago, driven, not by Chiron as many expected, but by the very promising driver from Clermont-

Ferrand, Louis Rosier, who had won the previous year's Albi GP in an old, rebodied 4-litre Talbot, and scored numerous creditable places elsewhere.

As Chiron's *monoplace* was also competing (the "Wily Fox" probably preferred his old, well-proven car to a new, untried example built under tricky labour conditions) it was possible to compare the old and the new cars. Externally they were very similar both in shape and dimensions, but the "Lago" was slightly lower, had a shorter, less comely nose with a wider grille, hefty twin exhaust pipes on the nearside of the car, and a circular carburettor air tube on the offside of the bonnet, rather marring the clean lines. These features were the clue to important under-bonnet novelties.

Although still basically the time-honoured six-cylinder sports-type engine, the Lago-Marchetti design team had replaced the single camshaft and angled pushrod system of valve operation with twin camshafts high in the crankcase, operating overhead valves inclined at 95 deg. to each other in a hemispherical head through short pushrods and rockers each side of the cylinder head. This was a system first used on the Belgian Pipe car back in 1904, by Riley for their very successful Nine in 1926, through Riley by ERA on their pre-war racing voiturettes, and by Talbot themselves since 1946 on their 4½-litre Lago-Record production Grand Touring model, thus once again emphasising that, where Tony Lago was concerned, "Today's sports-car was tomorrow's racing-car". The "high cam" system plus big valves provided excellent breathing with light reciprocating parts without the complication and cost of twin overhead camshafts driven either by gears or a shaft, and Marchetti's skilful adaptation to the existing 7-bearing lower end must have saved considerably on costs.

The alloy cylinder head was detachable from the alloy block, the bore and stroke were, as before, 93 × 110 mm., giving 4,482cc., and the power output in early 1948 form was *circa* 240 b.h.p. at 4700 r.p.m. on an 8:1 compression ratio. Carburation was by down-draught instruments this time, triple Zenith-Strombergs as before, but now mounted on the offside of the engine, with the circular air tube outside the bonnet also embodying a filter and a gauze flame trap. There were now two rocker covers instead of one, with the plugs in between; ignition was by Scintilla magneto, and dry sump lubrication was employed, as before, with the two finned oil coolers lying flush in the scuttle as on the *monoplace*.

Transmission was via a single dry-plate clutch to a Wilson 4-speed epicyclic gearbox, a heavy but favoured component which enabled the driver by use of a column-mounted lever to preselect the gear he requires at the next corner well before he gets there; a quick stab at the clutch pedal at the crucial point and the requisite gear is engaged without his hands having to leave the steering wheel. Correctly maintained, the Wilson box was a strong component, very useful also for providing braking power.

Behind the gearbox, the propeller shaft was offset considerably to the right by spur gears,

Theory: end section of the 1½-litre, 2-stage supercharged V-16 cylinder Talbot-Lago engine with roller-bearing crankshaft and twin "shoulder" camshafts. It was never built.

Practice: end section of the 4½-litre unsupercharged six-cylinder Talbot-Lago engine, showing the two "high" camshafts and pushrods.

Lagos and pre-Lagos; five Talbots storming out of Thillois during the 1948 French GP, Chiron's 4½-litre 1939-type monoplace *heading the Lagos of Etancelin and Comotti, the 1939 "offset" single-seater of Giraud-Cabantous, and Raph's Lago.*
(The Motor)

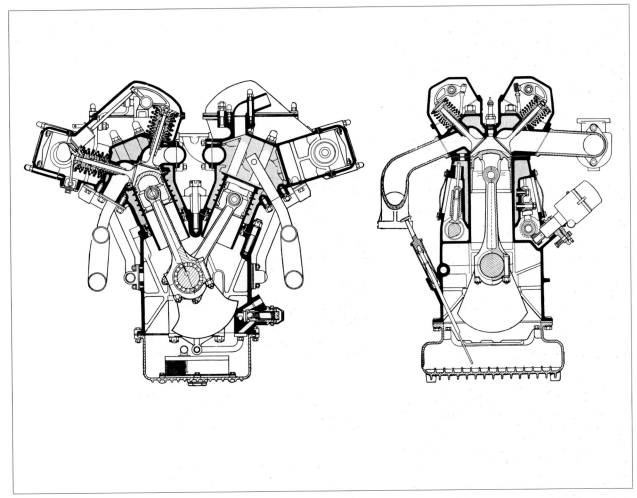

enabling the driver's seat to be set below the transmission line, the leather-covered tunnel actually serving as the right arm rest of the seat. The final drive differential housing was also off-set on the rear axle, still the old-fashioned "live" type with exposed semi-elliptic "cart springs". Ideally Lago may have yearned for a good independent rear suspension system, but he simply hadn't the capital nor the time to develop one; meanwhile the old time-tried system served well, was strong, and fortified his argument that he based his racing cars on Talbot production models.

The box-section frame and transverse leaf spring independent front suspension all re-appeared, but the car had Lockheed hydraulic brakes with 16 in. diameter alloy drums, and a more practical, if less graceful, appearance than the *monoplace* thanks to a shorter, blunter nose with wider radiator grille. The vertical slats in the grille had given way to simple wire mesh——not so elegant perhaps, but less delicate, cheaper, and easier to replace or repair if damaged.

The philosophy behind these cars was that, being supplied principally to private stables which would often prepare them themselves, they should be strong and reliable, and require less maintenance than the higher-stressed, more delicate supercharged cars. Lago and Marchetti endeavoured to keep the weight down, but the cars were frankly heavy at 18 cwt. unladen compared with their principal 1948 rivals, the all-conquering Alfa Romeo type 158 1½-litre blown straight-eights at 16.3 cwt. and the new Maserati 4CLT/48 blown 1½-litre fours at 15.2 cwt., but Lago was relying on two factors—reliability and low fuel consumption—to make the big blue cars from Suresnes competitive.

The new car did not do well first time out— they rarely do—and Rosier's Monaco GP ended after 16 laps with engine trouble emphasised by what a pre-diesel age *Autocar* called "a cloud of steam that would do credit to British Railways". But Chiron's gallant old *monoplace* more than atoned by finishing a strong 2nd to Farina's winning Maserati, with one of the 1939 offset GP cars driven by Yves Giraud-Cabantous adding to the legend of Talbot longevity by placing 6th.

Subsequent races saw this trio of Talbots in friendly rivalry, with interesting results. In the Paris GP at Montlhéry, Cabantous in the "offset" led all the way to win, Chiron in the *monoplace* came 2nd, while Rosier in the "Lago" duelled with him and passed, only to depart the race in a cloud of smoke heralding an engine derangement. They next went to Italy for the San Remo GP, where the "Lago" placed 5th, the *monoplace* 6th and the "offset" 9th, though none of them could cope with the latest 4CLT /48 Maseratis. At the GP of Europe in Switzerland Rosier's "Lago" was joined by a second example, just completed and driven by Gianfranco Comotti, the Italian who had won the 1937 TT in Britain for Talbot. Both he and Rosier retired early with broken oil pipes, whereas the older cars soldiered on to 6th and 8th, well behind the fierce supercharged cars.

Two more "Lagos" were ready in time for the

"Phi-Phi" Etancelin does his best to hold off the Alfa Romeo opposition in the 1948 French G.P. at Rheims, helped by live rear axle limitations.

French GP, one for the famous Philippe Etancelin, the other for the amateur "Georges Raph", whose real name was Béthenod de las Casas. Neither new nor old Talbots could do anything about the Alfa Romeos which romped home 1-2-3, but the "Lagos" were 4-5-6 in the order Comotti, Raph, Rosier, with Chiron's older car back in 9th position, while Etancelin retired. The "Lagos" now settled down to the role of "place fillers", Raph, Chiron and Rosier taking 2-3-4 behind a Maserati at Comminges, while "Phi-Phi" Etancelin and Rosier were 2-3 at Albi, where Raph unwisely mixed it with Chiron and suffered a spectacular inversion and a fractured skull, while Comotti fought enterprisingly with Villoresi for the lead, only to hit oil and spin out of the race.

At Monza for the Italian GP, Rosier, Comotti and Etancelin were 6-7-8 behind the blown cars. In the revived British GP (last held in 1927) at Silverstone Rosier was 4th, while Chiron, forsaking his beloved *monoplace* at last for a "Lago" acquired by the Ecurie France, retired with a seized gearbox. Then came the Coupe du Salon at Montlhéry and the first outright win for the Talbot-Lago; more than that, a 1-2-3 placing for Rosier, Levegh and Cabantous, albeit against somewhat spavined Maseratis and ERAs. Yet another driver, Eugene Chaboud, now joined the band of *Lago-istes*, placing 6th in the Monza GP and 5th at Garda, while for their final 1948 fling, Chiron and Rosier took 3rd and 4th places at Barcelona in the Penya Rhin GP. So the Talbot-Lago became a regular part of the GP scene, clearly no circuit-searing *bolide* but a good, tough slogger, its strength lying in its reliability, its frugal thirst of 9 m.p.g. of petrol-benzole against the blown cars' 3 or 4 m.p.g., and the fable of the hare and the tortoise.

O   3ft

O   1m

The 4½-litre, 6-cylinder Grand Prix Lago–Talbot in which Louis Rosier won the 1949 Belgian Grand Prix at Spa, at an average speed of 96.95 m.p.h. (154.92 k.p.h.)
James Leech © *Profile Publications Ltd.*

1949—Miracle year

The charm of motor racing lies in its uncertainty, although some things are more certain than others, one being that, when the fabulous Alfa Romeo 158s raced, they won. They won, in fact, 17 times and lost only 4 times between mid-1938 and the end of 1948, and had won every *Grande Epreuve* contested since July 1946, ten in a row.

It came as a surprise, therefore, and to some factions a relief, when Alfa Romeo announced their withdrawal from GP racing for 1949. They had lost their three top drivers, Wimille and Varzi in crashes, Trossi through illness; they were busy on a new production model, the 1900; and, it was said, dollar donors for postwar rehabilitation of Alfa were displeased at the amount being spent on motor racing. Whatever the reasons, their withdrawal threw Grand Prix racing wide open. The "also rans", the "place fillers", the Maseratis, Talbot-Lagos and the threatening new 12-cylinder supercharged Ferraris, all had a chance to win now, and with a new Argentine-sponsored Maserati team led by a man named Fangio also joining in, 1949 prospects looked decidedly bright.

None but minor changes were made to the Talbot-Lagos, which still churned out their *circa* 240 b.h.p. at 4700 r.p.m., and although the proposed batch of 20 cars was still incomplete, at least eight were now in circulation with more on the way from the Suresnes factory. Without embarking on an exhaustive race-by-race review of Talbot's 1949 fortunes, that season confirmed what was apparent in 1948—that the big, burly French cars, less accelerative than their blown rivals, were unhappy on twisting courses such as Pau or San Remo, and equally unhappy in races split into short heats and a final. Long-distance racing was their true element, the longer the better, for only then could their low fuel consumption, rugged reliability and milder tyre wear pay off.

Their first win was an easy one in the Paris GP at Montlhéry, where supercharged opposition was minimal, and 52-year-old Etancelin, 44-year-old Cabantous, and 32-year-old Claes, the Belgian, finished 1-2-3. 43-year-old Louis Rosier then gave a hint of things to come by placing 3rd in the 300-mile British GP at Silverstone, where he drove his heavy car for 3 hrs. 53 mins. 50 secs. non-stop, an indication of the stamina required in GP racing a little over 20 years ago. Then Etancelin took a fine 2nd to the Argentine prodigy Fangio in the Marseille GP despite a very wiggly and non-Talbot kind of circuit.

A Grand Prix for Rosier

The scene then moved to Belgium, where a quiet win in the Frontières GP at Chimay by a new *Lago-iste,* Frenchman Guy Mairesse, was followed a fortnight later by an outstanding victory for Louis Rosier in the Belgian GP itself. This was a 315-mile race on the famous Spa-Francorchamps circuit in the Ardennes, and three of the new 1½-litre supercharged V-12 Ferraris and five 4CLT/48 Maseratis opposed five Talbots.

It proved a race of attrition in which every Maserati but one retired, and three of the Talbots, too, dropped out. For the rest, although the Ferraris were far faster than the French cars, they wore out their tyres and had to change wheels as well as refuel. The competent, canny Rosier, well aware of all this, set a fast consistent pace and never stopped from start to finish 3¼ hours later to win at 96.82 m.p.h. from the three Ferraris of Villoresi, Ascari and Whitehead. In the words of *Autocar* it was "one of the best deserved and most popular victories in Spa-Francorchamps history".

So the Talbot-Lago had won a major Grand Prix, and Italian journals indignant at the defeat of their cars spoke of the "ponderous, ancient" Talbot which robbed them of their rights. The glow of this triumph sustained the Talbots through the Swiss GP at Berne, where Ascari and Villoresi avenged their Spa defeat by heading the "Lagos" of Sommer and Etancelin, and next on the agenda came the French GP at Rheims. And there, to the joy of the crowd, the "ponderous" Talbots did it again, rounding on the Italians to score another victory for racing blue.

This time Louis Chiron was the architect of victory, driving the 310 miles non-stop, and if Peter Whitehead, British driver of a blown Ferrari, was extremely unlucky to have gear change trouble when leading with 7 laps to go, allowing Chiron to pass, this ability of the Talbot-Lago always to be in close attendance to the faster cars was their *forte,* allied to the old master Chiron's heady skill in driving what began as a brand new and tight car, and ended up "nicely run in" after averaging 99.98 m.p.h. ! Other Lagos placed 4-5-7, and an unexpected Talbot pilot for the day was the Italian Farina, who retired after 12 laps before he really got the hang of preselector motor racing.

For that memorable French GP, the Talbot of "Phi-Phi" Etancelin had been fitted with a

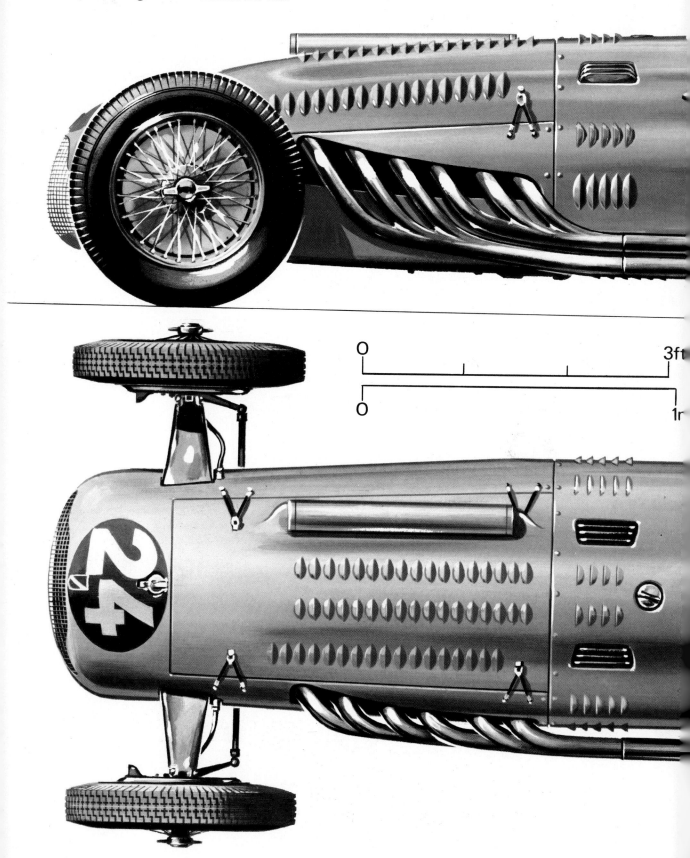

O 3ft

O 1r

new 12-plug head and twin magnetos. It availed him not, for he retired early, but his day was to come seven weeks later in the GP of Europe at Monza, Italy. This forceful and immensely popular French veteran, who won his first race in 1925 and was characterised by his cap reversed back to front, his gritted teeth and whirling elbows, put on a typical "tiger" performance on Ferraris' home ground, and though he could not master new star Alberto Ascari in the new 2-stage supercharged Ferrari, he got well ahead of everyone else in a fiery non-stop drive with his 12-plug Talbot to finish a fighting second.

A fortnight later a single Ferrari again denied Etancelin an outright win with his *vettura poderosa e anziana* in the GP of Czechoslovakia at Brno. This was a reverse of Talbot's French GP fortune, for this time Etancelin had taken the lead from Whitehead's Ferrari 6 laps from the finish; three laps later his motor began to misfire, and although he fought back, and repassed the Ferrari, he had to give best with two broken valve springs, nursing his car home to a brilliant second place. Said one Italian paper, "Both Whitehead and Etancelin deserved victory; Etancelin was the most spectacular driver and would well have merited the laurels. It was a pity his Talbot failed at the critical moment...". Talbot's "Rheims luck" had been redressed.

Nicely rounding off the "Lagos" best season, Raymond Sommer won the GP du Salon at Montlhéry, despite being involved in a lap 1 crash which put out two other Talbots and a Ferrari. He tore back into the race, broke the circuit lap record, and won at 92.38 m.p.h. in real Sommer style; followed home by two more "Lagos" driven by Harry Schell and Meyrat.

Two major GP wins, three lesser ones, two major 2nds and the French Championship (to Louis Rosier).... Tony Lago could spend a winter of content after these feats by his "sportscars in GP suits", were it not for the French post-war system of taxation which was badly restricting sales of Talbot production models.

He had, in fact, entertained hopes that year of building a new, supercharged V-16 1½-litre engine to fit into the Lago frame and transmission. Broadly following the pattern of the 3-litre 16-cylinder engine projected in 1939, it was to have a single overhead camshaft on the outside "shoulder" of each bank of eight cylinders, with pushrods across the head operating the inner valves through rockers. There was also to be two-stage Roots-type supercharging, but Lago could not obtain the financial support to build such an ambitious engine, and had to fall back on his trusty sixes (see page 31).

The year 1950 marked the return to the fray after a season's absence of the Alfa Romeo team, and the supercharged Ferraris found themselves eclipsed by these swift, mature performers. Whether to combat them with higher-boost, higher-stressed 1½-litre blown cars, or to try the unblown road taken by Talbot, was the Ferrari designer Aurelio Lampredi's problem, and after some initial rebuffs with the blown cars, he took Talbot's lesson to heart (Etancelin's 2nd place to Ascari's two-stage blown Ferrari at Monza in 1949 had particularly impressed him) and began development of unsupercharged engines.

Raymond Sommer the lion-hearted has his Lago ahead of at least one Alfa Romeo on lap 1 of the GP of the Nations at Geneva, 1950. His car has extra louvres cut in the nose to cope with hot weather.
(Louis Klemantaski)

Monaco melée on the opening lap of the 1950 race resulted when Farina's Alfa Romeo spun on a corner splashed by sea waves, eliminating nine cars at a stroke. Etancelin's Lago is seen squeezing through, followed by Bira's Maserati.

Talbot territory. The Lagos won four times at the Montlhéry circuit outside Paris. Here they lead away in the Paris GP of 1950, won by Grignard in No. 8, led by Sommer and Rosier who both retired.
(Keystone Press Agency Ltd.)

The Talbots, meanwhile, were a year older and little advanced, but Marchetti now fitted triple horizontal 50HN Zenith downdraught carburettors, raised the compression to 11 : 1, fitted a stronger crankshaft, and built some more twin ignition, 12-plug heads. 280 b.h.p. at 5000 r.p.m. was the result, at cost of a humpier bonnet, but these engines weren't ready until May, 1950. Rosier and Etancelin had meantime accepted an invitation to race at Mar del Plata and Rosario in the Argentine. An 8th and a 6th and two retirements was the modest result, despite "Phi-Phi's" elaborate precautions against South American summer heat of an iced cabbage leaf inside his helmet, a funnel on the scuttle directing cooling air through a rubber pipe on to his clutch foot, and a tin full of lemon slices in the cockpit.

But back in Europe at Pau in April, Rosier was one of four drivers who broke Mercedes' pre-war lap record for the tight street circuit, and he took a non-stop 3rd place, while a week later the first 1950 "Lago" win went to Georges Grignard in the Paris GP. With eleven starters and three finishers, this was clearly a survival of the fittest, and Sommer broke his Talbot after knocking 3½ secs. off his old lap record.

The new triple-Zenith 12-plug works car turned up at Silverstone for the GP of Europe, and driver Giraud-Cabantous outpaced Rosier and Etancelin to score 4th behind the inevitable Alfa Romeos, while at Berne in the Swiss GP Rosier drove the car to a brilliant 3rd place, all of which was encouraging.

Talbot radiator badge

1950 Le Mans winner: Louis Rosier's 4482 cc. sports-racing two-seater version of the Grand Prix Lago–Talbot, in which he won the classic 24-hour event at an average speed of 89.72 m.p.h. (139.55 k.p.h.) for 2153.2 miles (3445.12 km.)
James Leech © *Profile Publications Ltd.*

Le Mans interlude

From then on that year it was largely Rosier. This sage and crafty *Clermontois* saw the potential of the sturdy, frugal "Lago" in sports-car racing, and for Le Mans 1950 had one of the GP cars converted to a two-seater by fitting a widened body and offset steering. The compression was slightly lowered, and wings, lamps, a battery and a silencer were fitted. Louis Rosier nominated himself and his son Jean-Louis to drive the car, but in fact drove all but 20 minutes of the 24 hours himself, an impressive feat of physical endurance. Despite the loss of 25 minutes changing a broken rocker, they won Le Mans 1950 by 10 miles, and behind them came another Talbot, one of the 1939 offset cars bewinged and headlamped, driven by Meyrat and Mairesse. Moreover Rosier set the fastest lap at a record 102.83 m.p.h., making it a veritable joy-weekend for Lago.

Having struck a successful vein, Rosier kept it up. Back to Formula One the following weekend, he took another brilliant third between the Alfas in the Belgian GP, the race he won outright the year before. Hero of the day was tempestuous Raymond Sommer in another Talbot, who maintained such a pace that when the Alfas refuelled at half-distance he led the entire race for four laps. Then, alas, he blew up, and Alfa Romeo took up their customary victory formation with Rosier dogging them in the works car, now fitted with lightened brake drums and backplates. That Alfas were not infallible when pushed hard became evident when Farina's oil pressure began to wilt, and Rosier passed him, wearing, according to *Motor,* "an expression of great contentment" as he took third place.

The French GP at Rheims was not so good, the Talbots covering themselves in confusion and steam as one after another they boiled. 5-6-8 to Etancelin, Rosier and Cabantous was all they could manage, and it later emerged that new type radiator blocks, formed in two vertical halves butting against each other, did not register correctly so that the air passage through their honeycomb sections was impeded. Suresnes obviously got them right in time for the Albi GP, where Rosier went through to another of his surefooted victories, winning on the

Louis Rosier's winning Talbot at the pits, Le Mans 1950. The single-seater body has been replaced by a two-seater, but the Lago origins are obvious.

The Rosier Talbot at speed. How many modern GP cars could win a 24 Hours endurance race? (Louis Klemantaski)

Johnny Claes the Belgian with his yellow-painted Talbot-Lago in the 1950 Dutch GP. He won a race at Goodwood the following year with this car.
(Louis Klemantaski)

Raymond Sommer, fastest of the Talbot drivers, leading the 1950 Dutch GP at Zandvoort. This aspect shows the air tube for the triple carburettors.
(Louis Klemantaski)

This French GP line-up sums up the Formula 1 situation in 1950, the supercharged Type 158 Alfa Romeos hogging the front row, with the unblown Talbots and blown Maseratis behind.
(The Motor)

Hors de course— Louveau's Lago looks sorry for itself after running out of road at Berne during the very slippery 1951 Swiss GP; another Talbot passes by.
(Planet News Ltd.)

aggregate of two heats without winning either!

Once again the race hero was Sommer, who made a spectacular last-lap dash in Heat 1 to pass Fangio's Maserati on the very finishing line, the Talbot sliding madly and hitting the bales beyond so hard that it was too damaged to run again! Fangio also retired, so in Heat 2 cunning old Rosier sat just behind leader Gonzalez, whom he had beaten into 3rd place in Heat 1, secure in the knowledge that so long as he kept him in sight he could not fail to win on overall times. A week later he won the Dutch GP at Zandvoort, where the gallant Sommer built up a big lead over the rival Ferraris and Maseratis until a rocker broke, and non-stop Rosier moved ahead, his offside rear tyre minus most of its tread and saved only by a wet circuit.

In the Pescara GP in August it was Rosier, again who drove the highest-placed Talbot. With two refuel stops to allow for, the Alfa Romeos were much harassed by his pace—the Talbot clocked 166.5 m.p.h. through the flying kilometre—and when Fagioli's car had last-lap front suspension trouble the Frenchman nipped past to take second place. As Rodney Walkerley wrote in *The Motor*, "Even the Alfas cannot afford a moment's inattention with Rosier behind in his non-stop Talbot". In the Italian GP he and Etancelin were 4th and 5th, behind two Alfas and an unblown Ferrari, now becoming a real menace to the blown cars, and in the Spanish GP Etancelin placed 4th behind three of the unblown Ferraris, while Rosier for once had to retire. He became Champion of France just the same, for the second year.

A 500 Miles victory

The European season over, three Talbot-Lagos were shipped to South America to contest the Argentine 500 Miles race at Raffaela, staged over a very fast 5½ mile course, much of which was dirt-surfaced! The race, after two postponements, took place on December 24th, and Tony Lago had an extra Christmas present in a wire telling him of a Talbot 1-2 victory. Juan Manuel Fangio drove the winning car at the sizzling average of 111.05 m.p.h. in a race lasting over 4½ hours, while Louis Rosier followed in 1 minute behind. The third car, driven by Froilan Gonzalez, had to retire with ignition trouble. With dust and heat to contend with, this was an intensely gruelling race both for cars and drivers, and Rosier declared that it was "decidedly harder than Le Mans".

By 1951 the Talbots were verily becoming ancient as well as ponderous, and with the Alfa Romeo-Ferrari battle mounting to a climax, and the 1½-litre blown cars at last falling before the unblown 4½-litres' onslaught, the French cars which had pointed the way for Ferrari were well out of the hunt in the major Grands Prix. Yet there were still pickings to be had, and Rosier, whose skill has never been fully appreciated, carried off two more wins, in the Bordeaux and Dutch GPs, and three 2nds at Pau, Albi and Pescara, for the second successive year, this time behind the forceful Gonzalez in a 4½-litre Ferrari. It was Gonzalez who, earlier that year, had borrowed Rosier's 1950 Le Mans car and drove it, stripped of wings and other impedimenta to a fighting 2nd place behind Farina's Maserati in the Paris GP, while Rosier came third.

Another second place, albeit unofficial, was scored by a spectacular new *Lago-iste*, the British driver Duncan Hamilton, in the unique 1951 International Trophy race at Silverstone which was stopped by a tremendous rainstorm after 6 laps. Parnell in the Thinwall Ferrari and Hamilton got out ahead of the factory Alfa Romeos, and stayed there until the race was stopped. Hamilton took especial pleasure in passing Fangio in clouds of water and spray— "Never get another chance!" he chuckled, and the Lago-Talbot fulfilled his love for big, beefy cars. While his splendid story that "you could tell which gear you were in by looking at the height of the flames coming off the rear tyres!" spoke perhaps too well of Talbot-Lago acceleration, they could certainly generate plenty of wheelspin and rubber smoke under a heavy throttle foot such as Hamilton's, and he was always a popular performer with his green-painted Lago at Goodwood and elsewhere.

The irrepressible Duncan Hamilton with his Talbot in typical stance at Silverstone, 1951. (Geoffrey Goddard)

The newer unblown 4½-litre Ferraris leave the older unblown 4½-litre Talbots at the start of the 1951 Pescara GP in Italy——but Louis Rosier, the "old dependable", was second at the finish. (Planet News Ltd.)

Yves Giraud-Cabantous burns rear wheel rubber as he "powers" his Talbot-Lago out of Thillois, French GP, 1951. (Motor Sport)

The great Louis Chiron, winner of the French GP in 1947 and 1949 with Talbots, seen in the 1951 race at Rheims coming down the long tree-lined straight to Thillois. (The Motor)

The end begins

The somewhat abrupt decision late in 1951 to abandon Formula One for all major Grands Prix in 1952, and substitute Formula Two (up to 2-litres unsupercharged) brought a cry of anguish, not only from BRM of Britain, but from Major Lago too. *"C'est insensé"* he declared. At Suresnes, he said, they were preparing two new 4½-litre Formula One cars and two sportscars for Le Mans, as well as a 2-litre F2 racing car based on the abortive CTA-Arsenal built in 1947 and handed over to Lago for further development. This was a long-term development, however, he said, and all his hopes centred on the big cars; they had increased the power and saved about 150 kg. on the chassis. . . .

It was all in vain. The race organisers and the FIA were adamant, and at a stroke the 4½-litre Talbot-Lago was rendered even more obsolete than some critics declared it was already. A further blow came when their staunchest supporter, Louis Rosier, (who won the French Championship for the third time in 1951) forsook them to drive a 4½-litre Ferrari of 1951 type, and clearly the "Lago's" day was nearly done. Yet they appeared in the most unlikely places during 1952. At Buenos Aires Crespo took 4th place behind three Ferraris; at Piriapolis in Uruguay Maurice Trintignant took a 6th and a 9th; at Turin the *anziane* Talbots of Claes and Swaters placed 5th and 6th; at Helsinki the Belgian Roger Laurent won the Finnish GP; at Albi, that happy Talbot hunting ground, Cabantous and Crespo took 3rd and 4th; at Dundrod, Northern Ireland, Etancelin took 5th; at Boreham, Essex, now the home of the Ford Competition Department, the tireless Etancelin pipped Rosier's Ferrari for 3rd place; and in Australia, Doug Whiteford in the ex-Chiron "Lago" which won the 1949 French GP took first place in the Australian GP on the spectacular Mount Panorama circuit at Bathurst.

On the sports-car side, things began well with Pozzi and Vincent winning the Casablanca 12 Hours race from Ferrari, with Trintignant contributing fastest lap before retiring, but none of this could compensate for the bitter blow Talbot were to suffer at Le Mans in 1952. They had prepared two special cars with handsome up-to-the minute all-enveloping bodywork for Levegh/Marchand and Chaboud/Pozzi. The latter pair retired early, but Pierre Levegh had built up a 4-lap lead over two works Mercedes by ½-distance, and went on extending it.

Then the stubborn little Frenchman, eager perhaps to outdo Rosier's remarkable 23 hour 40 min. stint of 1950, made a bid to drive the entire 24 hours unrelieved, despite pleas from friends and colleagues to let Marchand take over for a spell. Alas, with 1¼ hours only between him and clearcut victory, Levegh's weariness caused him to mis-select a gear on the Wilson box; the revs. rose sky-high, a connecting rod broke—and France's victory fell to two Mercedes-Benz from Germany. Out of this tragedy, came an infinitely more terrible one. Mercedes were so impressed by Levegh's performance that when they sought drivers for their team of 300 SLRs at Le Mans in 1955, they offered him a place. Levegh accepted—and his was the car that, after colliding with an Austin Healey, hit a

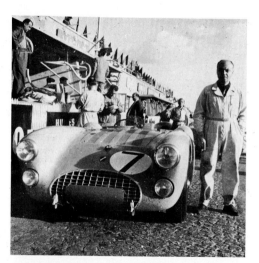

Pierre Levegh, who so nearly won Le Mans 1952 without a co-driver, seen with the same car a year later, when he finished 8th sharing the wheel with Charles Pozzi.
(Louis Klemantaski)

The Talbot-Lago six-cylinder three-carburettor unsupercharged engine.
(Louis Klemantaski)

bank and disintegrated, killing 81 people and Levegh himself . . . .

The Talbot twilight deepened in 1953, but there came last kicks from "Phi-Phi" Etancelin, who brought both himself and his trusty Lago out of retirement to finish a fighting 3rd to two works Ferraris in the Rouen GP before his fellow-*Rouennais*; and from Doug Whiteford and his ex-Chiron car down under, the combination winning their second consecutive Australian GP, this time on the Albert Park circuit in Melbourne. After duelling with Stan Jones' Maybach Special he looked like winning in typical Talbot non-stop style, only to be rudely interrupted by a burst tyre two laps from the finish. He won just the same. It was the Lago-Talbot's last success of any importance.

In sports-car racing, one of the Le Mans cars was sent to Morocco to try for a repeat of Talbot's 1952 win, but the works Ferraris also decided to go, so Etancelin and Levegh had to rest content with third place. Then Rosier temporarily rejoined the Suresnes fold and shared a Talbot with Cabantous for 2nd place in the Rheims 12 Hours, and at the end of the season he took the car to Mexico for the great Pan-American Road Race. Putting up a typical "stonewall" performance, Rosier let the fliers set the initial pace, preserving his car while the field thinned out, then placed 5th in the final three stages and 5th overall behind three works Lancias and a Ferrari—and with a basically 1948 car against the latest V6s and V12s, none could have done better.

Finis

By 1954 it was all over, even "Lagos" converted to sports-cars having a thin time against the modern flood of Jaguars, Ferraris, Maseratis, Aston Martins and Gordinis. Two of the big blue cars lurked for several years in the garages under the banking at Montlhéry, one served to pace Jose Méiffret, the famous racing cyclist, in an unsuccessful attempt on the cycle speed record of 109 m.p.h., the Talbot's shapely tail replaced by a vertical board to break the wind

pressure; others ended up in museums where one can admire the rugged build and functional shape of these Grand Prix cars of yesterday; while in Britain, where we are so fortunate to have vintage and historic racing, two Lago-Talbots can still be seen and heard in action, one a two-seater conversion, the other a genuine single-seater.

Talbot's last racing throes were at Le Mans, where they tried each year until 1957 for elusive success. A year later Automobiles Talbot was sold to the Simca concern, and Antonio Lago retired. Born of expedience under economic strictures, a design compromise which at least fitted it both for Grand Prix and sports-car racing, the Talbot-Lago did more than many far costlier cars. Five major Grands Prix, nine lesser ones, and the Le Mans laurels in 1950 . . . . Tony Lago in his retiring years could look back on a remarkable chapter of accomplishment, and in a decade marred by far too many fatal crashes he would say with special pride *"Jamais personne ne s'est tué dans une de mes voitures"*—"nobody was ever killed in one of my cars". He himself died at the age of 68 late in 1960.

Pierre Levegh the unlucky, leading Le Mans 1952 in the rebodied Talbot-Lago. He drove without relief for nearly 23 hours, then overrevved and broke a connecting rod. (Louis Klemantaski)

Henri Louveau waits patiently while his mechanic "reads" a sparking plug during practice for the 1951 International Trophy at Silverstone—the race that was drowned out by a tremendous freak storm. (Keystone Press Agency Ltd.)

Louis Rosier, the most successful Talbot-Lago exponent, won six Formula 1 races and the 1950 Le Mans 24 Hours GP d'Endurance with the Suresnes cars.

The Talbot-Lago X-rayed, showing the offset propeller shaft and final drive. It was the last Grand Prix car to employ semi-elliptic rear springing. (The Motor)

TALBOT-LAGO RACE VICTORIES

1948
Coupe du Salon, Montlhéry. (L. Rosier)

1949
Paris GP, Montlhéry. (P. Etancelin)
GP des Frontières, Chimay. (G. Mairesse)
Belgian GP, Spa-Francorchamps. (L. Rosier)
French GP, Rheims. (L. Chiron)
GP du Salon, Montlhéry. (R. Sommer)

1950
Paris GP, Montlhéry. (G. Grignard)
Le Mans 24 Hours Race. (L. Rosier/J.-L. Rosier)
Albi GP (L. Rosier)
Dutch GP, Zandvoort. (L. Rosier)
Argentine 500 Miles, Raffaela. (J. M. Fangio)

1951
Bordeaux GP (L. Rosier)
Dutch GP, Zandvoort. (L. Rosier)

1952
Casablanca 12 Hours (Sports-cars). (Pozzi/Vincent)
GP of Finland, Helsinki. (R. Laurent)
Australian GP, Bathurst. (D. Whiteford)

1953
Australian GP, Albert Park. (D. Whiteford).

SPECIFICATION OF 4½-LITRE TALBOT-LAGO GP CAR

ENGINE
Cylinders 6 in line
Cooling system Water; front-mounted radiator
Bore 93 mm. (3.66 in.)
Stroke 110 mm. (4.33 in.)
Capacity 4482cc. (273.69 cu. in.)
Valve gear Inclined o.h.v. operated by two high-set camshafts, pushrods and rockers
Compression ratio 8:1 (1948–49 cars); 11:1 (1950 onwards)
Carburettors 3 Zenith-Stromberg downdraught, later horizontal
Maximum power 1948–49 240 b.h.p. at 4700 r.p.m.; 1950 280 b.h.p. at 5000 r.p.m.

TRANSMISSION
Final drive Offset open propeller shaft
Clutch Single dry-plate
Gearbox Wilson preselector, 4 speeds

SUSPENSION
Front Independent by transverse leaf spring and "solid" top wishbones; hydraulic shock absorbers
Rear Non-independent by semi-elliptic leaf springs and rigid, one-piece axle, hydraulic shock absorbers

BRAKES
Make & type Lockheed hydraulic drum; 16 in. diameter

WHEELS
Type Rudge-Whitworth wire racing, quick-release hubs
Tyres—make Dunlop or Engelbert

DIMENSIONS
Wheelbase 8 ft 2.5 in. (250 cm.)
Track front 4 ft 6 in. (137 cm.), rear 4 ft 3.5 in. (130 cm.)
Unladen weight 18 cwt. (914.4 kg.)
Laden weight 22 cwt. (1117.6 kg.)

PERFORMANCE
Maximum speed 166.5 m.p.h. (Rosier, Pescara, 1950)

Nearly a winner first time out; Jack Brabham in the brand-new BT19 in the 1966 South African GP at East London

The Guv'nor — "Black Jack" himself, and Chief Mechanic Roy Billington pore over the brand-new BT19's Repco engine in the paddock at East London

The F1 Repco-Brabhams 1966–1968

by Doug Nye

The Formula One Repco-Brabhams won two double World Championships in 1966 and 1967, taking the Manufacturers' title in both seasons and adding Drivers' Championships for Jack Brabham himself, and in 1967 for his team-mate, Denny Hulme.

January 1, 1966, had marked the introduction of a new 3-litre Grand Prix racing Formula. These new regulations had been announced in November, 1963, when a Formula One capacity limit of only $1\frac{1}{2}$-litres was in force, and the two years' grace given before their introduction saw all the regular Grand Prix teams either designing and developing new engines, or casting around for suitable units from outside suppliers.

BRM in England and Ferrari in Italy both produced complex new multi-cylinder engines, but the backbone of Formula One racing had been the English "special builders", like Brabham, Cooper and Lotus, who built chassis around other people's engines. Throughout the $1\frac{1}{2}$-litre Formula (which ran from 1961–1965) the "other people" had been Coventry-Climax, but they would not be building 3-litre engines and so the hunt was on for alternative suppliers. Cooper went to Maserati, Lotus to Ford of Dagenham, and Brabham—eventually—found salvation 12,000 miles from their English base in Repco's Melbourne works, in Australia.

Genesis
Jack Brabham and Ron Tauranac met in Australia just post-war when they were racing against each other in national road events and

hill-climbs. Brabham had turned to road racing —first with a Cooper 500 and later with a Cooper-Bristol—from the rough-and-tumble of dirt track midget racing, and Tauranac built his own 500cc car with his brother Austin, combined their initials, and called it the Ralt Mark 1.

Although they were rivals on the track, Brabham and Tauranac worked together behind the scenes; Jack doing some of Ron's machining on his never-ending Ralt development programme, and Ron sorting-out the Brabham car's suspension. Both were regular customers of the Repco "Replacement Parts" service, and therein lies a tale....

Geoffrey Russell had founded Replacement Parts Pty Ltd in Melbourne in the 'twenties, and specialized in making parts for imported cars when such components were in short supply from overseas. His empire boomed, and when it went public in 1937 it adopted the Repco brand name (derived from "Replacement Parts") as its corporate title. Post-war, Repco was a friend in need to the Australian racing fraternity, and the group mushroomed to produce all kinds of original automotive equipment, and also entered the service, machine tool and textile fields.

In 1955 Brabham came to Europe and began an International race driving career which earned him a double World Championship with Cooper Cars in 1959 and 1960. On his return to Australia after his successful 1959 season, he talked Tauranac into joining him in England to set up their own racing car business. Ron and his wife Norma arrived at Easter, 1960, and he designed the first "Brabham" racing car which appeared in 1961 Formula Junior events as the "MRD"—initials for "Motor Racing Developments", which was the new Brabham-Tauranac business.

During the winter of 1961—62 the partners found premises in Victoria Road, Surbiton, and did a deal with Repco's UK marketing organization whereby Repco took over the warehousing facility, and sub-let production space to MRD for their first production batch of cars. The name MRD was dropped temporarily by the company (and permanently by the cars) because of its unfortunate connotations in French! In recognition of Repco's help the cars were renamed "Repco Brabhams"[1].

At this time Formula Junior was dominated by Ford engines, and so the new cars' complete title became "Repco Brabham-Ford", and when Climax-engined Tasman Formula cars were built they became "Repco Brabham-Climaxes". Repco had a big stake in Tasman racing, which demanded engines of not more than 2½-litres, and it was dominated by old ex-F1 Coventry-Climax FPF four-cylinder units. Repco made many parts for these engines and ran "down-under" sales and service with the Coventry firm's blessing. They eventually put Repco-Brabham name-plates on these engines, and technically speaking the cars then became pure Repco-Brabhams... but they mustn't be confused with the true Repco-Brabham Formula One cars.

Brabham as a manufacturer had entered Formula One racing in August 1962, when

The man behind Brabham's successes; Ron Tauranac, son of a boilermaker, whose family emigrated from England to Australia when Ron was three

Jack raced the original BT3 (Brabham-Tauranac type 3) under the MRD banner. A regular two-car team was instituted in 1963, and the last three seasons of 1½-litre F1 racing saw the works Brabham-Climaxes running under Jack's own Brabham Racing Organization colours. Tauranac had no share in this company, and Formula One became something of a chore for him. The arrangement was that MRD should design and build the F1 chassis, which were then sold to BRO who supplied the other basic necessities. But MRD's prime responsibility had to be towards the paying customers' production cars, and this meant that Formula One developments were often delayed but even so took up a lot of time which could more profitably be devoted to the production cars. Tauranac was unhappy with this state of affairs, and the production of new cars for the new Formula was in the balance.

Meanwhile, Coventry-Climax's promised last fling in Formula One racing—a 1½-litre flat-16 cylinder engine—had been still-born, and Brabham joined Cooper and Lotus in having chassis ready and waiting for the engine which never came during 1965. So the stage was set for the birth of the Formula One Repco-Brabhams....

An Engine is Born
The Repco V8 was conceived in February 1964 when the Melbourne management realized that supplies of Climax FPF bits and pieces would probably dry up within the life of the Tasman Formula. Chief Engineer Frank Hallam and Project Engineer Phil Irving were detailed to produce an engine to fit existing Repco Brabham chassis, and their answer was a new V8 using an existing GM Oldsmobile all-aluminium block.

[1] These non Repco-engined cars' names were usually rendered "Repco Brabham-Ford" without the first hyphen. Later F1 "Repco Brabhams" were often reported, but Repco themselves used the hyphen; thus "Repco-Brabham".

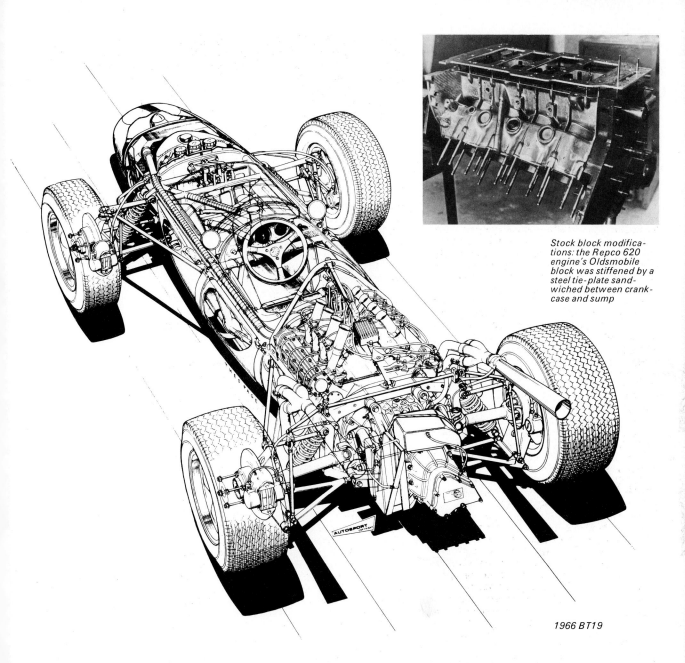

Stock block modifica-
tions: the Repco 620
engine's Oldsmobile
block was stiffened by a
steel tie-plate sand-
wiched between crank-
case and sump

1966 BT19

The obvious way to obtain more power from an unchanged capacity of 2½-litres was to use more cylinders, increasing piston area and crankshaft speed, hence the choice of a V8. It was then expedient to side-step a slow and costly foundry operation by using a proprietary block, and it so happened that General Motors in America had just shelved a suitable unit.

This Oldsmobile F85 had been developed as part of an enormously costly linerless alumin-ium engine programme for a 3½-litre Buick "compact". The linerless idea didn't work out, so a few units were produced with cast-in fer-rous liners, but that made the whole thing too fiddly for mass production, and GM cut their losses and scrapped the whole idea. Repco picked up the pieces, and turned commercial failure into a sporting Champion.

Irving found that the basic block could carry 2.5 to 4.4-litre internals, so could double as a Tasman Formula or Group 7 sports-car engine. It would need stiffening, and overhead cam-shafts would have to replace the standard cen-tre camshaft within the Vee which operated overhead valves by long pushrods. There were two basic parameters to observe; one, that frontal area should be minimised to maintain the existing Repco-Brabhams' excellent pene-tration, and, two, that overall width should be limited to fit existing chassis frames.

Irving consequently evolved simple mirror heads for each bank of cylinders, carrying par-allel valves in simple wedge-shaped combus-tion chambers, angled inwards at 10-degrees from the cylinder axis and operated by single overhead camshafts to keep the unit narrow,

51

and to reduce the length of unsupported drive chain to each shaft.

Basic work on the block filled all unwanted holes and spaces allowed for the original push-rod valve gear, and a ladder-formation stiffener plate in $\frac{3}{16}$-inch thick steel was then screwed to the sump flange to tie the crankcase crosswise. New main bearing caps were retained by long bolts which passed deep into the crankcase, and the existing 3.5-inch bores were reamed and fitted with 10-thou thick Repco cast liners. With a bore and stroke of 85 mm × 55 mm the capacity of 2.5-litres was achieved. Laystall in England machined new crankshafts, which ran in five Repco bearings, and another short-cut was taken when lightened and balanced Daimler $4\frac{1}{2}$-litre con rods were found suitable.

Repco pistons were cast in aluminium silicon alloy, with shallow valve clearance indents in their crowns, and Irving's new mirror heads were identical in every dimension to ease the spares situation; it was all good basic practical design.

The engine's internals were all-new, and two beautiful magnesium castings completed the conversion; a Y-shaped cover for the camshaft drive chains and a new $3\frac{1}{4}$-inch-deep ribbed sump which helped to stiffen the crankcase even more to accommodate its designed power increase. Adaptors were available to suit either Weber carburettors or Lucas fuel injection, and Repco even made their own specialized oil and water pumps to suit. Basic dimensions showed a length of $25\frac{1}{2}$-inches (excluding the Climax FWB fly-wheel), width across the heads of 21-inches, and height (excluding induction equipment) of 23-inches.

The prototype 2.5-litre engine coughed its way into the world on Repco's Richmond, Victoria, test bed on March 21, 1965, only 51 weeks after Irving and Hallam first put pen to paper. It was at about this time that Brabham and Repco began talking about producing an intermediate 3-litre variant for Formula One, and Phil Irving spent much of the summer in England, working closely with Jack himself on detail design of the new variant. They reverted to the standard 3.5-inch (88.9 mm) bore, and adopted a piston stroke of 60.3 mm, to give a

swept volume of 2,994cc. With Lucas fuel injection this new version gave 285 bhp at 8,000 rpm in early tests, and all Brabham had to do now was fit it into a chassis to have his 1966 Formula One car.

However, Ron Tauranac felt that MRD's lack of direct involvement with Formula One was most unsatisfactory, and it had then lasted for three whole seasons. Before work began on the new car, a new agreement was evolved with BRO, giving MRD their direct involvement and Tauranac the incentive which had been so lacking in the $1\frac{1}{2}$-litre days.

This arrangement was finalized as late as November, 1965, and a crash programme began to build up a new Repco-engined car for the first official race to the new Formula, the non-Championship South African GP at East London, on January 2.

The Brabham Cars 1966–1968

The last-minute nature of the 1966 Repco-Brabham programme has seldom been fully appreciated. When the "new deal" was forged between MRD and BRO there was only a month or so to go before the South African GP, and it was fortunate that the BT19 chassis (which had been built for the still-born 16-cylinder Climax engine) was lying in a corner of the workshop.

This was a simple multi-tubular spaceframe in the best Brabham traditions of simplicity, accessibility, ease of repair and sufficient rigidity to give good cornering and handling. While most of the opposition were building stressed-skin monocoque chassis, Ron Tauranac persisted with spaceframes. They were popular with private customers for the reasons above, and Jack Brabham practised what Tauranac's production cars preached by racing them in Formula One.

BT19 was typical, having a well-triangulated tubular frame although the use of oval-section tubes round the cockpit area was unusual. As Tauranac says; "I found there was some oval tube available, so I tried it to give some extra beam strength round the cockpit; always the weak point in a racing design".

The suspension was typically Tauranac, with

Repco engine development and assembly in the company's works just outside Melbourne. Photos show the 1967 Repco-block, centre-exhaust type 740 and the quad-cam four-valve per cylinder 860s of 1968

unequal-length unparallel wishbones at the front, composed of a transverse link with a trailing radius rod at the top, and a one-piece wide-based tubular wishbone at the bottom. Suitably-modified Alford & Alder uprights were used (from the Triumph Herald) and at the rear single top links, reversed lower wishbones and twin radius rods located specially cast uprights. In original form 13-inch wheels with 10½-inch diameter disc brakes were fitted (straight out of the 1½-litre cars), but as the season progressed so 15-inch rear wheels were adopted, carrying new square-shouldered Goodyear tyres, and housing 11-inch Girling discs. Later in its life BT19 carried 15-inch wheels all round. Co-axial coil-springs and Armstrong dampers were mounted outboard all round, and in early form the ''Old Nail'' as it came to be known, used a Hewland HD five-speed transmission, once again passed down from 1½-litre practise and not really man enough for engines of over 2-litres. Brabham made leisurely starts early on, but then commissioned Hewland to produce a heavier 'box, known as the DG, which was to become very popular in the 3-litre Formula.

The DG—picturesquely initialled after somebody had leaned over designer Mike Hewland's shoulder and asked, ''What's this, a different gearbox?''—used a ZF limited-slip differential and drove the wheels through one-piece solid drive-shafts, with inboard rubber couplings and outboard Hooke joints. The car was one of the lightest of the early 3-litre contenders, particularly since the Repco engine was very economical and 35 gallons of Esso premium grade were sufficient for a GP distance, but even so it was some 150 lbs over the 1102 lb minimum limit. Tauranac was far from satisfied with it, and regarded it as a ''lash-up''. It turned out to be the most successful lash-up in Grand Prix history.

With the BT19 running, work began on the true 1966 3-litre cars, the BT20s. These were to differ from the BT19 in using all round-section tubing, mostly in 18-gauge but with some 16- and some 20-gauge members. The main bottom chassis rails were revised and the cockpit area was double-braced with twin side tubes in place of the BT19's oval members. Tankage was similar to the 19's although small scuttle and behind-seat tanks were available for the long Italian GP, but were not required.

Horses for courses: for Monza Brabham tried this bubble canopy and also a gearbox cover in an attempt to reduce the BT24's drag. He suffered parallax problems with the canopy and ran standard bodywork in the race

Denny Hulme gives the original BT20 its first race at Reims. He finished third after a last lap stop out on the circuit. Note the 15-inch wheels all round, bulged side tanks and exhaust pipes wrapped around the upper radius arm

The suspension was also virtually identical to the BT19 but the geometry was revised to suit 15-inch wheels fore and aft. These allowed the first BT20 to use 12-inch brake discs in early races, but these were soon replaced by 11-inch units. Mechanically the BT19 and its two successors were identical, but the BT20 front and rear tracks were wider by 1-inch and $\frac{3}{4}$-inch respectively, and the wheelbase was $1\frac{1}{2}$-inches longer. The two BT20s differed from the BT19 externally in having vestigial two-piece engine covers in place of the original one-piece duck-tailed cowl, and in the exhaust manifolding, which was cramped within the rear radius arms of the BT19, and wrapped outside the upper arm in the BT20.

Early in 1966, before the BT20 was introduced, New Zealander Denny Hulme raced a 2.75-litre Climax four-cylinder-engined car for BRO. This was a rather mysterious device, known as a BT22, although officially only one BT22 was built, which belonged to a Scots club driver, who later sold it (crashed) to Jim Palmer in New Zealand. The Formula One "22" was a very good-handling frame, and Denny drove it in the 1967 Tasman series, using the prototype 740 engine. The BT21, incidentally, was the 1967 production F3 car.

For the 1967 Tasman Championship, Tauranac built-up a Formula Two-chassised Repco 740-powered car for Jack Brabham, and this was the prototype of the new year's GP cars which hit the minimum weight limit for the first time. This car was the BT23A, the first '67 F2 BT23 chassis frame of which nine more were to be made for the new 1600cc division. Ron used cast magnesium front uprights for the first time, replacing the Herald parts he had adopted in 1961, and produced a very compact and rigid spaceframe, modified about the engine bay to accept the $2\frac{1}{2}$-litre V8. The new car was very promising, and three similar new BT24 F1 cars were built during the season.

Tauranac regards these as his "... first real go at Formula One, apart from the BT3. We looked at the existing cars from end to end, slimmed and pruned everything to the minimum, used our own cast uprights all round and generally spent a lot of time designing just enough car to do the job. The amount of thought and time that went into producing a car as simple and light as that was tremendous —probably a lot more than if we had gone all complex and sophisticated. . . ."

The BT24s used the same wheelbase as the BT20, while front and rear tracks were down by $1\frac{1}{2}$-inches at the front and up by $\frac{3}{4}$-inch at the rear. Suspension was similar in general configuration apart from the new front uprights but the whole car was very neat and compact, with the BT23-type front body panel cut in half so that the nose cone detached to ease freight and stowage. A Hewland FT200 Formula Two transmission was fitted to the first car on its debut at Zandvoort, but it wasn't robust enough and was quickly replaced by a conventional DG300 five-speed and reverse unit.

The BT24s were fleet and forgiving, allowing their drivers to take liberties the opposition wouldn't look at, and Denny Hulme narrowly pipped Brabham himself for the Drivers' Cham-

Repco's family of Formula One V-8 engines, the 620, 740 and 860, were all effective and handsome pieces of machinery. They went just far enough to do the job, and even the unreliable 860 proved a match for the Cosworth-Ford V-8 opposition on its day, despite its apparent deficit in claimed power output

pionship, Jack having passed up the chance of Championship points to take all new development testing upon himself, leaving the proven and reliable cars to his team-mate.

In the 1968 Tasman Championship Jack ran a BT23E one-off, using the new 830 magnesium-block engine. The car had been ordered originally by New Zealander Feo Stanton's Rorstan Racing Team for Jochen Rindt to drive, but the deal collapsed and so the ultra-lightweight car was run by its co-constructor instead, proving the new short block.

Spanish sun greeted the 1968 BT26 quad-cam car's debut at Jarama in May. The car had been completed just in time to be airlifted to the Madrid circuit, but Brabham did very few laps before the engine wrecked itself.

Tauranac tried something new with the BT26 frame: "We tried to make a lighter but stronger frame by using alloy sheet panelling instead of tubular triangulation. This allowed us to use smaller-gauge, thinner section tubes for the basic frame, and the whole thing was built in a different way. Instead of making the bulkheads first and then joining them together in the jig, we laid down the bottom part of the frame on a flat bed, built the top deck immediately above it and then put the side members in between. We used similar main rails to the earlier cars, but with $\frac{5}{8}$-inch 20-gauge square tube carrying stressed panelling on the floor, around the cockpit deck, the sides and behind the seat and in the dash panel frame, around the driver's thighs. It worked OK, but it might have been cheaper to build a monocoque in the long run..."

The BT26 was a bigger car, with $1\frac{1}{2}$-inches extra wheelbase, 5-inches in the front track and $5\frac{1}{2}$-inches in the rear track. Suspension and bodywork were basically similar to the '67 car.

Ron was one of the first racing car designers to think deeply about aerodynamic downthrust on Grand Prix cars, and in the previous year's Belgian GP small trim tabs and spoilers had appeared on the BT24. In 1968 the BT26s tied with Ferrari by introducing strutted rear aerofoils at the super-fast Spa circuit, and as the year progressed the "wings" grew and multiplied, increasing traction without adding comparable mass, cutting lap times and keeping the still only moderately-powerful Repco-Brabhams competitively fast. But the Repco 860's problems were insurmountable, and Repco-Brabham failed in their attempt at a World Championship hat-trick—a feat yet to be accomplished by any manufacturer.

The Repco V8 1966–1968

In 1966, the Oldsmobile F85-based Repco-Brabham engine became known as the type 620, and engine numbers were all prefixed RB-620. This was a two-part classification, the 600 applying to the block and the 20 to the cylinder heads. Engine numbering began at RB 620—E1.

During the year the engine proved very reliable and produced sufficient usable power to make the light and good-handling Brabham chassis extremely competitive. At Monza for the Italian GP the BRO transporter disgorged three cars and an engine, newly crated from Melbourne, with "Monza 350 hp" stencilled

The new quad-cam Repco 860 V-8-powered BT26 for 1968 was beautifully made but had a string of problems which tended to be aggravated by the 12,000-mile gulf between racing shop and engine works. The spaceframe chassis used alloy sheet stressed skinning in place of tubular triangulation

on the crate. In fact engine E7 produced a peak of 298 bhp on Repco's test-bed, and after attention to the porting and a raise in compression ratio John Judd (BRO's ex-Climax engineer) saw 311 bhp at 7,250 rpm on the Climax dynamometer. There was more to come but at this point a piston burned out.

New developments were in hand for 1967, and during the following months a whole family of Repco V8 bits and pieces were developed, the blocks taking hundred-series numbers and the heads ten-series.

The basic deficiencies of the Oldsmobile production block and the complex operations necessary to bring it up to racing specification made the production of an all-new block a near necessity, and the 1966 World Championship success gave Repco the impetus to press on with its production. The 20-series cross-flow heads had also provided a low-level exhaust system which gave the chassis designer headaches weaving the pipes through his suspension system. So new heads were developed with their exhausts exiting within the Vee to clean-up the installation.

Repco engine developments were at this time being carried out by Repco-Brabham Engines Pty Ltd at Maidstone, outside Melbourne, where a four-man design team were working under general manager Frank Hallam, and with Phil Irving's strong influence their guiding light. The new team was headed by Norm Wilson, assisted by John Judd (down from England), Lindsay Hooper and Brian Heard.

The crankcase was redesigned to increase rigidity, and was cast in aluminium alloy. A change was made to wet liners and cross-bolted main bearing caps, and there was also a system of main bearing studs which distributed stress right through the new crankcase. These studs screwed into the bottom of the case, and continued right through it with reduced diameter, relieving stress concentrations through the top of the new block where they were provided with nuts, tightened down after the main bearing nuts had been tightened.

The new cylinder heads retained parallel valves, but they were now in-line with the cylinder axis—instead of at 10-degrees to it—and were flush with the head face. Camshaft centres were naturally changed to suit, and the original 20-series wedge-shaped combustion chambers were replaced by a "bowl-in-piston" arrangement. The all-new block took the 700 type number, and it represented a weight-saving of 30 lbs over the original Oldsmobile-based component. The new centre-exhaust heads were known as the type 40 . . . so what had happened to the type 30?

This was indeed the second design completed, but it retained the original cross-flow characteristics with outside exhausts, and mated that system to the new in-line valve/bowl-in-piston features. At the time it was felt that with parallel valves the gas had to make a pretty sharp turn as it left the cylinder, and it was immaterial to the gas which way it turned. The fallacy of this argument was proved when some serious tests were run with the 30-series heads, but when exhaust installation became of paramount importance the 30-series was

held over, and the centre-exhaust type 40 heads took their place in the 1967 type 740 engines . . . and another World Championship came Repco's way.

At the end of 1967 the Repco-Brabham range of V8 engines included the old Formula One 3-litre and sports-racing 4.4-litre 620s, and the new 740s in both 3-litre and Tasman 2.5-litre trim. Original 2.5 620s were still available, and new 4.2 and 2.8-litre Indianapolis engines were on the stocks (the latter with AiResearch turbocharging).

Highest output achieved from the F1 740s was only 330 bhp, but all Repco's horses seemed to be hard workers compared to the 408 claimed for the new Cosworth-Ford V8 and the 417 or so of the Eagle-Weslake V12. Nonetheless, something fairly drastic had to be done if the Repco-Brabhams were to be competitive in 1968.

There were two avenues of approach. One was for a short-stroke magnesium block engine, and the other was for a daring new cylinder head design, using a radial valve disposition. As it turned out a combination of the new and existing ideas was chosen, using aluminium short blocks with twin-overhead camshaft, four-valve per cylinder heads; without the complex radial layout, or short stroke.

Developments of the held-over 30-series heads had proved there was a power advantage to be achieved from cross-flow gas paths, and the radial layout type 50 heads aimed to exploit this advantage to the full. They were intended to use twin overhead camshafts per bank, each one driving inlet and exhaust valves alternately. The valves resided side-by-side in each half of a conventional pent-roof combustion chamber, exhausts and inlets being diametrically opposed across the chamber. This layout allowed very simple valve operation, compared to BMW's F2 Apfelbeck heads in which a radial valve layout appeared in hemispherical combustion chambers; the BMW valve stems protruded in all directions, like the horns on a sea-mine!

On the Repco test heads exhaust stubs appeared within the vee as a bunch of eight small-bore pipes, while four more appeared below the heads outside the vee on either side. Eight induction trumpets fought for space within the vee, and four more appeared on each side. One test engine was built-up using these heads and results were "most encouraging" but it was all a blind alley once again due to installation problems.

So the type 50 heads were shelved, and Repco (who had a lot of originality inside them, fighting to get out) adopted a more conventional 60-series design, using twin ohc and conventional four-valve per cylinder layout, with cross-flow gas-paths, neatly tucked-away outside exhausts and Lucas injection gear uncluttered within the vee. These heads were mounted on the new 800-series block, which was fully 1¼-inches shallower in the crankshaft centre-line to head interface dimension than its forerunners. It was considerably lighter, despite the use of a nitrided gear train to drive the new multiple camshafts, and was suitable only for 2.5 and 3-litre capacities. Part of this weight

1966 Repco-Brabham BT19. Jack Brabham won the 1966 French Grand Prix at Rheims at an average speed of 136·90 m.p.h. (220·31 k.p.h.) for 246·62 miles (398·48 kilometres), and thus became the first driver to win a World Championship event in a car bearing his own name.

Gordon Davies © Profile Publications Ltd

saving came from the use of new crankshafts with fewer balance weights, and the original 800-series block to be raced was cast in magnesium. It made its debut in the 1968 Tasman series, but in Formula One it eventually ran out of water and pulled out of line. It survives in John Judd's hands today in Rugby.

One short-stroke test engine was built-up using a 2½-litre crankshaft, bigger bore and a 5-litre sports-car head (a 700-series development of the 600-series 4.4-litre engine) carrying bigger valves to take full advantage of the extra bore. It showed no power advantage, and the short-block 800-series engines appeared in 3-litre form with shorter con-rods, using 5.1-inch centres instead of the original F85/620/740-type 6.3-inch-centre components. Time spent on these developments cost the quad-cam 60-series dear, and Brabham and Tauranac could have been forgiven for buying Cosworth-Ford engines as the 1968 season progressed from problem to problem. The Mexican GP saw Repco's last F1 appearance in a works car for the 12,000 miles between Melbourne and Guildford proved an insuperable obstacle to race development. Brabham drove a new Tasman car fitted with an 830 engine in the Tasman Championship early in 1969, and since then Repco have rested on their hard-won laurels, and have concentrated on service of their Tasman and Indianapolis V8s, and production of a successful Holden-based Formula 5000 engine.

The Racing Record
BT19 made its racing debut in the non-Championship South African GP at East London, on January 2, 1966. It was the only full 3-litre car in the race, qualified on pole position and led for 50 laps until the fuel injection pump seized, snapping its drive belt and retiring the car after it had set fastest lap.

Brabham then took the car to Australia for two Tasman races, using a 2½-litre 620 engine. Oil pressure disappeared and he retired on the manufacturer's doorstep at Melbourne's Sandown Park circuit, and then placed third at Longford in the car's first race finish.

The Syracuse GP was the first European 3-litre event, but Brabham retired early on with injection troubles. Then at Silverstone Jack took pole position, won easily and set a new lap record of 1m 29.8s, 117.34 mph.

This success was followed by the Monaco GP, opening round of the World Championship, but BT19 was out of luck, throwing the reverse idler gear in its gearbox and putting an already unwell Jack Brabham back into his hotel bed. Freakish rain storms made the Belgian GP a nightmare, and after frightening himself badly on the first lap (by helplessly sliding broadside towards a house at around 150 mph!) Brabham settled for fourth place to score his first three Championship points of the season.

The French GP followed at Reims, and Bandini's V12 Ferrari dominated it until its throttle linkage fell apart and "Black Jack" and BT19 swept by to score an historic first outright Championship round win for a driver in a car bearing his own name. Denny Hulme's third place in his brand-new BT20 made this

success all the more sweet, despite Denny stopping out on the circuit right at the end, apparently out of fuel. He lifted the nose of the car to swill the dregs back to the collector tank, his engine picked-up, and he made it to the line.

Back home for the British GP at Brands Hatch just winning wasn't good enough for the team. They qualified first and second on the starting grid, and finished in that order, Jack leading all the way and establishing the 3-litre lap record at 1m 37.0s, 98.35 mph. The Dutch GP one week later at Zandvoort saw the Repco-Brabhams first and second quickest once again, but Denny retired with ignition trouble and Brabham had a tremendous battle with Jim Clark's 2-litre Lotus-Climax, resolved only when the smaller car's crankshaft damper disintegrated. This left BT19 unchallenged to score a third consecutive victory. In practice for this race Hulme had a tremendous engine blow-up at the end of the main straight, throwing rods and wrecking the 620 block. A new bare block cost £11, and the Daimler rods were £7 each . . . inexpensive motor racing?

Rain made the German GP at Nürburgring a hard and daunting event, but Brabham led all the way to make it four in a row. A promotional trip to the Australian Surfer's Paradise circuit for a *Formule Libre* race followed, but it was completely wasted when the 3-litre engine sheared its distributor drive after only two laps!

Back in Europe Brabham retired from the Italian GP when an inspection plate on the timing chain case worked loose, let out the oil and forced another retirement. Championship rivals Stewart and Surtees also retired and a smiling Jack Brabham clinched his third World Championship and the first for his own cars right there in the pits. Hulme finished third.

The non-Championship Oulton Park Gold Cup was a complete Repco-Brabham demonstration as Jack and Denny finished first and second, and shared fastest lap at 1m 36.6s, 102.89 mph. The US GP saw Jack leading early on from pole position, until a cam follower broke, and Denny's V8 lost its oil pressure. In Mexico Jack led early on but couldn't hold Surtees' Cooper-Maserati once it had found a way past, and finished second. Denny was third again, and ended the year fourth in the World Drivers' Championship.

The 1967 Season
At Kyalami in January, the 1967 World Championship opened with Denny Hulme completely dominating the South African GP until he lost brake fluid, made a long stop and finally finished fourth. Jack also stopped, with misfiring, and rejoined with ice packed around his BT20's injection pump. He finished sixth.

The Tasman races followed, in which the new 40-series heads were introduced, and back in England the works BT20s had a poor Race of Champions, and then dominated the Oulton Park Spring Cup charity meeting in a carbon copy of their Gold Cup performance. Jack won again, using 40-series heads on a 600 block, Denny was second and they shared fastest lap. With an old 620 engine Brabham couldn't hold Parkes' Ferrari at Silverstone and finished second, and then came Monaco where

58

The 1966 Repco-Brabham BT19
which won the French Grand Prix of
that year.

Gordon Davies © *Profile Publications Ltd*

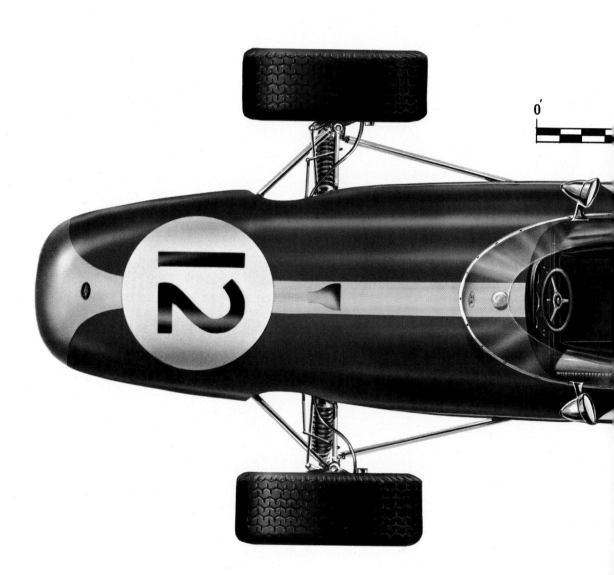

0ʹ

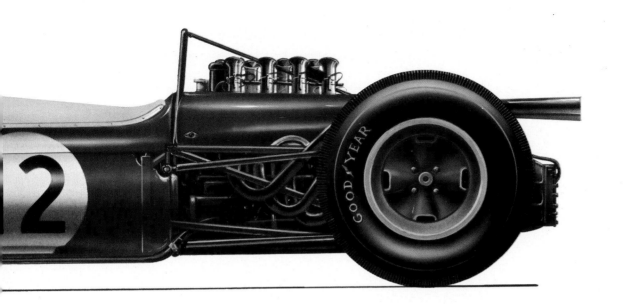

2′ 3′

BT19 in unfamiliar hands, driven by Denny Hulme in the '67 Belgian GP. The old car is fitted with 15-inch wheels all round, a late-model BT20 nose-cone with the enlarged radiator intake and a 740 engine. Trim tabs on the nose were forerunners of the aerodynamic revolution

Battle royal: Brabham's BT19 heads Hulme's BT20 as the pair fend off Jimmy Clark's 2-litre Lotus-Climax during the opening stages of the 1966 Dutch GP. Clark fought his way past Brabham on a slippery surface after Hulme retired, then made a stop to give Jack his third consecutive Grande Epreuve success

Hulme forces his BT24's nose ahead from the start of the 1967 German GP. He won after first Jimmy Clark and then Dan Gurney (Lotus and Eagle) retired. Brabham is on row two beside Surtees' great white Honda

he raced old BT19 with the first type 740 3-litre engine installed. It broke a con-rod on the opening lap, curiously kept running on seven cylinders, and Jack recovered from a spin to tour into the pits, larding most of the circuit with oil before realizing what had happened! Meanwhile Denny Hulme opposite-locked his BT20 to a superb victory, scoring nine Championship points to make up for his South African disappointment.

At Zandvoort BRO had four cars, the two BT20s, old BT19 and the prototype BT24, but Tauranac decided the new car was unraceworthy and Brabham drove the "Old Nail", fitted with the 24's type 740 engine, and finished second. Denny was third in his Monaco car, the last race appearance of a BT20 in works hands. Denny drove BT19 in the following Belgian GP, while Jack gave the BT24 its race debut, and the newer BT20 was shipped to South Africa for national champion John Love.
Spa saw both cars drown in their own oil with scavenge problems, and the French GP at Le Mans (a pitiful affair run through the car parks of the mighty 24-Hours circuit) saw the new Lotus-Fords dominant until both suffered transmission failure. Brabham and Hulme outdistanced the rest of the field—running two BT24s for the first time—and they scored a splendid one-two finish.

Guy Ligier, a French privateer, replaced his Cooper-Maserati with the older BRO BT20 in time for the British GP, where the works BT24s were second and fourth, with Denny ahead and setting fastest lap at 1m 27.0s, 121.12 mph. Brabham was criticized for baulking Amon's Ferrari, but he had a legitimate excuse for both his rear-view mirrors had fallen off.

In Germany the Lotus-Fords broke once again and Gurney's Eagle failed while leading, to give Hulme the race and Brabhams another one-two finish. In practice Jack had a nasty moment when a rear suspension bolt broke at 150 mph, and the car careered along on its belly for a very long way. Ligier was delighted with his new car, and took sixth place.

The Canadian GP at Mosport Park was run in torrential rain, and once again the Lotus-Fords had trouble while the well-prepared and easy-to-handle BT24s scuttled by to their third one-two finish of the season, Jack ahead again this time.

In Italy Brabham lost a fantastically dramatic race on the last corner, when he slid wide on spilt oil and allowed Surtees' Honda through to win by 0.2 second! Denny retired after leading when his car overheated, and at Oulton Park Brabham won yet again. Fellow Australian Frank Gardner drove BT19 in this event, but retired from second place.

Behind the glamour there's a lot of sweat and hard work. Denny Hulme helps John Muller and a Goodyear tyre technician lift his BT22's Repco 640 engine during the '67 Tasman series

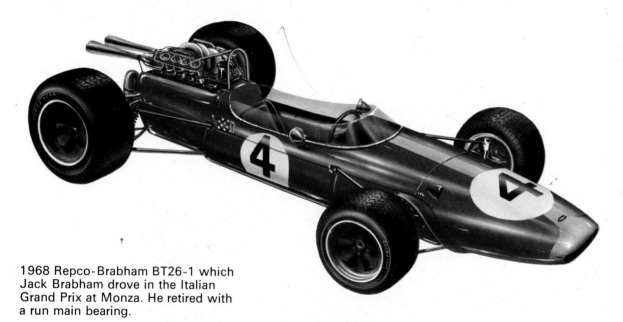

1968 Repco-Brabham BT26-1 which
Jack Brabham drove in the Italian
Grand Prix at Monza. He retired with
a run main bearing.

1967 Repco-Brabham BT24-2 which
Denny Hulme drove into 2nd place in
the French Grand Prix held on the
Bugatti circuit at Le Mans.

Repco-Brabham BT20 in 1967 form,
with the larger air intake opening in
the nose cone. A similar body
section was subsequently fitted to
BT19.

Gordon Davies © *Profile Publications Ltd*

At Watkins Glen Hulme was third and Brabham fifth and the Championship lay between them in the last race at Mexico City. Jack had to win to take the title, with Denny finishing lower than fourth, but Denny glued himself to the "Guv'nor''s tail, they finished second and third behind Clark's Lotus, and the rugged New Zealander took his Championship. Jack Brabham was runner-up and happy to have his cars winning another World Manufacturers' Championship title.

One Formula One race remained that season, the non-Championship event at Madrid's new Jarama circuit, in Spain. Brabham drove old BT19 there and finished third behind the works Lotus-Fords.

Late that season Denny Hulme raced Gulf McLaren sports-cars in the lucrative North American Can-Am series, and he signed with this team for Formula One in 1968, using the new Cosworth-Ford V8 engines. BRO signed-on Jochen Rindt, the Austrian driver who had dominated Formula Two racing in Brabham cars, and who was delighted to join the Formula One team after three fraught seasons with Cooper. Esso withdrew from motor racing sponsorship at this time, and Brabham gained new backing from the American Gulf Oil Corporation for 1968 and 1969. Unfortunately the last Repco-engined season was to be an unhappy one.

The 1968 Season
The old BT24s were raced in the opening Championship round in South Africa, where Jochen was a good third, and they were then sold to Team Gunston for Sam Tingle, and to the Lawson Organisation for Basil van Rooyen. Formula One regulations governed the South African and Rhodesian national championship divisions and many ex-works GP cars found good homes there during the 'sixties. Repco V8 engines also appeared in the InterContinental Brabham chassis driven by Dave Charlton and Luki Botha, and Love's Championship-winning BT20 was also still in harness. Botha had a terrible accident in Mozambique, however, burning-out his car and killing eight spectators, while Love eventually exchanged his trusty BT20 for an ex-works Lotus-Ford 49.

Meanwhile Brabham was racing BT23E-1 in Australia using a cross-flow 830 prototype engine, and when the European season began BRO were still awaiting delivery of their new quad-cam engines, and it was left to the Swiss driver Silvio Moser to fly the banner in his ageing ex-Ligier BT20, now owned by his compatriot, Charles Vogele.

The first BT26 quad-cam car appeared in practice for the Spanish GP at Jarama and blew-up when a valve insert dropped, leaving Rindt's BT24-3 to retire with no oil pressure in its 740 engine. He crashed the same car at Monaco, and its engine (127E) was an interesting "bitsa" which had been built up at BRO's Guildford racing shop from spares. It was later sold to Healey for their Le Mans car, John Judd's Engine Developments (Rugby) concern bought it back for John Cussins, and it is now used in Peter Voigt's British Hill-climb Championship Palliser.

Not this time: Brabham lost the '67 Italian GP to Surtees' Honda on the last corner, and finished a close second. Here the oil-covered BT24 hurtles into the Parabolica, showing its tail fins and air deflectors ahead of the front suspension. These created a low pressure area in the suspension "bays" which extracted hot air from the radiator

Birth of a new generation: Brabham's F2-based BT23A Tasman car leads Stewart's BRM and Clark's Lotus into the first corner at the 1967 Sandown Park round of the Tasman Championship. This car was the prototype for the Formula One BT24s

American moment; while new World Champion Jack Brabham leads Bandini's Ferrari at Watkins Glen, Peter Arundell's Lotus impedes Surtees' Cooper-Maserati as it spins while being lapped. Jack's BT20 retired with cam follower failure

Brabham retired at Monaco when a radius rod pick-up failed on the BT26 chassis, and in Belgium two quad-cam BT26s appeared for the first time. Rindt's leaked water and failed while Brabham's was put out by fuel feed problems. Jack had another valve insert detach during practice, and Repco decided that the material was shrinking, causing the problem. So Jack flew home overnight, while John Judd and Norm Wilson (over from Melbourne) collected a new engine from Heathrow. It was torn down overnight with the help of Chief Mechanic Roy Billington (who had been with BRO for years) and machinist Ron Cousins came in to fit the new parts. He had been with HRG who did all the original 620 work, and had joined BRO when HRG gave up. The new heads were cooked in Brabham's domestic oven, and Betty Brabham awoke the following morning to find her house full of acrid fumes!

At Zandvoort the wet Dutch GP saw Jochen on the front row of the grid, only 0.16-second slower than Amon's Ferrari, and Jack on row two, but they nearly didn't make it. Just after the transporter had left for Dover a message came from Melbourne saying there was not enough static clearance between the pistons and the valves in the 860 engines, and that the two would meet when started-up. So Jack Brabham bought a suitable wood chisel from a Guildford hardware store, and at Zandvoort the mechanics lifted the cylinder heads and chiseled the piston crowns down to provide the nec-

essary clearance. Both BT26's were also found to have dodgy alternator shafts, and so they were raced without the rotors in place. Brabham was still suffering fuel feed problems in his car, had to use the electrical pumps instead of the mechanical pump all the time (instead of just for starting), and flattened his battery—which of course was not being charged-up since the alternator was not functioning. He spun and stalled, and couldn't restart, while Jochen hated the rain and gave up. Dan Gurney drove the spare two-cam BT24-3 in this race, left the road, got some sand in the throttles and after some hairy moments with sticking slides gave up. Little Moser soldiered on through all this mayhem to take fifth place.

At Rouen the French GP was also run in heavy rain, but Rindt actually started from pole position, proving there was nothing wrong with the quad-cam BT26 in principle. Unfortunately his fuel tanks ruptured before he got into his stride, and Brabham's fuel feed problems persisted and finally put him out as well. It seems possible that when his tanks were crammed to the brim for the race itself, an air vent became blocked and the engine pumps did not have sufficient suction to overcome the vacuum they were trying to form within the tank.

The British GP at Brands Hatch saw Jack's engine losing the drive gear on the right-hand exhaust camshaft after one lap (an assembly fault), while Jochen's car caught fire after a pump failure. In Germany a cracked titanium

Brabham's BT24 was fourth in the British GP at Silverstone, narrowly beating Chris Amon's Ferrari. Amon complained of being baulked but for once Jack had a legitimate excuse—both his mirrors had fallen off as shown here!

valve spring retainer was located 1½-hours before the race, there was a spare engine in the transporter and in a mad scramble the two units' cylinder heads were swopped over. The car was back together with ten minutes to spare, and Jochen splashed round in the rain to finish third and Jack was fifth in the team's best race of the year.

At Monza the Italian GP saw Brabham's brand-new engine running the centre main bearing, and Rindt's breaking a gudgeon pin, which caused terrific damage. When Brabham's engine was stripped down one gudgeon pin in that unit was found in three pieces; he must have switched off literally a split-second before the engine destroyed itself.

Monza was dry and it was the first time that the Repco 860 engines had been run at anything like full-bore for any length of time. Judd adopted replacement pins from a Petter diesel engine, which Cousins again machined to fit and which cured the problem. Cam follower wear had been found on the Alfa Romeo-made components which had been used since 740 days, and this now became the quad-cam engine's latest bug-bear.

But in Canada Jochen took pole position yet again, only to have brake problems and overheating force him out of second place, and Brabham had another suspension failure; a front wishbone pick-up broke, and his exhaust system also fell apart.

For the lucrative US GP at Watkins Glen

Rindt's spirit and unusual reliability from the Repco 860 engine brought the BT26's best finish of the season; third place in a German Grand Prix held in near impossible conditions. Brabham brought his car to the finish in fifth place. Wings are growing taller . . .

. . . and they went forth and multiplied—Rindt's bi-plane BT26 took pole position for the 1968 Canadian GP, but retired yet again. The bi-plane arrangement had made its début in practice for the Italian GP, the two-piece rear wing hingeing in the middle and acting directly on the wheel uprights

Rindt at Rouen: Jochen Rindt's low-winged BT26 flashed round to take pole position for the French GP, but retired from the rainy race with ruptured fuel tanks. The fiery "Austrian" was very popular in the Repco-Brabham team, but they couldn't afford to counter other offers for 1969. He joined Lotus, and became racing's first posthumous World Champion for them in 1970

Last of the works Repco-Brabham road racers: Jack Brabham raced this Formula Three-based BT31 with a $2\frac{1}{2}$-litre type 830 engine at Sandown Park and Bathurst in 1969. He was third in the Melbourne race and won the Bathurst "100" in his last road race for Repco

Repco's 860 engine nestles in the rear of the first BT26 chassis, at Spa, while the strutted rear aerofoil developed by Ron Tauranac and Ray Jessop of BAC tied with Ferrari in kicking off the notorious "wings" craze of 1968 and early 1969. Gulf Oil sponsorship is evident on the aerofoil

After the 1968 South African GP both BT24-1 and BT24-2 were sold to local entrants. This is Basil van Rooyen in the original car, finished in its new STP colours, on test at Kyalami. The water pipes from the radiator have been run outside the cockpit and fitted with a heat exchanger for South African summer races, and Dunlop tyres replace the original Goodyears

Brabham refuses help from journalist Nick Brittan and photographer Michael Cooper after sliding into the fence at Zandvoort's Tarzan loop during the 1968 Dutch GP. He was unable to restart anyway for the battery was flat! Graham Hill, slithering by in the Lotus 49B, knocked two wheels off his car at the same spot later on, but other successes brought him the '68 World Championship

both drivers ran their engines 1,000 rpm down in an effort to conserve them, but Jack's broke a cam follower, and Jochen's threw a rod. The Mexican GP saw the BT26's final misery, for Jochen's engine broke after only two laps, and Jack soldiered into third place only to have excessive oil consumption dry his engine out before the finish. He stopped, but was classified tenth and last. In an effort to preserve the cam followers some of the oil drains from the head had been blocked, to keep more lubricant around them. Unfortunately this caused extra leakage down the valve guides, and the oil tank just wasn't big enough to last the distance.

This wasn't quite the end of the Formula One trail for the Repco-Brabhams, for in South Africa the Team Gunston BT20 and BT24 raced on through 1969 and both BT24s appeared early in 1970. Jochen Rindt went to Lotus in 1969, and became the sport's first posthumous World Champion in 1970. Brabham appeared at Sandown Park early in 1969 with a tiny Formula Three-based BT31 Tasman car with an 830 engine, and finished third. Later in the year he returned to race the car in the Bathurst "100", and won easily to sign-off the Repco-Brabham story on a high note.

The Author acknowledges his grateful thanks to Messrs Ron Tauranac, John Judd, R. C. Maclean and A. Robinson of Repco Ltd. and Duncan Rabaglatti of the Formula One Register for their assistance in the preparation of this Profile.

The illustrations were kindly supplied by the following:- Autosport; Alton Berns; Michael Cooper; Barry Curtis (Johannesburg); Geoffrey Goddard; David Holmes; London Art Tech; Phipps Photographic; Repco Ltd. (Australia); Nigel Snowdon.

SPECIFICATION OF 1966 REPCO-BRABHAM BT19

ENGINE:- Repco-Brabham 620.
Cylinders. V-8
Cooling system. Water.
Bore. 88.9 mm (3.5 in)
Stroke. 60.325 mm (2.4 in).
Capacity. 2995. 7 cc (182.82 cu in). †
Valve gear. Single overhead camshafts per bank.
Compression ratio. 11.5 : 1.
Fuel pump. Lucas petrol injection.
Maximum power. 315 bhp at 7,250 rpm.
† Repco's figure differs from generally quoted capacity of 2,994cc.

TRANSMISSION
Clutch. Borg & Beck diaphragm twin-plate 7¼ in-dia.
Gearbox. Hewland DG300 five-speed.
Final drive. ZF crown wheel & pinion to choice.

CHASSIS
Construction. Multi-tubular mild steel space frame in round and oval section.

SUSPENSION
Front. Independent by wide-based leading and trailing wishbones, outboard Armstrong dampers with co-axial coil springs.
Rear. Independent by reversed lower wishbone, single top link and twin radius rods with outboard Armstrong dampers and co-axial coils.

STEERING
Type. MRD rack and opinion.

BRAKES
Make & type. Girling AR (front) and BR (rear) calipers, solid discs.

WHEELS
Type & size. Brabham cast magnesium; 13 in dia. (front), 15 in. dia. (rear); 8 in (front), 10 in (rear) rims.
Tyres. Goodyear 5.00 × 13 (front), 5.00 × 15 (rear).

FUEL TANK
Capacity. 35 Imp gallons (159.109 litres).

DIMENSIONS
Wheelbase. 7 ft 8 in (233 cm).
Track. front 4 ft 5½ in (136 cm).
rear 4 ft 6 in (137 cm).
Weight. Approx 1252 lbs (568 kg).

PERFORMANCE
Maximum speed. Approx 175–180 mph.

1966 REPCO-BRABHAM BT20. As for BT19 except:-

Chassis. Multi-tubular mild steel spaceframe in round section 16, 18, and 20 swg tubing, no oval members.
Wheels. 15 in dia front and rear.

DIMENSIONS
Wheelbase 7 ft 9½ in (237.5 cm).
Track: front 4 ft 6½ in (138 cm).
rear 4 ft 6¾ in (138.5 cm).

1967 REPCO-BRABHAM BT24. As for BT19 except:-

ENGINE:- Repco-Brabham 740 giving 330 bhp at 8,000 rpm.

DIMENSIONS
Wheelbase. 7 ft 9½ in (237 cm).
Track: front 4 ft 5 in (135 cm).
rear 4 ft 7½ in (141 cm).
Weight. 1103 lbs (500 kg).

1968 REPCO-BRABHAM BT26. As for BT19 except:-

ENGINE:- Repco-Brabham 860 giving approx 375 bhp at 9,000 rpm.
CHASSIS. Frame untriangulated and instead panelled in 18-gauge aluminium alloy stressed sheet.

DIMENSIONS
Wheelbase. 7 ft 11 in (241 cm).
Track: front 4 ft 10 in (147 cm).
rear 5 ft 1 in (155 cm).

(NB The specifications listed here are typical of the cars, but naturally differed slightly from race to race, dependent on rim widths, individual engines fitted etc.)

THE FORMULA 1 REPCO-BRABHAM REGISTER

BT19 F1-1-65: Completed as F1-1-66 and renumbered F1-1-65 Italian GP '66—Brabham Racing Organisation retained the car until 1970 when it was completely refurbished by Motor Racing Developments and presented to Repco for their Melbourne show-rooms.

BT20 F1-1-66: Actually the second BT20 completed—Brabham Racing Organisation '66—to Performance Equipment Co (South Africa) for John Love '67—retained by Love under Team Gunston colours '68—to Jack Holme for Clive Puzey and John Rowe '69.

BT20 F1-2-66: BRO '66—Hulme's Monaco GP winner '67—to Guy Ligier (France) '67—to Charles Vogele (Switzerland) for Moser '68—Siffert collection of show cars '69.

BT24-1: BRO '67—to Team Lawson (South Africa) for Basil van Rooyen '68—to Gordon Henderson '70—believed to Eddie Pinto '71

BT24-2: BRO '67—to Team Gunston (South Africa) for Sam Tingle '68, rebuilt with smaller side tanks to accommodate him—written-off by Tingle at Killarney '70—remains to Eddie Pinto.

BT24-3: BRO '67–'68—to Frank Williams (Racing) late '68 for Piers Courage in Tasman series with 2.5-litre Ford DFW V8—to Silvio Moser with 3.0-litre Ford DFV V8 for F1—engine and suspension used in Moser's 1970 Bellasi F1 "special"—remains to Franz Albert (Austria).

BT26-1: BRO '68—to Williams Racing for Piers Courage with 3.0 Ford DFV V8 1969 via David Bridges—to Pieter de Klerk (South Africa) '70.

BT26-2: BRO '68—retained '69 as BT26A with 3.0 Ford DFV V8 engine, written-off in Jack Brabham's testing crash at Silverstone.

BT26-3: BRO '68—retained '69 as BT26A with 3.0 Ford DFV V8—to Gus Hutchison (Texas) for use in F1 class of national Formula A racing '70.

Two more BT26 frames were built, 26-4 built from the ground up as a Ford-powered car, now resides in the Wheatcroft Grand Prix Collection (England), and 26-5 was supplied as a spare chassis to Hutchison (Texas). The two privately-concocted South African 3-litre Repco Brabhams were as follows:

Jack's second successive win in the French GP came at Le Mans in '67, when he led Denny Hulme home in a brace of BT24s. Here the engine bay side cowls are clearly seen, but the tail tabs from Spa have been removed for the slower circuit

†F1-2-64: ('ghost' BT22) Jack Nucci (South Africa) '65 for Jack Brabham in Rand GP with 2.75 Climax FPF engine—to Aldo Scribante '66—'67 for Dave Charlton with Repco 620 engine—to Ivor Robertson '70.

†IC-5-64 (BT11) Jack Brabham '65 (as "F1-2-63")—to Jack Nucci '66 for Pieter de Klerk—dismantled and 2.75 Climax engine to John Love for Cooper/chassis to Luki Botha '67—Botha fitted Repco 620—crashed and burned-out Laurenco Marques '67—chassis to Steve Mellett, rebuilt with 2.75 Climax for Jack Pretorius '68/Repco engine to Sam Tingle for Team Gunston BT24-2.

† Both these cars carried the same numbers as earlier Brabham F1 cars, the "BT22" that of Gurney's BRO 1964 car which was sold to BMW and used as a test and record-breaking vehicle, and the Botha BT11 of Brabham's BRO 1963 car which was sold first to Rob Walker for Jo Bonnier (where it ran as "F1-1-63"), and then to Warner Bros for the film "Day of the Champion ... which was never completed.

THE F1 REPCO-BRABHAMS RACING RECORD
This list also includes particularly significant non-Formula 1 outings, notably in the Tasman Championship, in which new models made their first appearances . . .

1966 Event and Venue	Chassis type and number	Engine	Driver	Result
South African GP	BT19 F1-1-66	620	Brabham	Rtd/**FL/PP**
East London	BT22 F1-1-64*	Climax 4	Hulme	Rtd/**FR**
Exide Cup, Sandown Park, Melbourne, Australia	BT19 F1-1-66	620 2.5†	Brabham	Rtd/**PP**
South Pacific Trophy, Longford, Tasmania	BT19 F1-1-66	620 2.5†	Brabham	3rd
Syracuse GP, Sicily	BT19 F1-1-66	620	Brabham	Rtd
	BT22 F1-1-64*	Climax 4	Hulme	Rtd
International Trophy, Silverstone, England	BT19 F1-1-66	620	Brabham	**1st/FL/PP**
	BT22 F1-1-64*	Climax 4	Hulme	4th
MONACO GP, Monte Carlo	BT19 F1-1-66	620	Brabham	Rtd
	BT22 F1-1-64*	Climax 4	Hulme	Rtd
BELGIAN GP, Spa	BT19 F1-1-66	620	Brabham	4th
	BT22 F1-1-64*	Climax 4	Hulme	Rtd
FRENCH GP, Reims	BT19 F1-1-66	620	Brabham	**1st**
	BT20 F1-2-66	620	Hulme	3rd
	BT22 F1-1-64*	Climax 4	Bonnier	Unc
BRITISH GP, Brands Hatch	BT19 F1-1-66	620	Brabham	**1st/FL/PP**
	BT20 F1-2-66	620	Hulme	**2nd/FR**
	BT22 F1-1-64*	Climax 4	Irwin	7th
DUTCH GP, Zandvoort	BT19 F1-1-66	620	Brabham	**1st/PP**
	BT20 F1-2-66	620	Hulme	Rtd/**FL/FR**
GERMAN GP, Nürburgring	BT19 F1-1-66	620	Brabham	**1st**
	BT20 F1-2-66	620	Hulme	Rtd
Surfer's Paradise *Formule Libre*, Australia	BT19 F1-1-66	620	Brabham	Rtd
ITALIAN GP, Monza	BT19 F1-1-65**	620	Brabham	Rtd
	BT20 F1-1-66**	620	Spare car	—
	BT20 F1-2-66	620	Hulme	3rd
Gold Cup, Oulton Park, England	BT19 F1-1-65	620	Brabham	**1st** FL
	BT20 F1-2-66	620	Hulme	**2nd**
UNITED STATES GP, Watkins Glen	BT20 F1-1-66	620	Brabham	Rtd/**PP**
	BT20 F1-2-66	620	Hulme	Rtd
MEXICAN GP, Mexico City	BT20 F1-1-66	620	Brabham	2nd
	BT20 F1-2-66	620	Hulm.e	3rd

† For Tasman Formula races * 2.75-litre Coventry-Climax 4-cyl FPF-engined Inter Continental car.
** The second BT20 was completed just in time for this race, and since it was the second "true" 1966 car it took the number F1-1-66 from the BT19 to fall into line with the existing F1-2-66. BT19 then reverted to a more accurate F1-1-65 numbering !

Event and Venue	Chassis type and number	Engine	Driver	Result
1967 SOUTH AFRICAN GP, Kyalami	BT20 F1-1-66 BT20 F1-2-66	620 620	Brabham Hulme	6th/**PP** 4th/**FL**/**FR**
New Zealand GP, Pukekohe	BT22 F1-1-64	640 2.5†	Brabham	Rtd
Wills International, Levin, N.Z.	BT22 F1-1-64	640 2.5†	Hulme	Rtd/**FR**
Lady Wigram Trophy, Christchurch, N.Z.	BT23A-1 BT22 F1-1-64	640 2.5† 640 2.5†	Brabham Hulme	Rtd/**FL**/**FR** 3rd
Teretonga International, Invercargill, N.Z.	B.T.22 F1-1-64	640 2.5†	Hulme	Rtd/**PP**
Lakeside International, Brisbane, Australia	BT23A-1 BT22 F1-1-64	640 2.5† 640 2.5†	Brabham Hulme	2nd 4th
Australian GP, Warwick Farm	BT23A-1 BT22 F1-1-64	640 2.5† 640 2.5†	Brabham Hulme	4th Rtd
Sandown International, Melbourne, Australia	BT23A-1 BT22 F1-1-64	640 2.5† 640 2.5†	Brabham Hulme	Rtd/**FL** Rtd
Race of Champions, Brands Hatch, England	BT20 F1-1-66 BT20 F1-2-66	620 620	Brabham Hulme	9th Rtd
International Spring Cup, Oulton Park, England	BT20 F1-1-66 BT20 F1-2-66	640 620	Brabham Hulme	**1st** FL **2nd**
Rand Autumn Trophy, Kyalami, South Africa	BT11 F1-2-64*	620	Charlton	**1st**
Killarney, South Africa	BT11 F1-2-64	620	Charlton	2nd/Rtd(2 heats)
International Trophy, Silverstone, England	BT20 F1-1-66 BT20 F1-2-66	620 620	Brabham Hulme	2nd Rtd
MONACO GP, Monte Carlo	BT19 F1-1-65 BT20 F1-2-66	740 620	Brabham Hulme	Rtd/**PP** **1st**
Coronation "100", Roy Hesketh, South Africa	BT11 F1-2-64 BT11 IC-5-64	620 620	Charlton Botha	Rtd Rtd
DUTCH GP, Zandvoort	BT19 F1-1-65 BT20 F1-2-66	740 620	Brabham Hulme	2nd/**FR** 3rd
BELGIAN GP, Spa	BT24-1 BT19 F1-1-65	740 740	Brabham Hulme	Rtd Rtd
Taca Cid races, Laurenco Marques, Mozambique	BT20 F1-1-66 BT11 ICC-5-64	620 620	Love Botha	**1st***** W/O
FRENCH GP, Circuit Bugatti, Le Mans	BT24-1 BT24-2	740 740	Brabham Hulme	**1st**/**FR** **2nd**
BRITISH GP, Silverstone	BT24-1 BT24-2 BT20 F1-2-66	740 740 620	Brabham Hulme Ligier	4th/**FR** 2nd/**FL**/**FR** 10th
GERMAN GP, Nürburgring	BT24-1 BT24-2 BT20 F1-2-66	740 740 620	Brabham Hulme Ligier	**2nd** **1st**/**FR** 6th
CANADIAN GP, Mosport Park	BT24-1 BT24-2	740 740	Brabham Hulme	**1st** **2nd**/**FR**
ITALIAN GP, Monza	BT24-1 BT24-2 BT20 F1-2-66	740 740 620	Brabham Hulme Ligier	2nd/**FR** Rtd Rtd
Natal Winter Trophy, Roy Hesketh, South Africa	BT20 F1-1-66 BT11 F1-2-64	620 620	Love Charlton	**1st** Rtd
Oulton Park Gold Cup, England	BT24-1 BT19 F1-1-65	740 740	Brabham Gardner	**1st**/**FL** Rtd
UNITED STATES GP, Watkins Glen	BT24-1 BT24-2 BT20 F1-2-66	740 740 620	Brabham Hulme Ligier	5th 3rd Rtd
Rand Spring Trophy, Kyalami, South Africa	BT11 F1-2-64 BT20 F1-1-66	620 620	Charlton Love	**1st** 3rd
MEXICAN GP, Mexico City	BT24-1 BT24-2 BT20 F1-2-66	740 740 620	Brabham Hulme Ligier	2nd 3rd 11th
Spanish GP, Jarama	BT19 'BT24-3'**	740	Brabham	3rd
Rhodesian GP, Bulawayo	BT20 F1-1-66 BT11 F1-2-64	620 620	Love Charlton	**1st**/**FL** **2nd**

* The solitary BT19, F1-1-65, appeared in Spain carrying the chassis plate from 24-3, and was widely described in contemporary magazines as "an old BT20". In fact it was neither. † For Tasman Formula races.
*** Love was leading when the race was stopped after Botha's car crashed into the crowd.

Zandvoort was slippery for the '68 Dutch GP; as Silvio Moser in the ex-Hulme, ex-Ligier BT20 discovered. He finished fifth to take two World Championship points

Event and Venue	Chassis type and number	Engine	Driver	Result
1968				
SOUTH AFRICAN GP, Kyalami	BT24-1	740	Brabham	Rtd
	BT24-2	740	Rindt	3rd
	BT20 F1-1-66	620	Love	9th
	BT11 F1-2-64	620	Charlton	Rtd
Cape South-Easter, Killarney, SA	BT11 F1-2-64	620	Charlton	Rtd
	BT20 F1-1-66	620	Love	Rtd
International "100", Warwick Farm, Australia	BT23E-1	830 2.5†	Brabham	7th/**FL**
Australian GP, Sandown Park, Melbourne	BT23E-1	830 2.5†	Brabham	Rtd
Race of Champions, Brands Hatch, England	BT20F 1-2-66	620	Moser	Rtd
Rand Autumn Trophy, Kyalami, South Africa	BT24-1	740	Van Rooyen	Rtd
	BT 24-2	740	Tingle	Rtd
	BT11 F1-2-64	620	Charlton	2nd
Coronation "100", Roy Hesketh, South Africa	BT24-1	740	Van Rooyen	2nd/Rtd (2 heat)
	BT24-2	740	Tingle	Rtd/2nd (2 heat)
SPANISH GP, Jarama	BT26-1	860	Brabham	DNS
	BT24-3	740	Rindt	Rtd
MONACO GP, Monte Carlo	BT26-1	860	Brabham	Rtd
	BT24-3	740	Rindt	Rtd
	BT20 F1-2-66	620	Moser	DNQ
Republic Trophy, Kyalami, South Africa	BT24-1	740	Van Rooyen	2nd
	BT24-2	740	Tingle	3rd
BELGIAN GP, Spa	BT26-1	860	Brabham	Rtd
	BT26-2	860	Rindt	Rtd
DUTCH GP, Zandvoort	BT26-1	860	Brabham	Rtd
	BT26-2	860	Rindt	Rtd/**FR**
	BT24-3	740	Gurney	Rtd
	BT20 F1-2-66	620	Moser	5th
Natal Winter Trophy, Roy Hesketh, South Africa	BT24-1	740	Van Rooyen	1st
	BT24-2	740	Tingle	2nd
FRENCH GP, Rouen	BT26-1	860	Brabham	Rtd
	BT26-2	860	Rindt	Rtd/**PP**
BRITISH GP, Brands Hatch	BT26-1	860	Brabham	Rtd
	BT26-2	860	Rindt	Rtd
	BT20 F1-2-66	620	Moser	Unc
GERMAN GP, Nürburgring	BT26-1	860	Brabham	5th
	BT26-2	860	Rindt	3rd/FR
	BT24-3	740	Ahrens	12th
	BT20 F1-2-66	620	Moser	DNQ
Rand Winter Trophy, Kyalami, South Africa	BT24-1	740	Van Rooyen	2nd
	BT24-2	740	Tingle	4th (dead-heat)
	BT11 F1-2-64	620	Charlton	3rd
Oulton Park Gold Cup, England	BT26-1	860	Brabham	Rtd
	BT26-3	860	Rindt	Rtd
ITALIAN GP, Monza	BT26-1	860	Brabham	Rtd
	BT26-2	860	Rindt	Rtd
	BT20 F1-2-66	620	Moser	DNQ
False Bay "100", South Africa	BT24-2	740	Tingle	3rd
	BT11 F1-2-64	620	Charlton	2nd
CANADIAN GP, St Jovite	BT26-1	860	Brabham	Rtd
	BT26-3	860	Rindt	Rtd/**PP**
UNITED STATES GP, Watkins Glen	BT26-1	860	Brabham	Rtd
	BT26-3	860	Rindt	Rtd
Rand Spring Trophy, Kyalami, South Africa	BT24-1	740	Van Rooyen	2nd
	BT24-2	740	Tingle	5th
	BT20 F1-1-66	620	De Klerk	4th
	BT11 F1-2-64	620	A. Charlton**	DNS
MEXICAN GP, Mexico City	BT26-1	860	Brabham	10th NRF
	BT26-3	860	Rindt	Rtd
Rhodesian GP, Bulawayo	BT24-2	740	Tingle	2nd
1969				
Cape South Easter, Killarney, South Africa	BT24-2	740	Tingle	2nd
	BT20 F1-1-66	620	Puzey	5th
Sandown International, Melbourne, Australia	BT31-1	830 2.5†	Brabham	3rd
SOUTH AFRICAN GP, Kyalami	BT24-2	740	Tingle	8th
	BT20 F1-1-66	620	De Klerk	Unc
Coronation "100", Roy Hesketh, South Africa	BT24-2	740	Tingle	Rtd
	BT20 F1-1-66	620	Rowe	Rtd
Bathurst "100", Australia	BT31-1	830 2.5†	Brabham	**1st/FL**
Kyalami, South Africa	BT24-2	740	Tingle	2nd
1970				
Cape South Easter, Killarney, South Africa	BT24-2	740	Tingle	W/O
	BT24-1	740	Henderson	3rd

** Arnold Charlton, brother of Dave.
DNS, Did Not Start; DNQ, Did Not Qualify; Unc, Unclassified (too far behind at finish); NRF, Not Running at Finish; PP, Pole Position; FR, Front Row of Grid; FL, Fastest Lap; W/O, Written-off in crash.

Nürburgring, 1967.
(Michael Cooper)

The Chaparral 2, 2D & 2F *The Glassfibre Series*

by PETE LYONS

The Chaparrals were the most innovative American racing cars. They broke more technical ground, advanced the high-performance sciences farther, than any automobiles ever made there. They won races, they lost races, but more importantly they developed ideas. They pioneered new concepts in aerodynamics, in power units, in transmissions, in materials, and in testing procedures.

Their history exactly spanned a decade, a decade which saw tremendous increases in the speed capabilities of racing cars all over the world, and the big white roadrunners from the waste plains of Texas were in the forefront. It was an exciting period of applied science — science applied by the full, if clandestine, resources of General Motors.

Jim Hall was a rich boy but he was no playboy. He was foremost in that rare breed of driver-engineers, and approached his chosen vocation with total dedication. He surrounded himself with like-minded friends, started Chaparral Cars with their help, and some of those friends were in high places — GM's Technical Center at

Detroit. In time the small, remote racing team in Midland became a kind of secret proving ground for the latest high-performance GM thinking. Boxes full of exciting experimental hardware were shipped there to be tried in racing cars. Engineers were assigned to live and work there on a loose rotational basis. They were tightly linked to the northern base with teletype and computer lines. It was all supposed to be a back-door operation, kept strictly secret — indeed, it is still alleged that the highest corporate echelons never knew about it.

The whole thing died finally at the end of 1970 after 10 seasons of competition both domestic and international. The last Chaparral, the 2J "sucker", was outlawed, the third time such a thing happened to the firm. Hall himself had never fully recovered from a serious 1968 crash which left him with impaired legs and, perhaps, ability. In the background GM, together with all the automotive manufacturers of the world, were being forced to concentrate on the more prosaic aspects of their business. Economics were down, public rancour was up;

Front cover:
1967 BOAC 500 –
winning 2F.
(Michael Cooper)

it was no longer camshafts and camber curves, it was smog and safety. A miniature golden age was over.

Domestic automotive arts reached their Nader.

Chaparral evolution branched in 1966 into two distinct lines. This Profile deals with the parent line, which started with the first true model, the Chaparral 2, in 1963. It was developed for the informal series of North American ''big banger'' sports-car racing that flourished before the establishment of the CanAm in 1966. A new line of aluminium chassis was developed for this, and the glassfibre chassis were revised into FIA endurance racers — the feasibility of this having been demonstrated by winning the 12 hours at Sebring the year before. As type 2D they won the 1966 Nürburgring 1000 Kilometers, and as 2F they won the next year at Brands Hatch in the inaugural BOAC 500. All these models were essentially one-and-the-same automobile. To follow their evolution through five competition seasons is to appreciate the truly immense strides taken by automobile technology in a short period.

James Ellis Hall would probably have done it anyway, his oil money merely enabled him to do it right. At the California Institute of Technology (''Cal Tech'') in Los Angeles he trained himself in Mechanical Engineering. As soon as the Sports Car Club of America allowed he was racing, in a string of the latest European sports machinery. At that time he seemed to think of himself as a driver first, and he aimed at the top. In 1963 he arranged a season of Formula One in Europe, with a Lotus operated by the British Racing Partnership. He acquitted himself well, but during that season he began to realize ''it would take three years of strict concentration on Formula One to become World Champion''. He couldn't spare the time. Chaparral Cars was already established and deeply into development of an all-American sports-racer. It was a pivotal decision, and from that point he became more and more involved with the engineering side of things. He remained a superb driver, one always expected to see him toward the front of any grid. People who worked with him in his rôle as test driver still have nothing but praise for his ability.

His was an enigmatic personality. To his more gregarious associates he seemed aloof. He did not talk easily, particularly about himself.

Jim Hall — ''foremost in that rare breed of driver-engineers''.
(Geoffrey Goddard)

Beginnings — a youthful Jim Hall in the earliest version of his new, glass-fibre-chassised, world-beater.
(Michael Cooper)

Nassau, 1963: Hall's new ''roadrunner'' fending off the redoubtable A. J. Foyt's Scarab. The Chaparral 2's distinctive snowplough nose is an aerodynamic 'fix''.
(Michael Cooper)

He kept many things under close control, but he was evidently not good at dealing with people and there were storms. His demeanour was usually serious, a reflection of his single-minded drive toward Perfection. Not that he was a joyless sobersides: his career gave him deep satisfaction and he could use the word "fun". In an interview with *Autosport* he was asked, "What makes Jim Hall tick? Why did you get into race cars in the first place?"

"It's fun. I'm just a kid who never grew up! A big part of it is the challenge of making something work that nobody ever thought of."

The close liaison with General Motors meant that there were important rôles played in the Chaparral story by a large number of men, men of pride and unsimple character in their own right. The historian trying to piece together a single history of those halcyon days will run into contradictions, conflicts between the recollections and interpretations of different men. Much of the story has not yet come out. Perhaps some details *should* not come out.

What follows is a Profile concentrating on the nuts-and-bolts part of the story, the line of development that started as a "special" in a wealthy engineer's back yard and grew into a semi-works expression of the world's largest automobile manufacturer — and that on the way won international success.

Hatching The Chaparral

With his close friend James R. (Hap) Sharp, a petroleum engineer owning a couple of drilling firms, Hall had gained experience of the best in European cars. For the 1961 season they wanted a pair of American-made cars; it was time to show the world what home-grown technology could do. The Reventlow Scarabs were kings of the USA circuits in the late 1950s, and as a first step (although the mid-engined Coopers and Lotus were already on the scene) Hall and Sharp decided to follow their lines. They commissioned the Los Angeles specialist firm of Troutman and Barnes to build up-to-date versions of the Scarab, with a tubular space-frame housing a Chevrolet 5.4-litre engine in the traditional place. There were, Hall recalls, six built in all. He took the first two, brewery scion Augie Pabst had the next two, another ended a short career in a crash, and the last went overseas to carry the Detroit V8 faith to the British hillclimbs.

The car was named "Chaparral", or "Roadrunner"; that is, *Geococcyx californianus,* a ground-dwelling bird of the cuckoo family, a familiar, fleeting sight along roads in the southwestern deserts. Chaparrals run at furious speed. They catch and eat snakes (like fellow-Texan Carroll Shelby's Cobras!).

To nest these big new birds was built, on not-quite-flat scrubland six miles south of the oil-

Where it all happened: the magnificent Chaparrals were made in an unpretty, but totally functional, complex south of Midland in West Texas. There were later additions, but it looked like this in 1966. (Pete Lyons)

The Mexican Turn: few racing car factories have their own test circuit literally outside the back gate. Rattlesnake Raceway was one of the reasons why the Chaparrals were fast when they arrived at the real race. It was not just a track but was part of a computerised data-gathering system. (Pete Lyons)

A glassfibre chassis mould, or "buck", at the Midland works in 1966, showing a 1963-era chassis form being fitted with the 1966 type 2D windscreen and roof section.
(Pete Lyons)

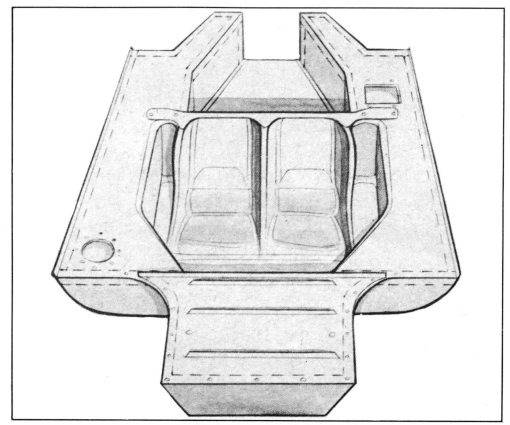

Chaparral sub-frame: "at the point of final assembly one had basically a top half and a bottom half, fastened together with a few rivets holding things together until the adhesive dried, with aluminium angle edging round the perimeter and vertically at the front corners".
(Autocar)

Mosport, 1964: a new nose and accompanying tail treatment make a more homogeneous racing car. Cooper wheels have replaced the earlier Lotus variety.
(Pete Lyons)

city of Midland, Texas, a facility that would have been a hobbyist's dream — were Hall and Sharp hobbyists. They weren't. They were determined to do everything as professionally, as big-business, as they knew how. They were not going to merely race their cars, they were going to develop them, scientifically extracting the ultimate performance. One thing was of first importance in the new venture: to excell. To win.

Within unlovely but sturdily functional metal buildings they set up, besides workspace and a well-equipped machine shop, a dynamometer cell (centrepiece: a British Heenan-Froude unit capable of registering 1000 bhp) and a tidy drawing office. Later there was another building devoted to work in FRP — Fiberglass Reinforced Plastics.

The racing cars could be driven directly from the compound out of the back gate to the test track, a genuine road circuit two miles round named Rattlesnake Raceway. It was a tricky lap, full of variable-radius curves and switchbacks over humps, plus a healthy long straight with an ultra-fast bend in the middle. There was installed an irrigation system for landscaping at the verges — and just possibly to simulate wet weather conditions. Photocells, buried at certain key points on "the line", were hooked into a recording/computer system; improvements on the cars weren't going to be assessed in anyone's seat-of-the-pants, they were going to appear in cold, clear graphic form. In a flat area touching an edge of the circuit a "skid pad" was paved which was marked off in concentric circles. By driving round smoothly in endless orbits right on the limit it was possible to develop a car to its ultimate cornering power. The "skid pad" was to become a tool of more importance than even the dynamometer.

The Chaparral was developed through two seasons, and began appearing with startlingly original body modifications. But the end of its basic configuration was being written in the records set by the new wave of nimbler mid-engined cars; even the Scarab was going mid-engined. With the facilities at their disposal the Midland Marauders could not help but join the trend — and try to go it one better.

The Chaparral 2 Described
The basic idea for the Chaparral 2 was *lightness,* coupled with strength and mechanical efficiency. Obviously expense would not be much of a barrier. After thought and study, it was decided to make the chassis structure primarily of FRP. Not strictly a new idea, for the world had grown used to the Lotus Elite, but the material being used to contain some 400 bhp in a circuit racer was innovative. For expertise Hall turned to one Andy Green, owner of a Dallas boatworks called Plas Trend. Together they worked up a structure that, in retrospect, looked startlingly like a dune buggy bodyshell.

The material had several attractive advantages. It was easy to make double-curvature surfaces, and to vary the thickness in areas requiring more local strength. Once completed there should be no permanent stresses locked into the structure. It would be easy to modify the chassis or add to it. In the event of damage it would not crumple but simply crack, so repair

should be straightforward. (This was in fact proven in service: a car crashed in 1964, was glued back together, and won Sebring in 1965.)

The design requirement was a chassis weight of 150 lbs and a torsional resistance, between axle-centres, of 3000 lbs/ft/deg. To achieve this stiffness, high for the era, Green made all his cross-sections as wide and tall as possible. The structure was essentially a grouping of individual "torque-boxes" glued together. At the point of final assembly one had basically a top half and a bottom half which, after installation of air ducts and other details, were fastened together with a few rivets holding things in place until the adhesive dried. Making the chassis of FRP was not a *stunt,* and where it was sensible there was metal taking localized loads. The entire perimeter of the two halves had aluminium angle edging, and there was more angle running vertically up the front corners; to these strong points were attached some suspension brackets. Steel crossmembers held more of the suspension, across the lower front and across the back both above and below the transmission. In fact, at no place was FRP alone asked to carry heavy loads. The bottom of the engine bay was an alloy sheet. The engine was mounted on lugs cast into the clutch housing and on its normal mid-block mounts — not on the alloy plates at the ends which became generally popular later.

Chassis aside, it was still a "special" and most of the other components were adapted from existing sources. Most of the suspension, including hubs, uprights, links, and wheels, came from Lotus; but the steering was from Cooper. The brakes were Girling and the transmission in those early days was a Collotti. It was expedient to buy such things, but also the fledgling bird-builders were humble: "We didn't think we could do things any better". *That* would change.

At some point Hall had made contacts in the GM Tech Centre at Warren, a town adjoining Detroit. Someone has said Jim just dropped by one day, en route to a race with car in tow, to say, "Come on outside and see what I've got." The entire engineering staff, most of whom were his own age and perhaps some even classmates at Cal Tech, clustered round. Inevitably one of them said, "Why did you do this this way, you should have done it this way", and a fruitful, far-reaching relationship was born.

Each party got full value from the new liaison. For Chaparral it was developmental resources, and priceless components, beyond the wildest dreams. For GM it was a stretching of mental muscles, a chance to involve a whole generation of young engineers in a project that really fascinated them. Beyond that, there was the chance to try new technical ideas in gruelling tests that could not be artificially devised. It was always a clandestine relationship, denied by all parties; many drawings for Chaparral transmissions, etc, were labelled "Future Corvette".

The aluminium engines came about through Roger Penske, who at that time was an eager young salesman with Alcoa, as well as a promising race driver. Somehow he connected his employers with casting patterns originally intended for Chevrolet's infamous Gran Sport Corvettes, and suddenly the Chaparrals were presented a weight saving of 110 lbs.

Block and head material apart, the engine was essentially the same "small block Chevy" that was a backbone of the domestic performance industry from its introduction in 1955 into the 1970s (F5000). The Chaparrals always used it as a "327", with a bore of 4 inches and stroke at 3.25 inches. (In metric terms, 5.36 litres, 102 mm by 82.6 mm). With its Weber carburation it offered horsepower above the 400 mark at just under 7000 rpm, and torque of about 380 at just over 5000. In those days of 1½-litre Formula One engines these were giant figures.

Jim Hall remembered as one of the landmarks of the whole Chaparral story the day "we set it on the scales, and we realized the car was really going to hold everything and be as light as it was and do everything we said it would do; that was a kind of high point for me".

The new car raced three times at the end of 1963, in FIA International events. At Riverside on October 13 gathered a remarkable field: Jim Clark, Dan Gurney, Graham Hill, Roger Penske,

John Surtees, A. J. Foyt, Pedro Rodriguez, Parnelli Jones, Roy Salvadori, Roger Ward, Frank Gardner, Richie Ginther, Lloyd Ruby, Augie Pabst, and Timmy Mayer. Jim Hall's homebuilt qualified fastest of all, started from the pole, and at flagfall showed its heels to everyone. In four laps it earned almost a half-mile lead — and then retired with an electrical fire.

The next week at Laguna Seca the roadrunner ran more conservatively and qualified fourth, but it ran the complete distance and finished third behind Dave McDonald's Cooper-Chevy and Foyt's Scarab-Oldsmobile.

In December the circus went to Nassau in the Bahamas for its annual end-of-season bash, and Hall was holding off Foyt in a preliminary event until he stopped with brake trouble. In the main race Penske's Cooper beat the Chaparral, which finally retired with broken steering.

Technical Developments, 1963–65
So the pattern was set: there were lots of new problems to solve but the car was fast. To describe the alterations carried out over the next two years, while the cars remained open sports-

Old and new: in mid-1965 at Watkins Glen, with the last version of the Chaparral 2, Jim Hall has Augie Pabst in his mirrors with one of the surviving Chaparral 1s. (Pete Lyons)

Moustaches and downforce: the car nears the end of its roofless development. By now it has its own wheels but the restless experiments with exhaust pipes continue. (Pete Lyons)

Nürburgring 1000 Kms, 1966: Bow and stern complexities of the winning 2D. Note the transparent ends to the ram air box above the carburettors for rear-ward vision via the over-head-mounted mirror . .

racers, we will select individual fields and treat them in one place regardless of the actual chronology of events.

AERODYNAMICS. The original body shape had appeared on the front-engined car, and was allegedly developed in a wind tunnel. On the track, however, it taught the lesson that everyone was having to learn in those days — and in days since — that what works in the tunnel may play peculiar tricks on the track. At relatively low speeds — 120 mph — the high-prowed nose was generating massive lift. The straightforward cure was a "cowcatcher" spoiler to prevent air going under the car, and this was kept for several races in various evolutionary forms. It was realized, however, that it was a kind of quick-and-dirty solution, and it seemed extremely sensitive to variations in the height of the nose above the road surface. Eventually a completely new nose profile was evolved (it bore a distinct family resemblance to certain Chevrolet styling exercises!) which remained through the 1966 season on the 2D coupé.

Fixing the nose taught the lesson of aerodynamic balance, and to get the tail to settle down in line with the nose an air-dam (seen first in 1961 on the Ginther-developed Ferraris) was needed across the back. Later, as engine and chassis and tyre improvements brought the working speed range higher and higher, the basically good shape had to be further refined. In May of 1965 the "moustaches" appeared, being at first simple plates below the body ahead of the front wheels; soon they were their full, distinctive shape. The adoption of Bruce McLaren's idea of venting radiator exit air out of the top of the nose into the natural low-pressure area there, which had the effect of reducing lift, seemed to lead logically to the pressure-relieving of *all* of the top body surface. In the latter part of 1965 louvres were set into the tops of all four wheel domes. The cars in this, their final open-bodied, form had an extraordinary appearance — sharp angles, scoops and vents, plates and dams, louvres like some wildly mutated shark, and 16 separate vertical engine pipes bristling from the rear. The Chaparral was not an *aesthetic* car, it was a *scientific* car.

SUSPENSION. The original proprietary components were for the most part just not men enough for their new jobs. Gradually, piece by piece, they were changed and changed again, until finally virtually every part was made from raw for Chaparral. The Lotus wheels gave way to Cooper wheels, and then special wheels were made in the distinctive web-spoke pattern that remained a sort of trademark to the end of the line. These were made up as separate pieces, bolted together. One of the ideas behind them was brake cooling, an early problem; the openings in the web had nothing to do with airflow but rather with allowing heat to escape from the discs as radiant energy. Although there was a flange to bolt the halves of the rims together there was no deep well necessary to mount the tyres, so the heat could radiate away all the more easily. The wheels were always 16 ins in diameter, which helped this also.

To further improve braking a new, wildly expensive aircraft fluid was adopted, which required special seals. The discs were ultimately

... and detail of the Chaparral cast-alloy wheel, which had an adjustable split rim to provide a choice of rim widths. (Autocar)

Chaparral 2D, Nürburgring, 1966: "... a very satisfying victory in its European debut". (Geoffrey Goddard)

made by Chaparral, while for the 2D the Girling calipers gave way to American Kelsey-Hayes units.

TRANSMISSION. The one feature that seemed to most distinguish the Chaparral was its successful use of an "automatic" transmission. Apparently it was embodied in the original planning of the type 2 but it was some months before it was judged safe to race. It first went into battle at Laguna Seca in May of 1964 — but no one noticed. At the next race people began to realize something about the sound was odd, but it wasn't until Mosport a month later that Dan Gurney took the bull by the horns and asked Hall about it. (Apparently the scheming Texans had wired a mercury switch into the brake light circuit, which made the lights go on at peculiar, confusing points!) For months and years thereafter the transmission was a deep mystery. No one would discuss it — unless they didn't really have anything to do with it, and *then* they were sure they knew all about it. Whenever it was necessary to remove the rear body section the back of the chassis was quickly covered with a tarpaulin; often mechanics were required to carry out work lying on the ground reaching under the tarpaulin. Anyone who looked into the expense (ie the expertise, the trouble) of making an automatic box

1967 Chaparral 2F 001 *(above)* as run in the BOAC 500 miles race at Brands Hatch and *(below)* as it appeared in the Targa Florio (see centre spread)

Collotti (Chaparral 2) . . .

. . . and Capparelli — the
ultra-secret General
Motors automatic trans-
mission was the
Chaparral trump card;
Chaparral 2D.
(Michael Cooper)

work in a road-racing car, (and Ford, with McLaren, and later Chrysler all looked into it), had to realize the Chaparral unit was a GM experiment pure and simple. But still the myth was fostered. When the 2D came to Le Mans in 1966, and the crewmen were presented with a recognition form containing a blank for "manufacture of transmission", they filled it in "Capparelli". That's Texan for "nuts!"

Many of the secrets have leaked out, though. While there may well have been different versions, it is essentially a simple device without any planetary gearsets or bands. It was laid out much like a Hewland, in fact, with two speeds at first — three later — and an hydraulic coupling, a torque-converter, instead of a clutch. The gears were simple straight-cut spurs engaged by sliding dog clutches; every second dog was cut back a little to assist the clutchless changes. The changes were all done manually, the driver easing his throttle foot to unload the dogs and snatching the gearlever as quickly as he could. It therefore wasn't really an "automatic" transmission, it was a fluid-clutch transmission. The engines were always started with a gear engaged, the driver preventing a lunge forward by firm pressure on the brake pedal with his left foot. At a certain rpm, something around 5000, the coupling was designed to lock up rigidly to prevent further slip and consequent power loss. Sensitive drivers could feel this happening.

The advantages of this transmission seemed to be worth the effort of development. From the driver's point of view the main benefit was in braking. He could concentrate on careful modulation of the pedal to achieve maximum retardation, and there was the further benefit that, should he ask the engine to help out by downchanging, the fluid coupling would lessen any tendency of the rear wheels to lock. Later on, of course, the existence of the two-pedal control system made possible the introduction of a third pedal controlling a variable-pitch aerofoil. From a mechanical point of view the fluid coupling absorbed many shock loads. There was much less chance, for instance, that a "yump" would break something in the drive-line. It was a success, and retained to the end.

GENERAL. During its three years as an open sports-car the Chaparral 2 gained somewhat in weight (stronger suspension, wider wheels and tyres, bigger body to suit and more aerodynamic appendages, etc) but at the same time it grew steadily faster. Better than that it became ever more predictable, more comfortable, "nicer to drive".

The 1964–66 Seasons

It was becoming an even better race vehicle as well, as its record through 1964–65 shows (see Table page 96). Usually running two cars (although three existed), with Penske joining in when either Hall or Sharp weren't there, the team entered 15 events the former year and 20 the next. From 24 vehicle starts in 1964 they scored 7 wins, with 8 retirements; in 1965 they started the type 2 34 times, from which it won 15 times and retired only 3 times. Granted, some of those races were SCCA club events not always fiercely contested, and Jim Hall's 1965 United States Road Racing Championship, while well-deserved, was not of world wide significance. However, during those two years 15 events were of FIA International status, and Chaparral won 8 of them. Indeed, at Sebring in 1965 Hall and Sharp ran superbly all through the 12 hours (plus a memorable, flooding rainstorm) to achieve an excellent victory. There were setbacks; the year before Hall crashed heavily at Mosport and was out the rest of the season with a broken arm. The incident did prove one of the original theories about FRP as a structural material, though: the same tub became the Sebring winner six months later. During that latter summer the team spent an interesting few days at Indianapolis trying the sports-car on the oval; it went a very respectable 144 mph and behind the scenes work was started on a single-seater. (This project was abandoned, emerging only six years later when the chassis was finished privately as a F5000).

With the 1966 season came the formal CanAm series, and it was deemed wise to lay down a new car for it. (It appeared at the end of 1965). To save weight — and perhaps expense — this revamped model was made with an aluminium chassis. It was called type 2C — there had been an earlier aluminium car called 2B, but it never appeared in public. Until that point there had been no numerical way to distinguish the several permutations of the original glassfibre cars. Now, as they entered a new career, they were relabelled. Roofs were grafted on and they went overseas to the long-distance wars as type 2D.

Sebring, 1967: the last appearance as a 2D, the 7-litre version is not gainly, nor is it successful, but it does demonstrate how one car and body can change and yet remain the same . . .

1967 Chaparral 2F 001. This car competed in the Targa Florio (No. 222) with a trim tab on the trailing edge of the wing, but Phil Hill and Hap Sharp retired when lying fourth. For the BOAC 500 miles race at Brands Hatch (211 laps), the car (No. 1) had its trim tab removed and the new front upper inlet for an oil cooler was added. Phil Hill and Mike Spence won in 6 hours 00 min. 26·0 sec. at an average speed of 93·08 mph (149·798 kph)

Gordon Davies © Profile Publications Ltd

0   1   2   3ft

It was the Ford era at Le Mans, and obviously the success at Sebring had fired the enthusiasm of General Motors; obviously too, Hall could look forward to going back to his old Formula One haunts with a spectacular machine of his own devising.

The Chaparral 2D

The 2D was a logical extension of the basic car. The body went back to its pre-louvre condition and the moustaches were removed (except for one reappearance in 1967). For the first race the tail was equipped with a low, body-mounted flipper taken from the 2C, but it was subsequently removed because it required too much pedal pressure. The roof and full windshield, complete with gullwing doors, were built on. The engine, which was nowadays capable of some 470 bhp, was allegedly cut back to 425 for longevity. Later, it breathed cool air drawn in from above the roofline through a prominent scoop.

The 2D had not too bad a career, although from seven starts in six events it retired six times. The single time it finished it won, at Nürburgring.

Its first race was at Daytona in early 1966, where Jo Bonnier and Phil Hill qualified it second fastest by a scant one-fifth second to a Mk II Ford. They jumped into an early lead, but after seven short laps were forced to pit with steering trouble. After two more long delays with the same problem the car was withdrawn at the 14 hour mark.

At Sebring that year were entered two 2Ds; the Daytona flipper tail had been replaced with a simple "ducktail". Hall and Sharp qualified 6th and Bonnier and Hill started 8th, and this

dim promise was fulfilled in the race. Both engines (or perhaps it was transmissions) developed a great thirst for oil and both were retired, the first car at least with transmission failure.

At the Nürburgring 1000 Kms race there was just one car, which Bonnier and Hill qualified second best by three seconds to a P3 Ferrari. That was driven by Surtees, who led the race until a damper broke. The Chaparral was left holding off a little Dino Ferrari. When a period of rain swept over the Eifel the American car stopped, changed to a distinctive set of hand-grooved full-flood tyres, and then, far from losing ground to the light Dino, the 2D pulled out 20 seconds. But the windscreen wiper had failed, and Hill had to work it by hand. Still the Chaparral lasted through and won a very satisfying victory in its European debut.

The car showed evidence of much development; the headlight system was different and there were additional aerodynamic "tweaks", and the rather ungainly rooftop scoop had been added to feed the engine air unmixed with warm radiator outlet flow.

The success story broke down at Le Mans. For the high speeds the body was streamlined a trifle with less rear "ducktail" and the twin bullet-mirrors were removed in favour of a single, faired mirror set into the roof. The accustomed driver pair qualified a reasonable 5.1 seconds behind the Ford Mk II pole winner. It started on rain tyres, and left the lead to be sorted out amongst the furiously scrapping Fords and Ferraris. At the first hour the Chaparral was holding 7th; it had filtered back to 12th by the third hour, and at nine o'clock was forced to retire with electrical problems.

The 2D didn't race again that year. Over the

Big win: Sebring 1965.
Holding off Rodriguez'
Ferrari on the way to
glory . . .

. . . and also vanquishing
one of Carroll Shelby's
snakes!
(Pete Lyons)

USRRC interlude, 1965:
Jim and Hap having a
nice Sunday afternoon
drive at Watkins Glen.
The McLarens didn't
invent anything!
(Pete Lyons)

Clean pair of heels: the
white bird from Texas
shows the red Italian
horse the way through
France; Le Mans, 1966.
(Michael Cooper)

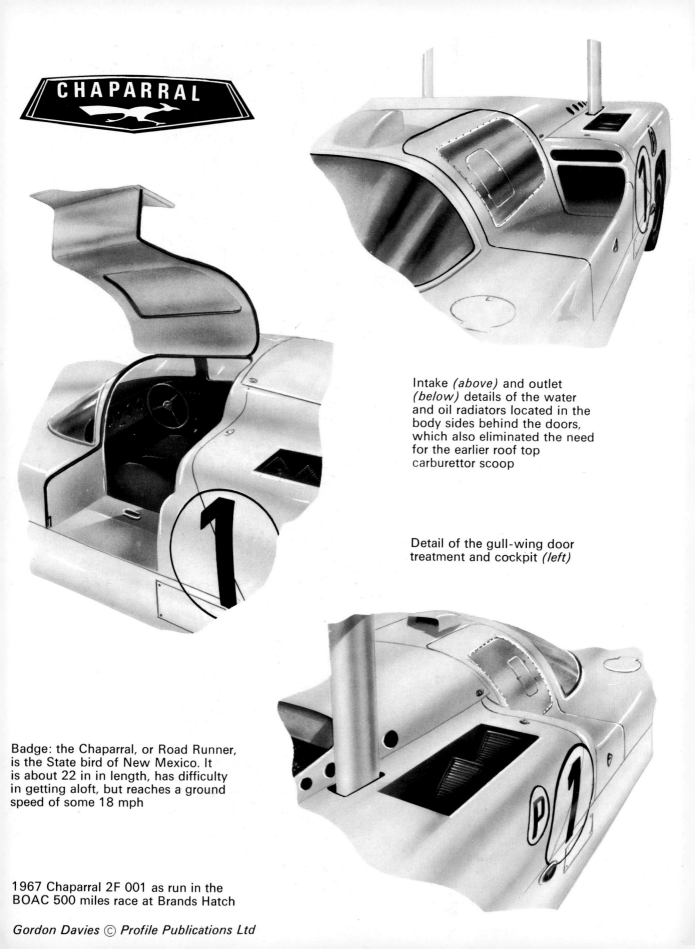

CHAPARRAL

Intake *(above)* and outlet
(below) details of the water
and oil radiators located in the
body sides behind the doors,
which also eliminated the need
for the earlier roof top
carburettor scoop

Detail of the gull-wing door
treatment and cockpit *(left)*

Badge: the Chaparral, or Road Runner,
is the State bird of New Mexico. It
is about 22 in in length, has difficulty
in getting aloft, but reaches a ground
speed of some 18 mph

1967 Chaparral 2F 001 as run in the
BOAC 500 miles race at Brands Hatch

Gordon Davies © Profile Publications Ltd

winter it was revised into the 2F, a spectacular car with exciting aerodynamic features, and a 7-litre engine. This conversion was done one-at-a-time; in early 1967 a 2D ran at Daytona fitted with a 7-litre and retired with its transmission gone after 12 hours. It was driven by Bob Johnson/Bruce Jennings, who had qualified 8th there. At Sebring they started from 4th spot and held their own during the early stages, but retired before half distance, apparently with more gearbox trouble.

Planning the 2F

In planning the 1967 endurance season, the Chaparral engineers didn't adopt the 7-litre engine simply to copy Ford, they made quite an interesting study of their options first. They had two choices: a 5-litre car weighing 700 Kg (1540 lb), based on the current aluminium CanAm chassis, or a glassfibre 750 Kg (1650 lb) car with the bigger power plant. The smaller engine was no problem, as the regular 5.4-litre unit could be destroked, or one of Chevrolet's experimental engines could be chosen — these included a six-cylinder based on the Corvair, a flat-eight ("boxer") based on the 5.4, and a 5.4 with 3-valve heads. Likewise a 7-litre engine was available, the modern, and efficient, staggered-valve ("porcupine") which was soon to go into series production; this was available, cast in aluminium, for such special GM friends as the boys in Midland. The big one offered just over 100 more bhp at a weight penalty of about 85 lbs.

By the use of aerial photographs and a topographical survey of the Daytona Speedway, plus what was already known about 2D performance, a computer was programmed to compare the various options of engine and weight. An electronic abstraction, the hypothetical race car scurried round and round inside, and the answers came out: the bigger, slightly heavier car should be about 1½ seconds faster.

So the glassfibre chassis were pressed into their fifth season of service. But the transformations they went through were extensive and

Promise unfulfilled: Phil Hill and Jo Bonnier came from the Eifel to the 1966 Le Mans 24-hours race as winners, but the Sarthe was less kind. Hill sweeps through the dusk toward nightfall and electrical trouble.
(Michael Cooper & Geoffrey Goddard)

The 1966 Nürburgring Chaparral 2D, showing the flow of cooling air to engine, brakes and driver, from the small high-pressure area ahead of the nose.
(Autocar)

VIC BERRIS

they emerged as virtually brand-new cars—
exciting cars.

Externally, only the central cab section looked
the same. A completely new body profile was
evolved, with a frontal section drooping close
to the road, in the form of a wedge, to generate
downforce. At the rear the body lines tapered
away to a low-drag spindle-shape with an effi-
ciently truncated stern. To balance the downforce at the front, the rear end adopted a device
proven the year before on the 2E CanAm car, a
large aerofoil mounted up above body turbu-
lence on tall struts bolted, not to the body, but
to the suspension uprights. This aerofoil was
connected hydraulically to a foot pedal in such
a way that pressure of the driver's left foot would
pivot it nearly flat for minimum drag on the
straights, but release of pressure for any reason
would flip it into maximum-downforce position.

Firestone had developed larger tyres which
called for wider bodywork, so to make things
come out neatly the actual chassis tub-cum-
fuel tank was covered by flat panels on either
side; these were simply skins, with empty space
between them and the old chassis. The water
and oil radiators were relocated to the body
sides just behind the doors. Among other advantages, this eliminated the need for the rooftop carburettor scoop.

The bigger engine was not that much more
bulky, so squeezing it into the available space
was not difficult, but right from the start the
existing transmission was expected to be a
problem. GM hadn't wanted to build a completely new gearbox; they hoped that stronger
internal parts could cope with the greater
torque. In retrospect it was an unfortunate
decision.

Such were the externally obvious features of
the 2F, but underneath there were many more.

Great attention was paid to weight, and the
car turned out to be a pleasant surprise—it was
lighter than the "model" in the computer. At
about 1750 lbs "wet" (but without fuel) it was
a good 600 lbs lighter than its great rival the Mk
IV Ford. This was due to a number of factors
both large and small; the FRP chassis was, of
course, as light as ever, and the engine was of
alloy rather than iron. Even the battery contributed—it was a stunningly expensive nickel-
cadmium device from the aerospace world.
(Jim Hall enjoyed ferreting out and using things
like that.) The body material itself broke new
ground. After exhaustive experimentation a
construction was found that was lighter than
beaten aluminium: a sandwich of $\frac{1}{4}$-inch thick
PVC foam between thin skins of "4-oz" cloth,
impregnated with Shell epoxy resin. This was
formed to shape in a vacuum-bag apparatus and
allowed to cure at room temperature, rather
than using the pressurized oven which cured
some other, earlier and later, body materials.
The aerofoil was similarly made, filled with
foam.

The whole car was made to the highest quality, aerospace standards. The electrical wiring
loom was made of teflon-insulated wires. The
halfshafts were of a steel that allowed as much
as 270 degrees of twist, to absorb shock-load-
ing, without failure. When the first car shunted a
wall in its first race a suspension wishbone,

"Faster up hill than
down...": far too much
animal for the 1967
Targa Florio. Aero-
dynamicists will note the
wing's trim tab, used on
fast circuits such as Spa—
but for the Madonie...?
(Geoffrey Goddard)

which should have crumpled or shattered,
merely warped. Steel-braided hydraulic line
was used everywhere, particularly on the brakes;
by resisting pressure-bulge they reduced the
required quantity of fluid, which allowed a
smaller master cylinder and thus lower pedal
effort. The Sylvania Company developed new
quartz iodide lights, using their own hand-
made bulbs in Marchal reflectors.

One of the most important details was buried
inside the nose shell, within the otherwise
superfluous "radiator" ducting. This duct had
nothing to do with cooling (beyond a fresh air
feed to the cockpit) but instead had everything
to do with aerodynamic balance. Inside was a
spring-loaded trap door. The problem it solved
had to do with the fact that the front of the body
generated downforce, but the back of the body
generated no downforce at all, perhaps even
some lift. The body, together with the whole
chassis, floated free on the road springs independent of any downforce generated by the
hub-mounted rear aerofoil. Therefore, the faster
the car went, the lower down on its springs was
pressed the nose. The whole body pitched forward, and the more it pitched the more downforce it generated. At something above 150
mph, still well below the expected maximum,

Downforce in detail: the tail section of the 2F was a study in pressure relief — mesh engine cover, holes and radiator outlets — all because of the work done by that big wing. (Michael Cooper)

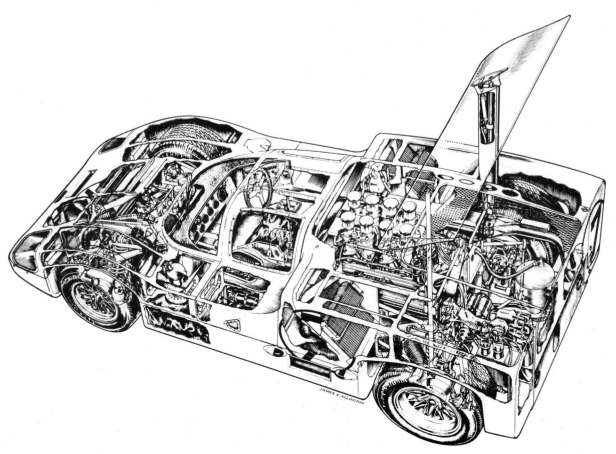

Exposé of the 1967 Chaparral 2F. (Courtesy of the Shell Oil Company)

Ball o' fire: the original 2F flames a warning (perhaps) to the Ford to keep its distance during their epic struggle at Sebring. (Pete Lyons)

Brands bangers: see the big tall American one lurking back in the crowd, trying to hide — but a few hours later all the British and Italian and German ones were trying to hide! BOAC 500 miles, 1967. (Michael Cooper)

So many times before: in seven races, seven disappointments. All that preparation and work and worry; each pit stop could be the last. But at Brands she went all the way. (Michael Cooper)

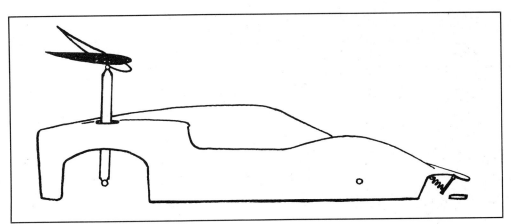

the nose actually compressed the suspension flat. To cure this, the spring-loaded trap door was arranged to start opening at about 140 mph. Air pressure building up within the duct was thereupon vented out underneath the belly-pan, and from that speed on upward the front of the car rose again. A driver who knew what to look for could feel this: over 100 mph the nose would start to dip, at 140 it would reach its lowest angle, and from then on the car settled back toward an even keel. This, it can be seen, encouraged a characteristic of progressive understeer at the higher speed ranges.

Of course, another solution to the pitching problem could have been a dam across the stern, as on the winged McLaren CanAm cars of two years later, but the trap door gave good handling characteristics without as great a drag penalty.

Although the original type 2 had built into its suspension considerable anti-dive and anti-squat geometry, the 2F had reverted to a straight-forward layout without such tricks. Apparently, it handled nicely and held the road well.

Those who drove the car still speak enthusiastically about it. Non-racing personnel—engineers trying out special ideas—say it was "like a street car to drive". The engine characteristics coupled with the clutchless transmission made it simple to handle, the plastic chassis absorbed noise so it was quiet, the rear-mounted radiators kept the cockpit cool. The difference was, "It would go to 160 mph before you knew what was happening—and at that speed it felt like 80 in a passenger car".

To America's World Champion Phil Hill, who drove Chaparrals in long distance events more than anyone else, the 2F was much like any good racing car to drive, ". . . only it was a hell of a lot more *honest*. It had better grip, it was more predictable—there were a lot of reasons for that. It had a lot more downforce than any other car at that time".

To watch a good driver's artistry with the wing pedal was enthralling. Jim Hall once remarked that his whole clutchless Chaparral concept "gives me more combinations". It sounded like a boxer talking about punches, but he was talking about the different ways to deal with corners and traffic.

An important factor about the wing, as Phil Hill pointed out, was that (providing it didn't fall off completely) it was "fail safe". Should

anything go wrong in the feathering mechanism, or should the driver suddenly need his left foot on the brakes, the wing instantly went into its full-drag, full downforce, maximum understeer mode.

Another point was that the whole car was a single integrated engineering whole; the two most prominent features, the transmission and the flipper, complemented each other—in fact the one led to the other.

The 2F was unquestionably one of the most significant and important racing vehicles in the history of the sport. Some of its features were not copied for years.

The 2F's Racing Record

Its racing record was spoilt by its overloaded gearbox. At Daytona in 1967, running for this first time with the rear flipper fixed in one position and the nose trap door inoperative, and double coil spring damper units at all four corners to cope with the banking, it missed by $\frac{1}{4}$ second getting the pole away from a Mk II Ford on "gumball" tyres. At the start it went into the lead, set fastest race lap, and continued to lead for four hours until a driving error put it on to loose material and hence into a concrete wall. A wishbone was replaced but a few more laps showed the suspension was bent too badly to continue. *Autosport* reported that the 2F was faster and more steady on the flat-out bankings than the Mk II, and thanks to its bigger brakes (inside bigger wheels) it could go deeper into the corners. (The light weight must have helped). Their reporter failed to appreciate the science behind the car, however: he said it was "the ugliest car yet seen". Had it won, however, it would probably have looked better to him!

For Sebring the flipper was made to flip and the nose-duct trap door was working. Because at Daytona the entire perspex back window had blown out, indicating extreme low pressure at that point, it was replaced with a porous screen and furthermore holes were bored in the after-body to either side of it. (Later, to get yet more air up into the low pressure area under the wing the radiator hot air outlets were directed up there as well, instead of continuing out to the tail above the rear wheels as in the original scheme). Mike Spence qualified second again, this time by a margin of 2.6 seconds to the Mk IV Ford. Phil Hill came down with appendicitis before race day so Jim Hall stepped in. From the Le Mans-style start Spence had trouble starting the car and it got away well down the field. At the one hour mark it was fourth but at three hours it was leading and into a furious dice with the Ford. Mike did the race's fastest lap, two seconds better than his qualifying time but the big white bird was smoking. The overloaded transmission was bursting its seals. Just after half distance, with the Ford only yards behind, out came a big plume of smoke and the Great Ford vs Chevy Race (for that's what it was and the crowd knew it full well) was over.

On to Europe, to the Chaparral base at Frankfurt, and a longer campaign than the year before. At Monza, using the second car converted to 2F specification, Spence won the pole and from flagfall settled into a stirring dice with a pair of P4 Ferraris (see Cars in Profile No 1). That came to an end after less than an hour when a U-joint broke.

A week later the first car was used at Spa. On this ultra-fast circuit a modification was needed for the wing — a small trim tab at the trailing edge. Normally a driver had to remember to push the wing pedal into feathered position under about 140 mph, as above that speed the aerodynamic pressures were too high. The trim tab acted to help him do this, so he was free to put the wing into downforce position in Spa's most thrilling curves, and get it flat afterward. This time Hill won the pole, by a margin of 3½ seconds from Ickx in a Mirage. But Sun-

day was pouring with rain and Phil recalls, "Ickx ate us alive". Spence started and settled into fifth place, until the refuelling stop when the car refused to restart for over nine minutes. At half distance it was in 8th place, and Spence had done another best race lap. Another blown transmission seal thereupon ended another race.

The Spa car was then taken way down to Sicily for the wonderful old Targa Florio. Spence was busy elsewhere, so Hap Sharp stepped in, but driving his 575 bhp winged "homebuilt" on those roads seemed to disturb his normal equilibrium. "The damn car is faster uphill than down!" he exclaimed, and went off to make a phone call back to Texas to tell Jim about it. Here Vaccarella's Ferrari P4 was faster by a minute and a half. There was trouble on the bumps with dampers, and the car never figured in the race. Near the end it was up to fourth, some 9½ minutes behind the leading Porsche, when a tyre went down flat near Collesano. Engine heat had made the spare unusable, but it was suspected by onlookers that the transmission was again giving trouble anyway.

The second car went to the Nürburgring 1000 Kms, where Spence chopped five seconds from the old sports-car record in practice and in fact set the first 100 mph lap by a sports-car, despite a new chicane which must have cost 10 seconds. Next fastest, by over seven seconds,

Le Mans, 1967: Hill/ Spence 2F at the pits with transmission troubles. (Geoffrey Goddard)

Bella Sicilia: it was more fun than testing on Texas *highways! Phil Hill at Caltavuturo, 1967 Targa Florio.* (Geoffrey Goddard)

was Surtees in a Lola. At the start Hill took time to put on full harness and came round after the first 14.7 miles in sixth place. On the 8th lap the 2F moved into the lead, vanquishing Jo Siffert's Porsche to the vocal distress of the local crowd, – and at 1½ hours into the race, it stopped at the pits a lap early, the damnable gearbox making bad noises. It tried to continue, but stopped on the circuit.

And so to the all-important Le Mans 24-hours, with six races done and six DNFs scored. Both cars ran here, and Hill/Spence missed by 0.3 seconds taking the pole away from a Ford Mk. IV. Johnson and Jennings were about 24th on the long starting row. Both cars got away late, but after one hour Spence was fourth and after two hours he was second. That was as far up as the "white team's" hopes rose, for the wing actuation had broken, robbing something like "30 or 40 miles an hour" according to Hill. After dark there were long pit delays to worry over the transmission, but at half distance the car was still in 3rd place. Then, in the pre-dawn hours, the Texans set to and spent three hours replacing the gearbox, but it was to no avail and they had to retire. The other 2F had quit earlier, reportedly with electrical failure.

The last race was the BOAC 500 miles at Brands Hatch, the shortest and tightest circuit of the series. Here the single entry, 001, qualified on the outside of the front row 0.8 seconds behind the Hulme/Brabham Lola, after half shaft trouble foiled a light-tank attempt at the pole. Hulme charged out to lead the race, and set best lap, but when he retired with a rocker broken Spence and Hill took over the lead from Stewart's and Amon's P4 Ferrari. A mid-race pit stop of 1 min 46 sec dropped the "Wing Machine" down to third, but it started carving back up by two seconds per lap. When the P4 was delayed, the Chaparral got ahead and there it stayed, carefully and regularly, and ran all the way to the end and took its first chequered flag. A winner at last!

Work had already begun on a 1968 version of the 7-litre car when the FIA dropped its controversial homologation bombshell limiting prototype cars to 3 litres, and requiring that 25 examples be built of cars of 5 litres capacity which, in effect, banned any Chaparral from further participation.

Epilogue
Thus the gallant overseas war came to an end. Chaparral Cars concentrated on their "sprint cars" for the North American series, which went on to introduce astonishingly imaginative concepts (so imaginative that three years later the FIA stepped in again and passed another ban that effectively shut down the whole operation!).

The big white coupés were retired to show and storage. They passed from the scene but they had made their indelible impression. Just how advanced they had been was demonstrated by the time delay before, cautiously and incompletely, other designers began to copy some of their principles: hub-mounted wings, downforce body shapes, midships radiators for weight distribution, penetration, and temperature control . . . .

No one ever copied the Chaparrals entirely, partly because of new restrictive legislation, and so they stand for all time as tall, white landmarks to engineering excellence. They stood for something, they proved something – and in their own right they were marvellous.

The Author and the Publishers gratefully acknowledge the assistance and co-operation of Messrs Jim Hall and Phil Hill, and former Chaparral engineers Messrs Don Gates, Paul Lamar and Paul von Valkenburg, in the preparation of this Profile. Autocar, Autosport and Road & Track were also useful sources of reference.

Fitting memory: how we shall always remember her.
(Michael Cooper)

SPECIFICATION OF CHAPARRAL 2F

ENGINE (Chevrolet manufacture)
Cylinders V-8
Cooling system Water; rear-mounted radiator
Bore 108 mm (4.25 in)
Stroke 95.3 mm (3.75 in)
Capacity 7000 cc (427 cu in)
Valve gear Single camshaft in V, pushrod-operated overhead valves with 2 valves per cylinder
Compression ratio 11:1
Carburation 4 Chevrolet 58 mm twin-choke down-draught carburettors of Weber pattern
Maximum power 575 bhp at 7500 rpm

TRANSMISSION

Gearbox General Motors "automatic", with torque converter; 3 forward speeds

CHASSIS AND BODY

Construction Semi-monocoque of fibreglass reinforced plastic

SUSPENSION

Front Double wishbone, coil spring and damper
Rear Two trailing link, single top transverse link, reversed lower wishbone

BRAKES

Make & type Kelsey-Hayes solid discs; 12 in diameter

WHEELS

Type Chaparral cast-alloy
Tyres Firestone; 10.10 x 16 (front), 12.10 x 16 (rear)

EQUIPMENT

Battery Nickel-cadmium 13.5 volt
Headlamps Sylvania quartz iodide with Marchal reflectors

DIMENSIONS

Wheelbase 7 ft 7 in (231 cm)
Track: front 4 ft 7 in (139 cm) rear 4 ft 10 in (147 cm)
Overall length 12 ft 11 in (394 cm)
Overall width 5 ft 10 in (178 cm)
Overall height (unladen) 3 ft 3 in (99 cm)
Weight (less fuel) 1750 lb approx (793 kgs)

SPECIFICATION OF CHAPARRAL 2 AND 2D

generally as for Type F above except:–

ENGINE

Bore 102 mm (4 in)
Stroke 82.6 mm (3.25 in)
Capacity 5360 cc (327 cu in)
Carburettors 4 twin-choke Weber 48 DCOE
Maximum power 415–475 bhp at 7000 rpm

TRANSMISSION

Gearbox 2 forward speeds at first, 3 speed later

BRAKES

Make & type Girling calipers on Type 2 only

RACING RECORD, CHAPARRAL 2, 2D, 2F.

1963 – 3 starts: one 3rd, 2 DNF

*Riverside	Hall, DNF – electrical fire
*Laguna Seca	Hall, 3rd
*Nassau	Hall, DNF – steering

1964 – 24 starts: 7 wins, 8 DNF

Augusta	Hall, 2nd
Pensacola	Hall, 1st; Sharp, DNF
Riverside	Hall, DNF – crash
Laguna Seca	Hall, 1st; Penske 3rd
Kent	Sharp, 2nd; Hall, DNF
*Mosport	Penske, 12th; Hall, DNF
Watkins Glen	Hall, 1st; Penske, 2nd
Greenwood	Hall, 3rd
Meadowdale	Hall, 1st; Penske, 2nd
Mid-Ohio	Sharp, 1st; Hall, 2nd
Elkhart Lake	Hall, DNF
*Mosport	Hall, DNF – crash (broken arm)
*Riverside	Penske, 2nd; Sharp, DNF
*Laguna Seca	Penske, 1st (1st, two heats)
*Nassau	Sharp/Penske, 1st; Penske, DNF

1965 – type 2. 34 starts: 15 wins, 3 DNF

*Sebring 12 hr	Hall/Sharp, 1st; Hissom/Jennings, 22nd
Pensacola	Hall, 15th; Sharp, DNF
Riverside	Hall, 1st; Sharp, 2nd
Laguna Seca	Hall, 1st
Bridgehampton	Hall, 1st; Sharp, 2nd
*Mosport	Hall, 2nd OA (1st in heat 1)
Elkhart Lake	Hall, 1st; Sharp, DNF – crash
Watkins Glen	Hall, 1st; Sharp, 2nd
*St. Jovite	Hall, 2nd; Sharp, 3rd
Kent	Hall, 1st; Sharp, 2nd
CDR (Colo.)	Sharp, 1st; Hall, 4th
Mid-Ohio	Sharp, 1st; Hall, DNF
Elkhart Lake	Hall/Sharp/Hissom, 1st; Sharp/Jennings/Hall, 2nd
*Bridgehampton	Sharp, 1st
*Mosport	Hall, 1st
*Kent	Sharp, 2nd; (Hall 1st in 2C – new model)
*Laguna Seca	Sharp, 2nd; (Hall in 2C, DNF – crash)
*Riverside	Sharp, 1st; (Hall in 2C, non-start – susp.)
*Las Vegas	Sharp, 1st; (Hall, 3rd)
*Nassau	Sharp, 1st; (Hall, DNF)

1966 – type 2D, 5 starts: 1 win, 4 DNF

*Daytona 24 hr	Bonnier/P. Hill, DNF
*Sebring 12 hr	Hall/Sharp, DNF; Bonnier/P. Hill, DNF
*Nürburgring 1000 Km	Bonnier/P. Hill, 1st
*Le Mans 24 hr	Bonnier/P. Hill, DNF

1967 – types 2D and 2F. 11 starts: 1 win, 10 DNF

*Daytona 24 hr	2F 001, P. Hill/Spence, DNF	
	2D,	Johnson/Jennings, DNF
*Sebring 12 hr	2F 001, Hall/Spence, DNF[1]	
	2D,	Johnson/Jennings, DNF
*Monza 1000 Km	2F 002, P. Hill/Spence, DNF	
*Spa 1000 Km	2F 001, P. Hill/Spence, DNF	
*Targa Florio	2F 001, P. Hill/Sharp, DNF	
*Nürburgring 1000 Km	2F 002, P. Hill/Spence, DNF	
*Le Mans 24 hr	2F 001, P. Hill/Spence, DNF	
	2F 002, Johnson/Jennings, DNF	
*Brands Hatch BOAC 500 mile	2F 001, P. Hill/Spence, 1st	

*Indicates FIA International event.

[1] P. Hill practised at Sebring but withdrew because of appendicitis and Jim Hall stepped in for the race.

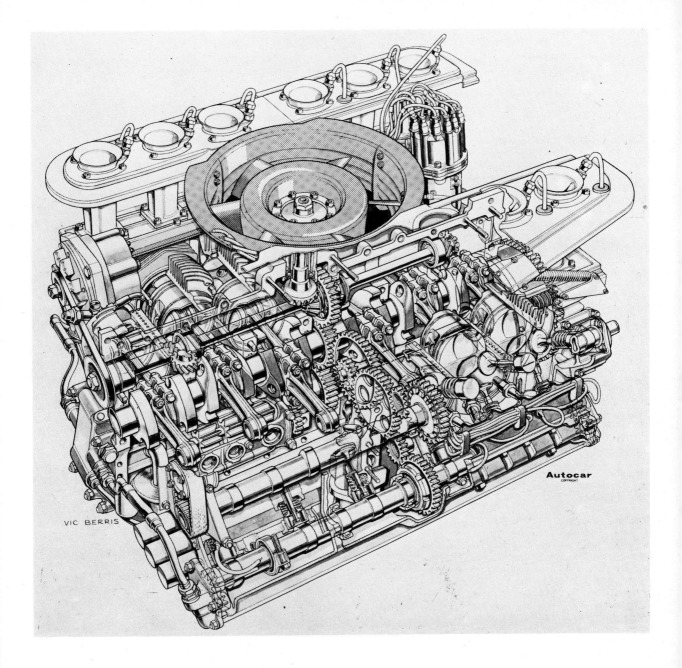

The Porsche 917

by Paul Frère

In April 1968, on the occasion of one of my visits to the Porsche factory, Dipl-Ing Ferry Piëch, Dr Porsche's nephew, who was then the head of the factory's Research and Development Division and responsible for racing car design, told me: 'If we had known earlier that cars with an engine capacity of 5 litres would be allowed to take part in the major races counting towards the Manufacturers' World Championship, with the proviso that 25 identical units had been made, we would have made a car of this type, instead of developing a 3-litre (ie the type 908)'.

As it was, the CSI's decision had been taken much too late and even the 908 would never have been ready to race in 1968 if Porsche had not anticipated the 3-litre limit imposed on Sports Prototypes, which had been announced in October 1967 to come into force on the 1st January 1968. Nevertheless, the Porsche engineers never really accepted the fact that they had not taken advantage of the opportunity which had been left open by the CSI—strictly with an eye to allowing existing cars like the Ford GT40 and the Lola T70, powered by tuned American push-rod V-8 engines, to prolong

The complexity of the flat-12 engine, which takes over 200 hours to assemble. Note the auxiliary oil pumps driven by the lower camshafts to scavenge the cam boxes. ('Autocar')

their racing careers. Surely someone was bound to rise to the occasion, so why should not Porsche be the first to do so?

So it came about that, in July 1968, design work was started on the 917 project, which was easily kept secret as nobody suspected Porsche, who had always specialized in comparatively small-engined cars, of preparing a car in the 5-litre class, while the flat-12 engine was cunningly given the 912 project number, a type number already borne by a production model, but only after a dispute with Peugeot who objected to the actual project numbers 901 and 902 being given by Porsche to production models (which consequently became known as 911 and 912).

Among those who *should* have known, many just would not believe that it was possible to build a successful air-cooled racing engine of that size at all: one of them was Enzo Ferrari who was later to learn better at his own expense!

By this time Porsche had become really expert at light-weight design. They had built a 2-litre, 272 hp Spyder, weighing less than 900 lbs on the starting line, for the European Hill Climb Championship and, at Le Mans, where all cars are carefully weighed, their 3-litre open models were 300 lbs lighter than their Ferrari, Matra and Alpine rivals. For ultra-fast circuits they had developed highly streamlined 'long-tail' cars, thus allowing them make do with somewhat less power than the opposition if the large-sized air-cooled engine really could not be developed to produce the same specific output as water-cooled units of the same capacity. In fact, Porsche never had any problem in matching the power of the only 5-litre opponent who eventually came up to challenge them: the Ferrari 512.

The 917 Engine

At the time the 917 design was put in hand, however, there was no opposition in sight and moreover, Porsche were convinced that they could produce their car to the minimum weight required by the rules for 'Sports Cars' of over 3 litres, ie 800 Kg (1763 lbs). This gave them such a tremendous advantage over the 3-litre opposition that, to start with, they did not even bother to bring the engine up to the full 5-litre capacity: in order to speed up its development, the flat-12 unit used the same reciprocating parts, the same bore and stroke and the same valve and port sizes as the current 3-litre type 908 eight-cylinder engine. This gave a capacity of 4494 cc with a bore and stroke of 85 x 66 mm. All the fuel injection settings and the valve timing could also be directly taken over, the only modification made being a slight reduction in the included valve angle which was reduced from 71° to 65°, in the interest of a more compact combustion chamber design, the inlet valve being inclined 30° from the cylinder axis and the exhaust valve 35°. This was considered to be the narrowest angle compatible with sufficient cooling air passages between the valves, more than two valves per cylinder being ruled out on that account.

Nevertheless, apart from this, the flat-12 is anything but a type 908 flat-8 with four cylin-

ders added. This concept would have led to an unacceptably long crankshaft and brought insurmountable problems of crankshaft torsional vibrations. In order to keep critical periods above the normal revolution range of the engine, and also in order to reduce the vibrations at the power take-off, this is located in the middle of the crankshaft rather than at one of its ends. The long crankshaft thus becomes, in fact, two half length crankshafts having their flywheels bolted together. In this case, however, the flywheels are just a gear in mesh with another gear on the output shaft running parallel to, and under, the crankshaft. Moreover, the power take-off being in the centre of the crankshaft, it also coincides with the node of fundamental torsional vibrations (which are the more severe ones), where the amplitude of the vibration is nil. For the same reason, all the timing and accessory drive gears are also driven from the crankshaft centre.

A flat six can be fully balanced only if each connecting rod has its own crankpin. On a flat-12 the same full balance can be obtained with two connecting rods per crankpin and advantage has been taken of this to reduce the number of crankshaft webs and thus make the engine shorter without loss of bearing surface (see drawing page 99). Since the central driving gear is supported on both sides, the crankshaft has a total of 8 main bearings. And further to increase the useful bearing surface while keeping the engine short, the oil fed to the big end bearings comes from both ends of the crankshaft through an axial drilling, in order to avoid the ridge in the bearing shell necessary if the big ends are to be lubricated from the oil supplied directly to the main bearings. This has also made it possible to reduce the maximum oil pressure to as low as 35 lbs/sq in and thus reduce the power absorbed by the lubricating system. The main and big end bearings are the only plain bearings in the unit.

Originally, the central power take-off gear was in one piece with the crankshaft, both the gear and the crankpins and journals being case-hardened, but when an electronic beam welding machine was acquired by the factory, the case-hardened gear was usually welded to the two crankshaft halves, of which the crankpins and journals were induction hardened. From then on such built-up crankshafts were used for most of the 4.5-litre units. The power output shaft is driven at 32/31 engine speed and its 31 teeth gear also drives the triple gear-type oil pump with two chambers scavenging each half of the flat-12 engine and one chamber feeding the bearings under pressure. There are four additional small oil pumps driven by the exhaust camshafts to scavenge the cam boxes. Another shaft running symmetrically above the crankshaft drives the two distributors of the twin electronic ignition system, the cooling blower running at 0.895 engine speed, and the belt-driven alternator, while the timing gears to the twin ohc per bank are located each side at crankshaft level. The Bosch fuel injection pump is cog-belt driven from the left hand intake camshaft.

Even in its original form, the 917 engine had

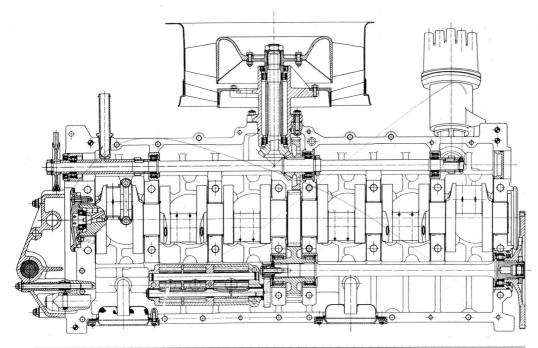

917 engine, longitudinal
section: the absence of
the cushioned cooling
blower drive indicates
the 1969 model.
(Porsche)

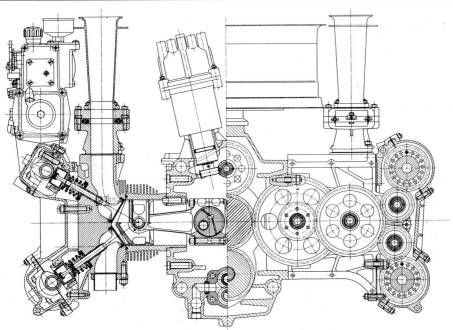

Cross section of the 917
engine.
(Porsche)

very few steel or iron parts: the crankcase, vertically split along its centre line, the cam covers
and the timing gear casing were magnesium,
the cylinder heads were aluminium and so were
the individual cylinders which had chrome-
plated bores (the so-called Cromal cylinders).
Titanium was used for the connecting rods and
their bolts as well as for several spindles,
brackets, linkages etc, while the cooling blower
and most of the air ducts were of plastic. In the
course of further developments, many of the
remaining steel parts were replaced by either

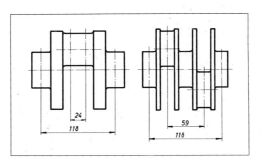

Two connecting rods
per crankpin permit
increased bearing and
flange width.
(Porsche)

light alloy or titanium. Both were used for some of the timing and other gears and titanium was used for the auxiliary drive shaft and was even successfully tried for the main output shaft. Even titanium inlet valves and valve springs were developed successfully. The total engine weight was originally 528 lbs, of which 156 lbs or 29.5% were magnesium.

Concurrently with the engine, a completely new gearbox and final drive had to be designed to take the torque of 376 lb/ft developed by even the original version of the flat-12 engine.

This gearbox also had a magnesium casing and the five-speed unit had full Porsche-type synchromesh. A wet sump was used, but additionally, the oil was circulated by a pump and fed to strategic points by jets. The friction-type ZF limited slip differential had a 75% locking factor and the clutch was a 3-disc Fichtel and Sachs.

Even though the chassis was largely a takeover from the existing 3-litre type 908, suitably reinforced and with the cockpit moved forward to make room for the larger power unit in the

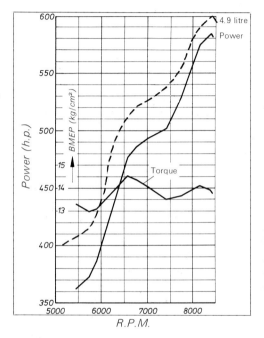

Engine installation in an early 917: the (raised) plastic engine cover indicates a 1969 car. (Geoffrey Goddard)

Power (Ne) and torque (Pme) of the 4.5 litre engine, and power curve (dotted line) of the 4.9 litre engine. (Porsche)

The accessories shown here include the engine oil tank, auxiliary fuel supply tank, fuel pump and filter. The rough finish of the plastic wheel arch and of the welds is typical of the Porsche 'function-before-beauty' attitude. (Geoffrey Goddard)

unaltered 90 in. wheelbase, it was a fantastic achievement that the first example of the new car, on which design had started in July 1968, was exhibited to a startled world at the Geneva Motor Show on the 10th March 1969 and that by the end of April the 25 units required by the CSI for recognition as a 'Sports Car' had been built and homologated. In May, the car ran in its first race, retiring after only one lap at Spa, but finishing 8th two weeks later in the Nürburgring 1000 Kilometres race, and in mid-June it led the Le Mans 24 Hours Race for the first 20 hours!

By that time, the 4.5-litre engine already developed 580 hp at 8400 rpm and right from the start the car was just about as light as the rules would permit, ie 800 Kg, which made its performance vastly superior to anything seen on the tracks before.

The 917 Chassis
As we have seen, the chassis of the 917 was largely a take-over from the 908, suitably re-inforced as required. After some successful experiments with a 907 and a 908 in 1968, all Porsche racing models were built around a welded aluminium tube spaceframe in 1969 and the 917 was, of course, no exception. The proportions had to be considerably altered, however, to accommodate the big engine, so that the pedals were actually ahead of the front wheel axis, while the spare wheel (fitted with a Goodrich 'Spacesaver' tyre) was moved back, over the gearbox. As with all other Porsche

The first 917 to be built was the talk of the 1969 Geneva Motor Show. It was exhibited with its bolt-on long tail, and was listed at 140,000 DM (about £14,500 at the time). The very con-servative figures of 520 hp and 200 mph were claimed.
(Geoffrey Goddard)

Two-row fuel injection pump by Bosch.
(Porsche)

racing cars, the frame had to withstand over 600 miles hard driving over the rough 'Destruction Course' of the factory's own proving ground at Weissach. Even then, the complete frame, with all brackets welded on, weighed only 103 lbs. In order to get a quick check on possible cracks, all the tubes were interconnected (except those frame tubes used for piping the oil between the engine and the front oil cooler, where leaks would have shown up anyway) and a tyre valve was fitted in a convenient location, so that the frame could be 'inflated' and a check for pressure losses, indicating a crack, made with a tyre pressure gauge.

Magnesium, aluminium and titanium parts were widely used for the running gear. Among unusual applications were titanium ball- and spherical joint housings throughout the suspension and steering, titanium hubs, suspension springs, gear lever, steering column etc., an aluminium steering rack in a magnesium housing and, of course, magnesium uprights and wheels, while the central wheel locking nut was aluminium.

The suspension geometry was very similar to the 908 forerunner, except that a 50% anti-dive geometry was originally incorporated at the front by angling the upper and lower wishbone pivots to each other, and even the relatively narrow rims sizes were the same as for the 3-litre: 9 x 15 front and 12 x 15 rear.

In this connection, it must be recalled that Porsche's favourite testing ground, considered the ultimate test of handling, is the Nürburgring. This has many bumps and dips calling for a rather long suspension travel and relatively soft and well-damped suspension. With such suspension, considerable camber variations are necessary to keep the outside wheels more or less perpendicular to the road surface under high cornering forces causing the car to roll, and with such a geometry, comparatively narrow tyres with a slightly rounded tread section are necessary to accommodate normal suspension movements and still keep the largest possible tread surface on the road. As it turned out, however, it soon became evident that the full power could not be exploited with the rims and tyres originally fitted.

The coupé body, made of fibreglass reinforced polyester, was certainly not the least interesting part of the car. Its final design was a result of extensive wind tunnel tests and two

alternative, interchangeable, bolt-on tails were offered: a short one for normal circuits and a long one for very fast circuits, the drag factor being reduced from $C_W = 0.4$ to $C_W = 0.33$ by the use of the long tail. With the latter, a speed of 236 mph was reached on the Le Mans straight in 1969.

At such speeds, stability is largely a matter of aerodynamics. It is essential that some aerodynamic downthrust should be exerted to keep the car firmly in contact with the road surface. Unfortunately, the downthrust is very dependent upon the angle of incidence of the vehicle. If the front is raised, even only slightly, downthrust can be considerably reduced and even change into lift, which will cause the vehicle to take off—the sort of accident that has happened before. To prevent this, both the 917 long-tail and short-tail cars were not only fitted with front spoilers creating downthrust, but they were also given mobile rear flaps connected with the rear suspension in such a way that if the suspension was compressed, the flaps would create an aerodynamic force tending to raise the tail, while if the suspension was extended, the flaps would angle up to push the tail down. Immediate correction was thus obtained to keep the speeding car as near its designed posture as possible.

In 1969, these mobile flaps gave rise to some intense discussion at Le Mans because, only two weeks before the race, any sort of mobile aerodynamic devices were banned by the FIA. As the cars were proved to be undriveable without the mobile flaps and these were part

There is not an ounce of excess weight in this 917 cockpit. (Geoffrey Goddard)

Early type 917 aluminium tube chassis frames. The one on the right is incomplete. Weight of complete frame: 103 lbs. (Porsche)

of the homologated model anyway, the matter was finally settled by an agreement between all entrants, but they could not be used in later races. Twenty-five of these bolt-on long tails were made to comply with the homologation rules, though only two or three of them were ever used.

Early Developments

The first race for which the 917 was entered was the Spa 1000 Kilometres race in May 1969. Up to then, there had hardly been any time for testing it and sorting out the suspension and it was brought along mainly as a development exercise. Unfortunately nothing could be done, as it rained during all the practice sessions and a valve broke on the first race lap—possibly following over-revving at the start. So practically the only testing the car got under racing conditions before Le Mans was in the Nürburgring 1000 Km race, later in May. It ran, of course, in short-tail form and was taken around the track in practice by Dieter Quester in 8 min 37.8 sec, but in the race it was driven by the British pair of Frank Gardner and David Piper who brought

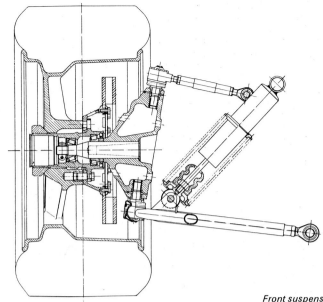

Front suspension and brake, early 1970 version, with fixed stub-axle. In later cars, the stub-axle turned with the hub in larger bearings held in the upright.
(Porsche)

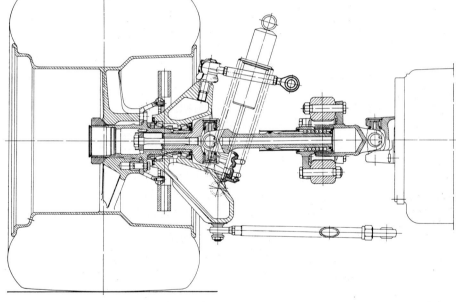

Rear suspension and half-shafts.
(Porsche)

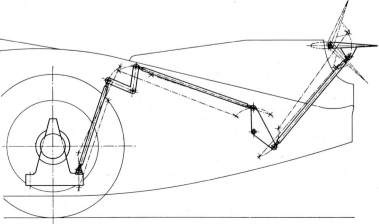

Linkage actuating the rear mobile flaps of the 1969 Le Mans cars.
(Porsche)

it home 8th. The car was said to be very difficult to drive and very unstable at speed, and as a first measure before Le Mans, the front anti-dive geometry was modified to give only 5% rather than 50% anti-dive.

Otherwise, the cars which ran at Le Mans were practically unchanged. From the 542 hp it produced on its first testbed run, the engine had been developed to give some 580 hp, and those who think an air-cooled racing engine loses too much power in driving its cooling blower will be interested to know that this absorbed only 17 hp at peak revs (580 hp is a net figure at the output shaft, with the blower running). This is, of course, much less than the power required to drive a large water radiator through the atmosphere at over 200 mph.

It would certainly be untrue to say that the drivers were delighted with the way the cars handled at Le Mans, but with their mobile flaps they were stable enough to be driven flat-out on the long straight and this gave them such an overwhelming advantage that they were far faster around the course than any of the other cars. If Stommelen's furiously driven car did not last very long, the biggest surprise for everyone concerned was that the more gently driven 917 of Elford and Attwood led the race until the 20th hour: a win was not to be however and it finally stopped with a cracked bell housing. This was the race in which the only surviving works Porsche, a 908, which had had a 20 minutes pit stop to change a front wheel bearing, lost the race by 2 seconds after 24 hours racing to the Ford GT40 of the Gulf-Wyer team . . .

Except at Le Mans however, the 917 was still not really competitive, and during the following autumn and winter the development people really got down to sorting it. Track testing, wind tunnel tests and steering pad tests all played their part, but the most important contribution was probably the track tests carried out on the Austrian Zeltweg circuit where, a few days earlier, a short-tail 917 fitted with wider wheels and tyres and driven by Siffert and Ahrens, had scored its first victory in the Austrian 1000 Kilometres race where the competition was admittedly rather weak. Zeltweg is a very fast track where lap speeds of some 130 mph were reached at that time and the importance of aerodynamics was emphasized by the fact that modifications to the body shape alone, partly inspired by John Wyer and his team who were to race Porsches on behalf of the factory in the following year, improved the lap times by some 4 seconds or 3.5%. The main modifications consisted in raising the waistline on the doors and raising the tail, to give the car roughly the profile of a wedge. The modification brought about a 15% drag increase to $C_W = 0.46$, but the rear of the body being left open, the total body weight was reduced by 33 lbs to 150 lbs.

Testing showed that with the power available, wider rims and tyres were definitely beneficial and, as the 917 was not used by the factory on the Nürburgring anyway, and as most other tracks were smoother, they were finally adopted, after steering pad tests had also shown them to be advantageous. Simultaneously stiffer

Two of a kind at Zeltweg, 1970. No 23 has the additional small rear aerofoil, first used on the John Wyer cars at Le Mans. The other car, fresh from its victory at Le Mans, has the standard 1970 short-tail, which was replaced in 1971 by the lower, finned tail.
(Geoffrey Goddard)

How the original 917 tail of 1969 was experimentally modified to become the wedge tail of 1970.

Front brakes, 1969 and 1971 versions. The 1969 cars had a full diameter ventilated cast-iron disc with radial vanes bolted to the titanium hub. Several stages of development led to the use of extensively drilled, lightened discs with curved vanes reduced to a ring bolted to a drilled aluminium cone carried by the titanium hub. The saddle carrying the aluminium (here Girling) brake cylinders is also made of titanium.
(Porsche and Geoffrey Goddard)

1970 Le Mans winner: driven by
Hans Herrmann and Richard Attwood,
this 4.5-litre 917 K (short-tail) car
entered by Porsche-Salzburg won the
classic 24 hours race, covering
2,863.14 miles (4,607.81 kilometres),
an average speed of 119.3 m.p.h.
(191.99 k.p.h.).

Terry Hadler © Profile Publications Ltd

0   3feet

springs were used to reduce the suspension movements and attitude changes under braking and acceleration, but no changes were made to the suspension geometry itself. Additionally a bag-type safety fuel tank was fitted as required by the 1970 regulations, which also allowed a maximum capacity of 120 litres (26.39 gallons).

For the moment, the engine was largely left alone, but the exhaust system was modified to direct all the pipes towards the rear of the car, instead of having the exhaust system of the front cylinders coming out at the sides where they tended to overheat the fuel system and create vapour lock. As the Fichtel and Sachs

An open version of the 917, called 917 PA, was built for Jo Siffert to drive in some of the 1969 Can-Am races. It was very reliable but not quite fast enough. (Porsche)

In its first two races, the 917 ran in short-tail form with a fixed rear spoiler. The front spoilers were not only inelegant but very vulnerable. Here the car is seen in the Nürburgring 1000 Kilometres race of 1969 when it was driven by David Piper and Frank Gardner. (Porsche and Geoffrey Goddard)

For 1970 the transmission casing was stiffened up by heavy ribs. The rear chassis pyramid is shown partly dismantled for access to the transmission. (Geoffrey Goddard)

clutch had not been very satisfactory, it was
replaced by a Borg and Beck unit of three-disc
pattern with sintered metal linings and, as a
lesson from Le Mans where the two 917s had
suffered bell housing failures, the whole gearbox and clutch housing was reinforced.

To get experience of some of the modifications made and to further develop the type 917,
a single car called 917 PA (PA stood for
Porsche-Audi as the car was called in the
U.S.A.) was built with an open body and sent
to America for Jo Siffert to drive in the
Canadian-American Championship series as a
private entry. This car still had the front exhausts on the sides but it used 10.5 in wide
rims at the front and 15 (later 17) in rims at the
rear. It had also been further lightened to some
extent, the ventilated cast-iron brake discs
being reduced to a crown bolted to a titanium
cone to which the titanium hub was bolted.
Later aluminium was used for this cone because
of better heat transfer from the disc to the wheel
and it became a standard 917 part notably
reducing the unsprung weight. This car, which
had a larger tank capacity, was actually quite
successful: though it was not fast enough to
compete with the current 7- and 8-litre engines
used in the Can-Am races, it finished second in
one of them and took 4th place in the Championship, although it only competed in 6 out
of the 11 races of the series.

The 1970 Season
For 1970, Porsche's racing activities were re-
organized and though the factory continued
with the development of the cars, their preparation and the actual race organization was entrusted to two independent set-ups: the Gulf-
sponsored John Wyer Organization and
Porsche-Salzburg, a firm run by Dr Porsche's
sister Luise Piëch, and dealing with Porsche
and Volkswagen interests in Austria. Only for
the Targa Florio and for Le Mans were the cars
still prepared and run by the factory itself.

*John Wyer—a typical
picture of the boss at
work.
(Geoffrey Goddard)*

*A fleet of 917s being
prepared at J. W. Auto-
motive Engineering at
Slough. The different
pattern of the orange
central stripe on the car's
nose made it easier to
distinguish between a
car driven by Siffert
(nearest the camera) and
one driven by Rodriguez
(No 15).
(Nigel Snowdon)*

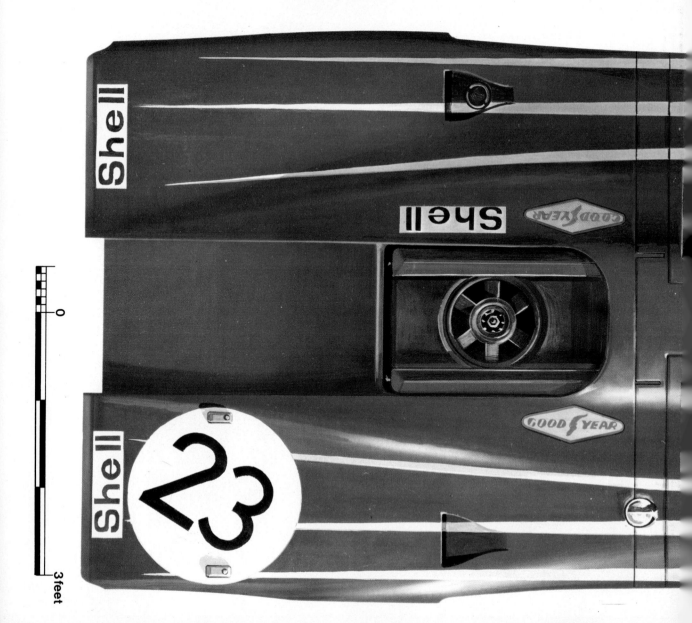

1970 Herrmann-Attwood 4.5-litre 917 K, winner of the
Le Mans 24 hours race.

Terry Hadler © *Profile Publications Ltd*

With all the development now behind the 917s, they proved almost unbeatable in 1970, losing only one of the races in which they were entered. This was the Sebring 12 Hours race in which a new, and insufficiently tested, type of front hub with larger bearings (introduced to reduce pushing back of the brake pads on bends) failed on all the cars, giving the rival Ferrari 512 S, which had been hastily developed to counter the Porsche attack in the 5-litre field, its only victory. Apart from this, the 917 won every race for which it was entered. They were not used for the Targa Florio and the Nürburgring 1000 Kilometres race however, for which the lighter and smaller new 3-litre Type 908/03 was a more suitable car, which it proved by winning both races.

Throughout the 1970 season, except at Le Mans, the 917s were run with a four, rather than a five-speed gearbox, the torque of the engine being considered sufficient to bridge the slightly wider gap between the gears.

view of the anticipated Ferrari onslaught. Except for its bore and stroke dimensions of 86 x 70.4 mm, this engine was practically identical with the 4494 cc unit and used the same cylinder heads, valves and camshafts. But the power was raised to 600 hp and the torque went up by 10% to 415 lb/ft. Using this new engine in a short-tail car, Jo Siffert won the Spa 1000 Kilometres race and Pedro Rodriguez set up a new lap record at an average speed of 160 mph, the fastest speed ever reached on a road-racing circuit and to be beaten only the following year, at 162 mph, by Siffert on another 917. This still stands as the absolute record for the Spa-Francorchamps circuit.

Meanwhile at the factory the development work now centred around the long-tail cars to be run at Le Mans. It was not an easy task to combine a low drag factor with good high-speed stability and acceptable handling, without having recourse to the mobile rear flaps used in 1969 which were now definitely

First lap at Mulsanne corner in the 1970 Le Mans 24 Hours race. Vic Elford in the long-tail car is leading the two short-tail cars of Jo Siffert and Pedro Rodriguez. (Geoffrey Goddard)

Another successful step was the introduction of perforated brake discs, with the holes matching up with the cooling vanes to establish a forced circulation. They lowered the disc temperature by over 100 °C in addition to reducing the disc weight by nearly 4 lbs. As a result of comparative rig tests, Girling brake calipers were found to be better than those made by Ate which were normally used by Porsche. Following these tests, the cars run by the Wyer team used Girling calipers, but for patent reasons, they could not be used on the Porsche-Salzburg cars.

Except for the addition of a rubber spring hub in the cooling blower drive, to reduce inertia loads on the driving gears, the engine was practically unchanged until, on the occasion of the Monza 1000 Kilometres race (the third race in the Championship series) some cars were fitted with engines brought up to 4907 cc in

banned, and two cars were completely destroyed in the course of the development tests, fortunately without too serious injury to the drivers. The issue was not simplified by the fact that, whereas in dry weather the short-tail 917s were now running mostly on 10.5 or 12 in wide front rims and 17 in wide rear rims, 10.5 and 15 in rims were used for the long-tail cars in order to reduce the frontal area and the concomitant total drag. But the major problem of reducing the lift variations induced by attitude changes was eventually solved—at the cost of some increase in drag from $C_W = 0.33$ to $C_W = 0.36$ — by giving the front and rear upper decks a slightly concave shape, a solution which was arrived at in cooperation with the French SERA design office. In view of the much wider speed range of the long-tail cars, which were about 20 mph faster than the short-tail models, they were fitted with a five-speed version of the reinforced gearbox. Two long-tail cars were entered for the race: one, fitted with the 4.9-litre engine, was run by Porsche-Salzburg while the other, a 4.5 litre-engined model was entrusted to the private Martini Racing Team, as John Wyer had refused to run the long-tail cars which, in his opinion, were too tricky: on his own initiative he added a small adjustable wing at the back of his short-tail cars. Neither of the 'long-tails' had much luck: the 4.9-litre driven by Elford and Ahrens retired with a broken valve whereas the car which had been given the 4.5-litre engine for the sake of its proven reliability was plagued by misfiring during the many thunderstorms which made the event look more like a speed boat race than a car race. Driven by Larrousse and Kauhsen, it eventually finished 2nd to the short-tail car of Herrmann-Attwood which had run like clockwork throughout.

Looking Ahead

By the beginning of 1970, it had become known that no cars of more than 3-litres capacity would be allowed to compete for the World Championship of Makes after 1971 and that, for that last year, 5-litre cars would be accepted without homologation, which meant that existing cars could be modified as required without 25 identical units having to be made. For Porsche, this meant that any sort of experiment could be carried out on the 917 during 1971 and also that, as far as Europe was concerned, the cars could be scrapped by the end of that year. Having developed a very successful 3-litre car weighing only 545 Kg (1201 lbs) (in Targa Florio trim, 1970), neither were they keen on taking part in a Championship for 3-litre cars in which a minimum weight of 650 Kg (1433 lbs) was required, light weight having become a sort of a religion in Zuffenhausen. Consequently, and following the comparative success of the 917 PA Spyder driven by Siffert in the Can-Am series, the decision was taken, early in 1970, to get on with the development of the 917 with a view to its banishment from European sports-car racing. Development work was immediately started on the engine, two lines being considered: adding four cylinders to the existing unit to make it a 16-cylinder, and, secondly, turbo-charging the flat-12. For size and weight reasons, the second solution was finally preferred and, by mid-1971, a turbo-charged car was running on the Porsche test-track in Weissach.

Notwithstanding all the time devoted to the new project, the development of the European version of the 917 which was to defend Porsche's title in 1971 did not lag behind. The Stuttgarters were determined to leave the European scene in a blaze of glory with both the Championship of Makes, and Le Mans, in their pockets. The short-tail body was further improved following track and wind tunnel tests which led to a slightly lowered back and two tail fins, the drag factor being lowered from $c_W = 0.447$ to 0.386 at a penalty of a 20% reduction in downthrust at the rear but probably better behaviour in side winds. The finned tail raised the maximum speed by some 6 mph and was used for most of the 1971 races, though

Three vintages of long-tail cars at Le Mans: 1969—No 14 of Stommelen-Ahrens cornering at Mulsanne. Note the asymmetric positions of the mobile tail flaps as the car rolls. (Geoffrey Goddard)

1970—No 25, driven by Elford-Attwood, was much more stable, despite its fixed rear wing and absence of front spoilers. The concave nose and unswept tail are notable features. (Geoffrey Goddard)

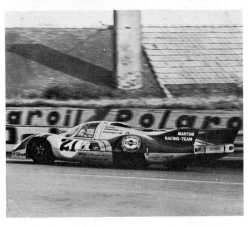

1971—The last version of the long-tail 917, No 21 of Elford—Larrousse had a flatter bow, lower front wings, and rear wheel spats. (Geoffrey Goddard)

The battered 917 L of Elford-Ahrens leading the 1970 Le Mans race under appalling weather conditions. It set up a new lap record but a broken valve caused its retirement. (Geoffrey Goddard)

The J. W. Automotive-entered 5-litre
917 K of Pedro Rodriguez and Jackie
Oliver won the 1971 Monza 1,000
Kilometres race in 4 hours 14 min
32.6 sec, an average speed of
146.54 m.p.h. (235.88 k.p.h.).

The psychedelically-decorated
4.5-litre 917 L (long-tail) car of
Gérard Larrousse and Willi Kauhsen,
entered by the Martini Racing Team,
came second in the 1970 Le Mans
24 hours race.

Terry Hadler © Profile Publications Ltd

in some cases the older tail was fitted.

At the end of the 1970 season, Ferrari produced an improved version of his 512 S, called 512 M, which had more power, less weight (but still some 220 lbs more than the Porsche) and better streamlining, and one of them, driven by Ickx and Regazzoni, beat the privately-entered, but works-prepared 917 of Siffert-Attwood in the non-championship Kyalami 9-Hours race, which certainly made Porsche sit up and take notice. Their answer, in addition to the improved body, was a full 5-litre engine, the cylinder bore being increased from 86 to 86.8 mm. In itself, this 90 cc capacity increase should not have produced a worthwhile boost in power, but at the same time a change over was made from Cromal to Nikasil cylinders, which means that instead of being chrome-plated, the bores of the aluminium cylinders were formed by a nickel-silicon layer similar

ment, combined great rigidity with extremely light weight. It had already been used with great success for the ultra-lightweight 908/03 which won both the Targa Florio and the Nürburgring 1000 Kilometres race in 1970, and the Nürburgring race, again, in 1971.

The Final European Season
As Ferrari had decided not to enter his 512 M in the Championship races of 1971 and had sold most of them to private owners, who were not really a force to be reckoned with by the fully factory-backed Porsches of the Gulf-Wyer and Martini Racing Teams (the latter having replaced the Porsche-Salzburg Organization for the 1971 racing season), any further development of the 917 was not really essential to secure the Manufacturers' World Championship for Porsche for the third consecutive year, but the Porsche engineers now looked upon

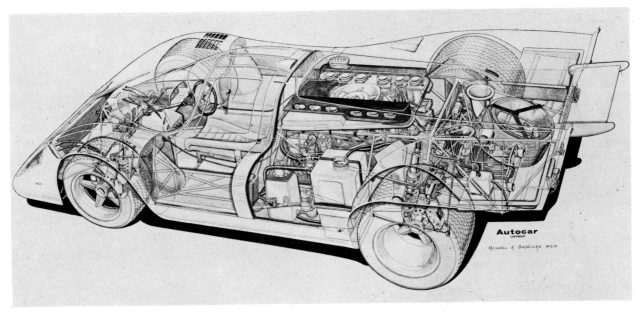

to that used by NSU for Wankel engine trochoids. Rather surprisingly, this change of material in itself produced a noticeable increase in power (possibly due to quicker bedding-in of the piston rings), so that the average power output of the full 5-litre (exactly 4998 cc) engine came out at 630 hp at 8300 rpm. As a matter of interest, the cooling system having been left unchanged, this makes the 17 hp absorbed by the cooling blower come out at only 2.7% of the total output.

To go with this engine, the gearbox was further reinforced, mainly by the use of larger diameter shafts.

For the 1971 season, new rules came into force, making stronger roll-over bars compulsory and requiring central, large capacity, fire-extinguishing equipment which added some weight to the vehicles. To compensate for this, a new epoxy material was used for the body, the moulded panels of which were a comparatively thick foamy material sandwiched between two glass-hard outer skins. This material, developed by Porsche's own plastics depart-

this last European season of the 917 as a development exercise for the 'Can-Am' version they were preparing for 1972.

Perhaps the most interesting aspect of this activity was the development of a chassis frame made up of welded magnesium tubes. Compared with aluminium, this promised a further substantial saving in weight, but it proved to be a very difficult task. Tests on the Weissach destruction course proved very discouraging, but in the end a chassis made of larger diameter tubes successfully withstood 620 miles driving on the destruction course, just after having taken part in the preliminary practice session at Le Mans, in April 1971. To get an unbiased judgement on the behaviour of the car using the new frame, the drivers were not told of its existence and, as it wore a rather old and shabby body, they were far from suspecting anything unusual, especially as the other short-tail car, with the current aluminium frame, brought along for comparison, looked much the newer of the two. So when Siffert lapped faster with the magnesium-frame car than with the standard model

A 917 K as used by J. W. A. Engineering at Le Mans in 1970 and later that season, with an adjustable aerofoil between the rear wing extensions. The front radiator is, of course, an oil cooler. ('Autocar')

and passed a better overall judgement on it, everyone was very pleased.

In order to obtain further test data on this type of frame, which was to be used on the following year's Can-Am car (as no minimum weight is specified for Group 7 cars), a new short-tail car was made with a magnesium frame and entered for the Le Mans 24 Hours race, where it was entrusted to the junior members of the team, Dr Helmut Marko and Gijs van Lennep, who eventually won the race! This was certainly not because of any particular merit of the magnesium frame, as the rules did not even allow the car to take advantage of its lighter frame and despite all the Le Mans supplementary equipment, the car had to be fitted with a 12 Imp. gallon oil tank which was filled as much as was necessary to get the weight up to the minimum 800 Kg (1763 lbs) required! At the time the drivers did not even know they were driving a car that was strictly experimental.

Although it did not look as if much competition would be forthcoming at Le Mans, it was essential for Porsche to make quite sure that the World Championship title, gained for the third consecutive year even before the French race was run, would not be spoiled by a defeat at Le Mans, as it had been in 1969. Consequently, further development work was done on the long-tail body which was further refined to give improved stability without impairing the drag factor, notwithstanding the fact that 17 in. wide wheels were now to be used at the rear. Externally the most obvious changes compared with the previous year's cars were the sharply cut-off front with a flat and horizontal front undershield to reduce the amount of air rammed under the car, and the partly shielded rear wheels. At last, the full benefit of the low drag body was gained, as with this shape and the lighter body material notably reducing the weight of the overhung tail, the drivers were unanimous in saying that the cars handled just as well as the short-tail models, this being reflected by the fastest-ever Le Mans lap achieved by Jackie Oliver in 3 min 13.6 sec in the course of the April preliminary practice, when his car was officially timed at 240 mph on the Hunaudières straight, using a 4.9-litre engine.

While the long-tail cars were being further developed, an attempt was made to obtain an equally low drag from a car not exceeding the length of the normal short-tail model. This led to the design of a very wide body with considerable side overhang to reduce the wheel arch interference, but the car, called a 917/20, was not really successful, being slower and less stable than the long-tail cars which, of course, had many years of development behind them. In the race itself, all cars used the 4.9-litre engine because of its now-proven reliability, rather than the 5-litre, and all used a 5-speed gearbox which, in fact, was another reason for not using the full 5-litre engine with which the five-speed transmission had never been endurance tested. But by a strange stroke of coincidence, none of the special Le Mans cars—three long-tail cars and the 917/20 internally known as the 'Big Bertha' (or less reverently as 'the Pig')—reached the finish. Big Bertha crashed;

one of the long-tails broke the cooling blower drive; one seized its engine following the breakage of an oil pipe and, on the third, the engine crankcase split. So once again it was up to the short-tails to save the day by finishing first and second, breaking all existing records. This should not detract from the merits of the long-tail cars which were found to be approximately 5–6 seconds per lap faster, when fully extended, and which had a notably lower fuel consumption: practice checks by the John Wyer team indicate that their short-tail car averaged 5.4 mpg while their long-tail models did 5.9 and 6.3 mpg, an improvement averaging some 12%

Those present at Le Mans in 1971 cannot have failed to notice the strange way in which the 'Big Bertha' was painted when she came to the starting line. There is a story behind this, such as could only happen in a family business (which the Porsche Company in fact is, as the entire capital is in the hands of Ferdinand Porsche Senior's successors) in which the contacts are more informal than is usual in a concern of such importance.

When it was decided to try and design a car which would combine the merits of the long- and short-tail models, two separate groups got down to it: Porsche's own Experimental Department and the SERA Design Office. But Porsche's Styling Office thought they too were quite competent enough to produce a worthwhile project and they eventually came up with their own design. As it turned out, the final design—not a particularly elegant one, one must admit—was really a combined effort of Porsche Experimental and the French technicians, while the project of Porsche Styling was not taken into consideration. To compensate for this, the stylists were asked to participate in the project by at least painting and decorating it according to their own ideas. That is when they got their own back! They thought the car looked just like a pig and they enthusiastically combined their efforts to make it look even more like one. They had it sprayed in pigskin pink and wrote down all the comestible parts of the animal on the car, suitably contoured, to make quite sure everyone knew how they felt about it!

The 917 Becomes a Group 7 Car

With Le Mans in the bag, all the factory's efforts now centred around the evolution of the 917 into a Group 7 'Two-seater Racing Car', to use the official description. Backed by the experience they had gained in the 1969-70 Can-Am series, a new open-bodied car, known as the type 917/10 was built and raced by Jo Siffert in four of the Can-Am races in which he took two 2nd, a 3rd and a 5th place before his fatal accident in a Formula One car. Private owners of 917 coupés were also given the opportunity of having their cars modified to Group 7 specifications with an open body. Mainly for their benefit, the engine was further developed to take 90 mm bore cylinders thus raising the capacity to 5.4 litres with an appreciable benefit in torque, though the maximum power was not increased to the same extent, the valve sizes and timing being still the same as for the original 4.5-litre engine.

The 1971 Le Mans winner, driven by Marko and van Lennep, had many experimental features including a magnesium tube frame. (Geoffrey Goddard)

Le Mans, 1971: the Elford-Larrousse 917 L. The sharp lower edge of the nose, the concave front deck and the extensively louvred front wings are clearly seen. (Nigel Snowdon)

Big Bertha, the Truffle Pig of Zuffenhausen, painted by the Porsche Styling Department with a series of lines indicating the various joints of meat, each cut being named in German; Le Mans, 1971. Note the transmission oil cooler and regulation 'luggage boxes'. (Porsche)

The 5-litre turbo-charged engine. Except for the two turbo-chargers (right) it is outwardly identical with the normal type 912. (Porsche)

Here George Follmer is leading the pack at the start of the 1972 Road Atlanta race, the first to be won by the open-bodied 5-litre Porsche 917/10. He subsequently went on to win the 1972 Can-Am Championship outright in this car, while Leo Kinnunen in a very similar 4.5-litre turbo-charged 917/10 won the 1972 Interseries Championship. (Porsche)

By that time however, an agreement had already been reached with the Roger Penske Racing Organization to run a turbo-charged 917/10, to be driven by Mark Donohue in the 1972 Canadian-American Championship series and most of the development effort went into this project.

As the gasket width would probably be critical with the 5.4-litre engine, most of the development tests were made with the 4.5- and 5-litre units. No major change was made to the power unit itself and even the cooling blower size has remained unaltered, though its speed has been increased slightly. But instead of being led into the atmosphere, the exhaust gases of each bank of cylinders are now ducted to a small Eberspächer turbocharger, consisting of an exhaust gas-driven turbine and a centrifugal blower feeding air to the corresponding bank of cylinders. Much development work was necessary to reduce the time lag in the throttle response inevitable with exhaust-driven superchargers and this has, among other things, involved the replacement of the throttle slides of the aspirated engine by butterfly valves located as near the ports as possible. Maximum governed blower pressure is around 20 lbs/sq in. As soon as this is reached, a valve opens to by-pass some of the exhaust gases directly into the atmosphere. At the maximum governed boost pressure, the power obtained from the 5-litre engine, weighing 600 lbs with the blower, was over 900 hp at 8200 rpm as the car started its career in the Summer of 1972. Turbo-charged 4.5-litre engines, producing 850 hp, were also released to some private entrants, both in Europe and in America.

A completely new, stronger 4-speed transmission had to be designed to take the torque not far short of 700 ft/lb produced by the turbo-charged engine. It is pump lubricated and the oil is circulated through a radiator located above the transmission. The titanium half-shafts had to be reinforced too, and the splined joint accommodating length variations was deleted, these being accommodated by the 'doughnut'. The stub-axles, the hubs and the cones carrying the brake discs are titanium, front and rear, as developed in earlier 917s from which the weight-saving techniques have been taken over, and Porsche have developed their own, heavily-ribbed aluminium brake calipers for this car.

The tail end of the chassis had to be slightly redesigned to make room for the turbocharger installation and the wheelbase is increased by $\frac{5}{8}$ in to take care of the slightly more rearward position of the differential output shafts in the new transmission. Extensive testing led to some revisions of suspension geometries aiming at reducing camber changes induced by suspension movements, while the front anti-dive effect was increased. In the Can-Am car, with nearly 1000 hp available, the over-ruling factor has become to keep the tyres as perpendicular to the ground as possible when the car is under full acceleration or is being heavily braked, both in order to improve the grip and to prevent local overheating of the tyres. To reduce the handicap this would impose on cornering, rather stiff (titanium) springs and anti-roll bars are

used and lateral accelerations over 1.6 g were measured on the 580 ft diameter Weissach steering pad, the corresponding speed being around 90 mph, when the downthrust effect is still quite moderate.

Considerable development, both on the track and in the wind tunnel, went into the body shape. With close to 1000 hp on tap, and as none of the circuits used for the Can-Am series have very long straights, drag takes second place to downthrust and these are the factors which have led to a body shape in which the concave shape of the front, which was first seen on the Le Mans long-tail cars of 1970, has been accentuated to the extreme and a large, overhung rear aerofoil is used. The large louvres in the front wings, aiming at reducing the brake temperature are also a take-over, on an increased scale, from earlier 908s and 917s.

917/10s sold to private owners all have their frames made of aluminium tubes and those delivered in view of the 1972 'Interseries' and 'Can-Am' races have used the atmospherically-aspirated 5-litre, or 5.4-litre, engine or the turbo-charged 4.5-litre. Due to the various reinforcements that have had to be incorporated into the chassis to make it resist the stresses fed into it by the immensely powerful turbo-charged engine, the weight of the 1972-vintage 917/10 aluminium frame has risen to 60 kg (133 lbs)—which is still astonishingly light if you think of the forces set up when the car is accelerated fully in the lower gears. But the development of the magnesium frame used with complete success for more than 3500 miles practising and racing at Le Mans in 1971 was brought to its logical conclusion by its inclusion in one of the two 'works' cars run in America by Roger Penske.

Of those two cars, one intended to be the actual race car and the other a spare, the race car had a magnesium frame—so difficult to weld that only two specialists in the factory could be entrusted with the work—bringing a further weight saving of 32 lbs to make it virtually a round 100 lbs complete with all the attachment brackets.

Porsche's agreement with Penske is very similar to the one that linked the Gulf-Wyer Team to Porsche for the 1970–71 seasons: he is entrusted with the preparation of the cars and the actual racing organization, but gets his engines—in this case the 5-litre version of the turbo-charged flat-12—straight from the Experimental and Racing Department (a single unit at Porsche, so that any new experience gained in racing is immediately available for production development, and vice-versa), while most of the development work is left to the factory on the basis of reports from Penske, and of the Porsche engineers who are sent from Stuttgart to America on the occasion of every major race.

Unfortunately, the original magnesium-frame 917/10 was destroyed at Road Atlanta, when practising for the second race of the 1972 Can-Am series. It flew off the road when the improperly secured rear part of the body came off and Mark Donohue was lucky to escape with only serious leg injuries. But even in its first race at Mosport, Donohue had proved it to be the fastest car on the track. This was later

confirmed by George Follmer deputizing for Donohue, won the Can-Am Championship outright in the aluminium frame spare car, bringing to an end the six year long domination of the Chevrolet-engined McLarens, while Leo Kinnunen won the European 'Interseries' Championship in a turbo-charged 4.5-litre, with Willy Kauhsen second.

*   *   *

In 1969, when Porsche lined up 25 complete (if not raceworthy) 917 coupés in the factory forecourt for homologation as Group 5 'Sports Cars' by startled CSI officials, and also offered the model to private customers at 140,000 D-Mark (around £14,500 at the time, which was no doubt well below cost price), it was generally thought that more than half of the batch produced would never get as far as a race track, due to lack of customers or lack of opportunities for them to be raced, and that Porsche had just invented a very expensive way of securing supremacy in the Manufacturers' World Championship series.

In fact not many of the first series 917s were sold—one of them being the car which John Woolfe crashed with fatal results on the first lap of the 1969 Le Mans race—and following the complete body redesign for 1970, most of the original bodies and more than 20 of the bolt-on long-tails were scrapped without ever having been used. However, all the engines, transmissions and most of the mechanical parts incorporated in those cars which were never raced were certainly used, while most of the chassis were updated when the model was developed further, so that, in the end, not all that much was wasted from that first batch of cars. While it originally seemed that 25 units of such a powerful model could never be used, by the end of 1971 the total number of 917s produced amounted to something like double that original batch of twenty-five.

The Porsche 917 has become an all-time classic sports-racing car, and with more and more emphasis being laid on—and more and more money being poured into—Group 7 racing, its fourth successful racing year will certainly not be the last.

SPECIFICATIONS OF PORSCHE 917s

COMMON SPECIFICATIONS 1969-1972

ENGINE: (Type No. 912) Air-cooled flat-12 cylinders.
Magnesium crankcase vertically split along its centre line. 8 plain main bearings formed by two crankcase halves.

Power take-off by pinion between the two middle main bearings to layshaft running parallel to crankshaft in lower part of crankcase and supported by roller bearings. 32 tooth pinion on crankshaft meshing with 31 tooth pinion on layshaft.

Triple main oil pump driven off layshaft incorporating two gear-type scavenge pumps and one main pressure pump. Four auxiliary gear scavenge pumps, driven by the exhaust camshaft.

Dry sump lubrication. Big ends lubricated from axial oil feed at both ends of crankshaft. Oil pressure 35 lbs/sq in.

Auxiliary drive shaft parallel above crankshaft, driven from central crankshaft gear and driving cooling blower, ignition distributors and (via V-belt) alternator.

Four overhead camshafts, gear driven from central crankshaft gear. Camshafts and timing gears running in ball bearings.

Two sodium-filled valves per cylinder, operated through inverted cup tappets. Inlet valves inclined 30° from cylinder axis exhaust valves inclined 35° from cylinder axis.

Two plugs per cylinder. Electronic ignition with twin distributors.

Cylinder heads interchangeable. Material aluminium.

Ignition timing: Fixed advance 27° before TDC. Valve data: Inlet 47.5 mm dia. Lift 12.1 mm. Opens/closes 104° bTDC/104° aBDC. Exhaust 40.5 mm dia. Lift 10.5 mm. Opens/closes 105° bBDC/75° aTDC.

Aluminium cylinders: 'Cromal' (bores chromium-plated) on 4.5 and 4.9 engines 1969-1971. 'Nikasil' (bores nickel-silicium layer) on 5-litre and 5.4 litre engines, also on all turbocharged engines.

Forced air cooling by plastic axial blower (with cushioned hub from 1970) running at 0.895 times engine speed (1.12 times engine speed in 4.5- and 5-litre turbo-charged engines, 1972).

12-plunger Bosch fuel injection pump, cog-belt driven from l.h. exhaust camshaft. Fuel output controlled by three dimensional cam, sensitive to throttle position and engine speed. Injectors in inlet tracts. Injection pressure 255 lbs/sq in.

CHASSIS

Frame Tubular space frame. Material aluminium except No 917 051 (purely experimental, never raced), 917 052 (1971 Le Mans pre-practice), 917 053 (1971 Le Mans winner) and 917/10/003 (original Penske Can-Am car), which had a magnesium tube frame.

Suspension Front transverse wishbones with lower trailing radius rod. Anti-dive geometry on 1972 917/10. Rear transverse wishbones (lower inverted V) with trailing radius arms (aluminium). Magnesium uprights. Titanium hubs.

Springs Taper section, progressive rate titanium coil springs.

Shock absorbers Bilstein light alloy telescopic, co-axial with spring.

Anti-roll bars Tubular, adjustable front and rear.

Steering Rack and pinion. Housing magnesium, rack aluminium alloy. Ratio 11.4 to 1 (type 920 steering 13.6 to 1) around central position. Rh drive.

Brakes Hydraulic, ventilated discs front and rear. Adjustable front/rear braking ratio.

Wheels Magnesium casting with centre aluminium lock nut. 15 in diameter front and rear.

TRANSMISSION
Casing material Magnesium.

Clutch 3-disc, dry.

Gearbox Fully Porsche-synchronized 4- or 5-speed gearbox with individually interchangeable gears. Same casing used with 4 or 5 speeds, except for 1972 type 917/10 which had reinforced box taking 4 speeds (and reverse) only.

Differential (1969–71) Disc-type limited slip. Up to 75% slip limitation.

Drive shafts Titanium. Incorporating a sliding joint, two universal joints and a cushioning 'Giubo' rubber joint ('dough-nut'). No sliding joint in 1972 917/10.

FUEL TANKS
Carried by frame, below door sills. Two tanks with a total capacity of 31 Imp. gallons in 1969. One flexible safety bag-tank of 26.5 Imp. gallons capacity on 917 coupés 1970–1. Two safety bag tanks of 42 gall capacity on 1969 917 PA Spyder. Two safety bag tanks of 66 Imp. gall total capacity on 917/10 Spyders.

BODY
Fibreglass bonded to chassis. Two seats, two doors. Moulded epoxy material on some 1971 coupés and all 917/10 Spyders.

INDIVIDUAL SPECIFICATIONS ACCORDING TO YEAR AND TYPE

ENGINE
4.5-litre (first used Spa 1000 Km race, May 1969). Used on works-sponsored cars 1969-1970.

Bore x Stroke 86 x 66 mm.
Capacity 4494 cc.
Compression ratio 10.5 to 1.
Net Power output 580 hp at 8400 rpm.
Max torque 52 mkg (376 lbs/ft) at 6600 rpm.
Weight 528 lbs.
Cromal cylinders.

4.9-litre (first used Monza 1000 Km race, April 1970). Used on works-sponsored cars 1970–71.

Bore x Stroke 86 x 70.4 mm.
Capacity 4907 cc.
Net power output 600 hp at 8400 rpm.
Max torque 57.2 mkg (415 lbs/ft) at 6400 rpm. Otherwise as above.

5-litre (first used Brands Hatch 1000 Km Race, April 1971). Used on works-sponsored cars in 1971.

Bore x Stroke 86.8 x 70.4 mm.
Capacity 4998 cc.
Net power output 630 hp at 8300 rpm.
Max torque 58.5 mkg (425 lbs/ft) at 6400 rpm.
Nikasil cylinders.
Otherwise as above.

5.4-litre (first used 1972 for privately-owned Group 7 cars 917/10 on 17).

Bore x Stroke 90 x 70.4 mm.
Capacity 5374 cc.
Net output 660 hp at 8300 rpm.
Max torque 63 mkg (456 lbs/ft) at 6400 rpm.
Nikasil cylinders.
Otherwise as above.

4.5-litre turbo-charged (first used 1972 for privately-owned Group 7 cars 917/10 only).

Bore x Stroke 85 x 66 mm.
Capacity 4494 cc.
2 Ebersprächer exhaust-gas driven turbo-chargers.
Net power output 850 hp at 8000 rpm.
Max torque 85 mkg (615 lbs/ft) at 6600 rpm.
Boost pressure (max) 20 lbs/sq in.
Weight 600 lbs.
Nikasil cylinders.

5-litre turbo-charged (first used Mosport Can-Am race, June 1972 in magnesium frame 917/10 works-sponsored car).

Bore x Stroke 86.8 x 70.4 mm.
Capacity 4998 cc.
Net power output approx. 950 hp at 8000 rpm.
Max torque approx 95 mkg (690 lbs/ft) at 6400 rpm.
Otherwise as 4.5-litre turbo-charged.

CHASSIS
Brakes 1969 Ate aluminium calipers. 1970 Girling aluminium calipers on cars run by JW Racing Team, Ate on cars run by Porsche-Salzburg. 1971 Girling calipers on most factory sponsored cars (JW and Martini). Perforated ventilated discs used on most occasions in 1970-71. Standard on 917/10 Spyder. Chrome plated copper alloy discs on aluminium vanes used experimentally in Daytona 24 Hours 1970, on rear brakes only. Porsche-designed aluminium caliper with titanium bolts standard on 1972 917/10 Spyder.

WHEELS
Rim width front:	1969:	9 in (917 PA Spyder 10.5 in).
	1970–71:	10.5 or 12 in.
	1972:	12 in (10.5 for rain tyres).
Rim width rear:	1969:	12 in (end of season 15 in) (917 PA 15 or 17 in)
	1970–71:	15 or 17 in.
	1972:	17 in. (15 in for rain tyres)

DIMENSIONS

Wheelbase 2.30 m (90 in) all models, except 1972 series 917/10 which have 2.316 m (90 ⅛ in)
Track, all 917 coupés (depending on rim width used);:
1969: front 1.488 m (58.8 in)
rear 1.457 m (57.5 in) with 12 in rims
1.533 m (60.4 in) with 15 in rims
1970–71: front 1.526 m (60.2 in) with 10.5 in rims
1.564 m (61.7 in) with 12 in rims
rear 1.533 m (60.4 in) with 15 in rims
1.584 m (62.7 in) with 17 in rims
1969 917 PA Spyder: as 917 coupé on 10.5 in front and 15 or 17 in rear rims.
1971–72: 917/10 Spyder:
front 1.620 m (64 in) with 12 in rims.
rear 1.586 m (62.7 in) with 17 in rims.

TRANSMISSION
Clutch Fichtel and Sachs in 1969, Borg and Beck thereafter.
Weight All coupés were only just above the 800 Kg (1763 lbs) minimum weight required by CSI for Group 5 cars of the 5-litre class. Even long-tail 1971 Le Mans cars with full supplementary night equipment and two batteries were only 25 kg (55 lbs) above limit. Magnesium car was under the limit and had to have 12 gallon oil tank part-filled to comply. John Wyer-prepared cars were usually 25-30 kg (55-66 lbs) heavier than cars prepared at factory.
1969 917 PA Spyder: 750 Kg (1653 lbs).
917/10 Spyder, unsupercharged: approx 734 Kg (1618 lbs)
917/10 Spyder, turbo-charged:
750 Kg (1653 lbs) with aluminium frame. 735 Kg (1620 lbs) with magnesium frame.

THE PORSCHE 917 RACING RECORD IN EVENTS COUNTING TOWARDS THE WORLD CHAMPIONSHIP OF MAKES

1969

Aug. 10 Austrian 1,000 Kms., Osterreichring

| 1st | J. Siffert/K. Ahrens | 917 K–4.5 litre | 115.7 mph (186.3 kph) |
| 3rd | R. Attwood/B. Redman | 917 K–4.5 litre | |

1970

Feb. 1 Daytona 24 hours, Florida

| 1st | P. Rodriguez/L. Kinnunen | 917 K–4.5 litre | 114.8 mph (184.8 kph) |
| 2nd | J. Siffert/B. Redman | 917 K–4.5 litre | |

Mar. 22 Sebring 12 hours, Florida

| 4th | P. Rodriguez/L. Kinnunen | 917 K–4.5 litre | |

Apr. 12 BOAC 1,000 Kms Brands Hatch

1st	P. Rodriguez/L. Kinnunen	917 K–4.5 litre	92.1 mph (148.3 kph)
2nd	V. Elford/D. Hulme	917 K–4.5 litre	
3rd	R. Attwood/H. Herrmann	917 K–4.5 litre	

Apr. 25 Monza 1,000 Kms., Italy

| 1st | P. Rodriguez/L. Kinnunen | 917 K–4.5 litre | 144.5 mph (232.6 kph) |

917 K = Short-tail car   917 L = Long-tail car

THE PORSCHE 917 RACING RECORD IN EVENTS COUNTING TOWARDS THE WORLD CHAMPIONSHIP OF MAKES

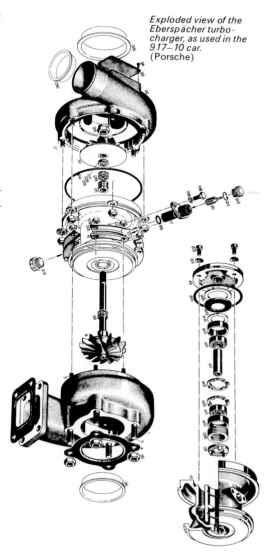

Exploded view of the Eberspächer turbo-charger, as used in the 917—10 car. (Porsche)

1970
917 K = Short-tail car   917 L = Long-tail car

May 17 Spa 1,000 Kms., Francorchamps

1st	J. Siffert/B. Redman	917 K–4.9 litre	149.3 mph (240.4 kph)
3rd	V. Elford/K. Ahrens	917 K–4.5 litre	

June 13/14 Le Mans 24 Hours, Sarthe

1st	H. Herrmann/R. Attwood	917 K–4.5 litre	119.3 mph (192.0 kph)
2nd	G. Larrousse/W. Kauhsen	917 L–4.5 litre	

July 11 Watkins Glen 6 Hours, U.S.A.

1st	P. Rodriguez/L. Kinnunen	917 K–4.9 litre	117.8 mph (189.6 kph)
2nd	J. Siffert/B. Redman	917 K–4.9 litre	
4th	D. Hulme/V. Elford	917 K–4.9 litre	

Oct. 11 Austrian 1,000 Kms., Osterreichring

1st	J. Siffert/B. Redman	917 K–4.9 litre	121.6 mph (195.7 kph)
4th	V. Elford/R. Attwood	917 K–4.9 litre	

1971

Jan. 10 Buenos Aires 1,000 Kms., Argentina

1st	J. Siffert/D. Bell	917 K–4.9 litre	115.6 mph (186.2 kph)
2nd	P. Rodriguez/J. Oliver	917 K–4.9 litre	

Jan. 31 Daytona 24 Hours, Florida

1st	P. Rodriguez/J. Oliver	917 K–4.9 litre	109.1 mph (175.7 kph)

Mar. 20 Sebring 12 Hours, Florida

1st	V. Elford/G. Larrousse	917 K–4.9 litre	112.5 mph (181.1 kph)
4th	P. Rodriguez/J. Oliver	917 K–4.9 litre	

Apr. 4 BOAC 1,000 Kms., Brands Hatch

3rd	J. Siffert/D. Bell	917 K–5.0 litre	

Apr. 25 Monza 1,000 Kms., Italy

1st	P. Rodriguez/J. Oliver	917 K–5.0 litre	146.5 mph (235.9 kph)
2nd	J. Siffert/D. Bell	917 K–5.0 litre	

May 9 Spa 1,000 Kms., Francorchamps

1st	P. Rodriguez/J. Oliver	917 K–5.0 litre	154.7 mph (249.0 kph)
2nd	J. Siffert/D. Bell	917 K–5.0 litre	
4th	W. Kauhsen/R. Jöst (private entry)	917 K–4.5 litre	

June 12/13 Le Mans 24 Hours, Sarthe

1st	H. Marko/G. van Lennep	917 K–4.9 litre	138.1 mph (222.3 kph)
2nd	R. Attwood/H. Müller	917 L–4.9 litre	

June 27 Austrian 1,000 Kms., Osterreichring

1st	P. Rodriguez/R. Attwood	917 K–5.0 litre	123.0 mph (198.0 kph)

July 24 Watkins Glen 6 Hours, U.S.A.

2nd	J. Siffert/G. van Lennep	917 K–5.0 litre	
3rd	D. Bell/R. Attwood	917 K–5.0 litre	

RECORD OF THE 917/10 (5 litre) CAR ENTERED FOR JO SIFFERT IN FOUR CAN-AM RACES OF THE 1971 SERIES

July 25 Watkins Glen, 304 Kms.–3rd

Aug. 22 Lexington, 309 Kms.–2nd

Aug. 29 Elkhart Lake, 322 Kms.–2nd

Sept. 12 Donnybrooke, 338 Kms.–5th

RECORD OF THE 917/10 (5 litre) TURBO-CHARGED CAR IN 1972 CAM-AM SERIES

June 11 Mosport			*Sept. 17 Donnybrooke*		
2nd	M. Donohue		4th	G. Follmer	
July 9 Road Atlanta			*Oct. 1 Edmonton*		
1st	G. Follmer		1st	M. Donohue	3rd G. Follmer
July 23 Watkins Glen			*Oct. 15 Laguna Seca*		
5th	G. Follmer		1st	G. Follmer	2nd M. Donohue
Aug. 6 Mid-Ohio			*Oct. 29 Riverside*		
1st	G. Follmer		1st	G. Follmer	3rd M. Donohue
Aug. 27 Road America					
1st	G. Follmer				

Alfa Romeo Monoposto Type B (P3)

by Peter Hull

1932—The first Season with 2.6-litre Cars
The new 2.6-litre Monoposto Alfa Romeo
Grand Prix car, also known as the Type B or P3,
made its debut in the five hour Italian GP at
Monza on June 5th, 1932. Following the Alfa
Romeo tradition of first appearance Grand Prix
wins already instituted by the P2 in 1924 and
the 'Monza' in 1931, the new Monoposto,
driven by Tazio Nuvolari, duly won the race at
an average speed of 104.13 mph. This was
within an ace of the lap record by the 2-litre P2
in the 1924 GP at Monza of 104.24 mph and
only slightly slower than the 1931 Italian GP
lap record put up by the 2.3-litre 'Monza' model
on the same circuit at 105 mph. The lap record
in the 1932 race, however, was at 112.2 mph,
put up by Luigi Fagioli's big 4.9-litre 16-
cylinder Maserati (which was powered by two
8-cylinder engines geared together) and this
car, which finished 2½ minutes behind
Nuvolari's, might have won the race but for
inefficient refuelling stops. A second Monoposto Alfa in the race, driven by the veteran
Campari, came in fourth behind Borzacchini's
'Monza', so the new cars did not have it all their
own way.

On July 3rd the five hour French Grand Prix
was held on the Rheims-Gueux circuit, a proper
road course which had formerly been used for
the Grand Prix de la Marne, and here the new
Alfa Romeos truly triumphed against 4.9- and
2.3-litre Bugatti and 2.3-litre 'Monza' Alfa
Romeo opposition, for the complete Monoposto team finished in the first three places in
the pre-arranged order of Nuvolari, Borzacchini
and Caracciola.

It was the same story for the German Grosser
Preis at the Nürburgring on July 15th, the
Bugatti opposition, headed by the Type 51s,
being completely outclassed by the three
Monopostos of Caracciola, Nuvolari and
Borzacchini, who finished in that order, the
first two actually lapping fourth man Réné
Dreyfus's Type 51 Bugatti twice.

Three Italian races of lesser importance then
fell to Nuvolari's Monoposto, the Coppa Ciano
at Montenero, the Coppa Acerbo at Pescara
and the Coppa Principe di Piemonte at Avellino
against Bugatti, 'Monza' Alfa Romeo and
Maserati opposition.

Only two Monopostos contested the
Czechoslovakian GP at Brno on September 4th,
Tazio Nuvolari and Baconin Borzacchini being
the drivers, and this was a race that the new
Alfa Romeos actually did not win. Nuvolari at
first led the race, which was held in pouring

*Caracciola testing a P3
with an unusual radiator
cowl in early practice for
the Monza GP, Septem-
ber 6th, 1932*

rain, until he was held back by ignition trouble. Then Borzacchini, who had held second place, retired with a broken differential, and in the end Nuvolari finished third to Chiron's Bugatti and Fagioli's Maserati.

At the Monza GP meeting on September 11th Caracciola won the 20 lap final in his Monoposto at 110.8 mph, and Nuvolari, who was third behind Fagioli's big Maserati, after being delayed by loss of fuel pressure, put up identical record laps both in his heat and in the final of 112.7 mph.

The following week-end inefficient pit control caused another Monoposto defeat, this time at the hands of a privately-owned 'Monza' Alfa Romeo driven by the Frenchman Raymond Sommer. This was at the Miramas track in the Camargue (now used for tyre testing) on the occasion of the GP of Marseilles where Nuvolari drove the sole works-entered Monoposto and allowed the privately-entered 'Monza' to go into the lead due to a slow pit stop. As soon as the situation was realised he set off after the slower car, but then burst a tyre, and the 'Monza' won from him by some 40 secs at 109.80 mph after Nuvolari had been lapping at 125 mph.

The Design Analysed

The Alfa Romeo which is the subject of this Profile is known by three names—the Monoposto, the Type B or the P3. *Monoposto* is simply the Italian word for the English 'single-seater' or the French *monoplace*, and it has come to be written with a capital letter in the case of the P3 because both the P1 and the P2 which preceded it had two-seater bodies, and the P3 was the first European car built to a GP formula, and which ran in a GP, with single-seater bodywork in which the driver was placed centrally in the chassis. There is a slight qualifi-

Nuvolari won the 1932 Italian GP at Monza on the P3's first appearance. (Alfa Romeo)

cation to this last statement, as this was also a feature of the Monoposto's immediate predecessor, the Alfa Romeo Type A, but the Type A was never seriously campaigned as a Grand Prix car.

Already we have seen that the 16-cylinder 4.9-litre Maserati of Luigi Fagioli, powered by two side-by-side 8-cylinder engines, was a force to be reckoned with, and in the early 'thirties Bugatti was also racing a car suitable for fast circuits, the 8-cylinder 4.9-litre Type 54. Previously Bugatti had also built the less-successful Type 45 of 3.8 litres, with two 8-cylinder blocks side by side with geared crankshafts in a common crankcase which was used for hill climbs in 1928–30. Alfa Romeo's reply to the 16-cylinder Maserati, which had first

Nuvolari on his way to winning the 1932 French GP at Rheims in a 2.6-litre Monoposto. (Alfa Romeo)

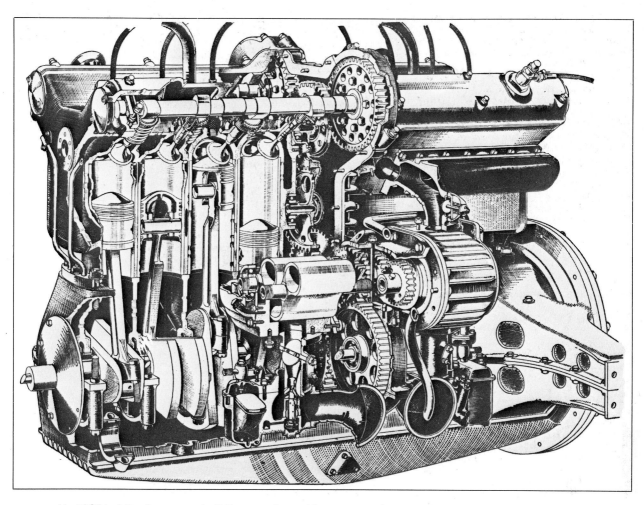

Cut-away drawing by
L.C. Cresswell of a 2.6-
litre engine.
(IPC Ltd)

appeared in 1929 in 4 litre form, was the 3.5-litre Type A of 1931. This had two developed versions of the supercharged 6-cylinder 1750 cc sports car engine side by side in the chassis, with the crankshafts geared together and, more remarkably, two gearboxes and two propeller shafts to the back axle, which was fitted with two differentials. There is evidence that the design of the Type A influenced that of the Type B, and although the early car was nothing like so successful as the Monoposto, it had a very definite moment of glory at Pescara in August, 1931, where Campari drove one to victory from Chiron's Type 51 Bugatti, with third place and fastest lap going to Nuvolari in a second Type A.

Vittorio Jano (1891–1965) could be termed Italy's greatest designer of high performance cars, for what other Italian could claim to have evolved so many classic designs, not only the P2, P3 and Type C 8C-35 and 12C-36 Alfa Romeos and D50 Lancia and Lancia/Ferrari Grand Prix cars, but also great road cars like the 1500, 1750 and 2.3-litre Alfa Romeos and the Lancia Aurelia?

Back in 1923 Giuseppe Merosi, Jano's distinguished predecessor at Alfa Romeo, had brought out the GPR or Gran Premio Romeo Alfa Romeo which was called the P1 for short. Although never actually raced, the P1 in super-

charged form was used as a test bed in the development of Jano's first and favourite Grand Prix design, the immortal P2, which was victorious in its and its constructor's first appearance in GP racing in the French Grand Prix at Lyons in 1924, Giuseppe Campari being the driver.

Jano's next Grand Prix car, the 'Monza', was developed from his new 8C 2300 sports car and not from the old P2, whilst the Type A was also a breakaway from what had gone before. It was thus logical that the new Monoposto, following on from the 'Monza' and the Type A, with which it had definite links, should be called the Type B, but old traditions die hard, and by 1933 it was being referred to as the P3 in a race programme in Italy, and convenience and common usage soon conferred the name P3 upon it.

The heart of a car is its engine, and in the case of the P3 this was clearly a follow-on from that of the Monza, though apparently with a glance at a remarkable 1100 cc racing Salmson engine which had appeared in 1928 and which was the work of the French designer Emile Petit. An intriguing question that will never be answered is whether Jano was even aware of the existence of the Salmson engine, let alone influenced by its design.

The original twin overhead camshaft P3 engine of 2.6 litres had 8 cylinders in line, each measuring 65 x 100 mm (2654 cc) compared

123

with the 65 x 88 mm measurements of the 2336 cc 'Monza'. The cylinders were in two blocks of four, for a feature of the straight-eight Alfa Romeo design was the camshaft drive in the centre of the engine to cut down torsional stresses. Thus the 2-4-2 layout crankshaft, which ran in ten bronze-backed white metalled bearings, was made up of two halves with two helical gears bolted between them in the centre, one driving the camshafts through two intermediaries, and the other the superchargers, magneto, oil and water pumps. On the 'Monza' the crankcase was of light alloy, on the P3 it was elektron, but a more important

difference was that, though both engines had alloy blocks with steel cylinder liners, on the 'Monza' the cylinder head was detachable, whereas on the P3 it was fixed. At the same time on the P3 the exhaust was on the right hand or offside of the engine, and the inlet was on the nearside, which was opposite to the arrangement on the Monza and sports car engines.

The final main difference between the two engines was that instead of the large capacity supercharger and single carburettor of the 'Monza', the P3 had two smaller capacity Roots-type blowers, each with its own carburettor, giving a boost of about 10 lbs compared with the *circa* 8 lbs of the 'Monza'. On the P3 the ratio of the drive to the superchargers, normally about 1.1 times engine speed, could be altered fairly easily. The compression ratios on the two engines were the same, 6.5 to 1, but the valve angle was 104 degrees on the P3 and 90 degrees on the 'Monza', and the P3 had bigger valves, which were 34 mm in diameter for both inlet and exhaust as against 29 mm, running direct in the head, with no valve seat inserts. Official output figures were 165 bhp at 5,400 rpm for the Monza and 215 bhp at 5,600 rpm for the P3.

The 49.9 x 70 mm (1085 cc) Salmson engine design of 1927, though but little raced and never developed by the Société des Moteurs Salmson due to a change in policy, nevertheless achieved some successes in private hands in the early 'thirties and had the same method of drive to the twin overhead camshafts, and the

Detail of the ½-elliptic rear suspension showing the double friction type shock absorbers and the housing for the crown-wheel and pinion of the nearside propellor shaft

Cut-away drawing by L.C. Cresswell of a 1932 car.
(IPC Ltd)

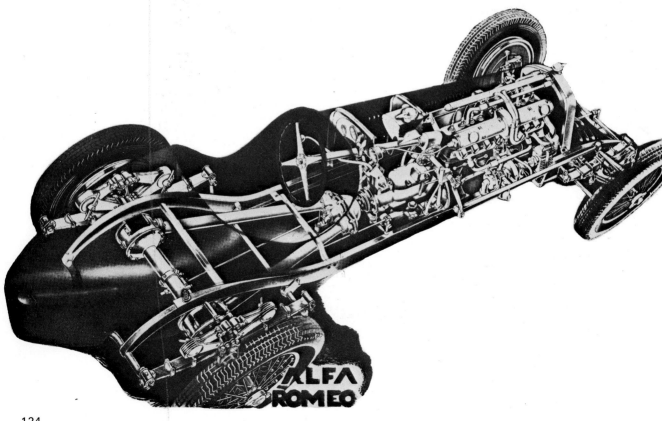

same twin supercharger arrangement on the nearside with exhaust on the offside, as the P3. There the similarity ended, however, for the Salmson crankshaft was a 4-4 running in 5 roller and ball bearings, and the connecting rods were also roller bearing, unlike the plain bearing two bolt rods of the P3. The Salmson engine, which used Cozette vane-type superchargers, whereas Jano's Roots blowers were of his own design, also had desmodromic tappets, but the P3 used the well-known adjustable mushroom tappets which had first been introduced on the 1500 and 1750 sports cars. The Salmson engine gave a remarkable and reliable 140 bhp at 8,000 rpm, outstanding for an 1100 cc engine.

In all but one respect the chassis of the P3 was conventional for its day, though narrower, of course, than its contemporaries. The width was 2 ft 2 ins, and as the body was the same width as the chassis, large cutaways were provided for the driver's arms. The wheelbase of 8 ft 8 ins was the same as that of the 'Monza', as was the 4 ft 7 ins track of the front axle, but the Monoposto had a narrower track back axle of 4 ft 5 ins, the 'Monza' having the same 4 ft 7 ins track at the back as at the front.

The early 1932/33 P3 had semi-elliptic springing all round, with two radius arms preventing the front axle twisting under braking, and there were double friction shock absorbers at the rear, single at the front. The unladen weight was down to 13 cwt 90 lbs (701 Kg) thanks to light alloys used in the engine and for brake drums and shoes, shock absorber arms

etc, and the P3 Alfa weighed no more, and probably less, than a smaller 2.3-litre Type 35 Bugatti or straight-8 1½-litre Delage of the previous decade.

The 15¾ inch diameter brake drums and the rod-operated braking system was the same as on the 8C 2300 sports cars, and another saving in manufacturing costs was made in the adoption of the four-speed gearbox from the sports cars. The clutch, too, was the sports car one, but with the linings omitted and extra plates and alloy rings substituted to deal with the higher torque.

It was, however, in the remainder of the transmission that the P3 Alfa Romeo differed from any other racing car, for the drive to the rear wheels was entirely novel. The differential, instead of being in the back axle, was attached to the rear of the gearbox and was thus virtually part of the unsprung weight of the car. Behind the differential two propeller shafts enclosed in torque tubes came out to form a V, and each of these led to a small bevel gear in a light alloy housing just inboard of each rear wheel.

Why this form of transmission was adopted is a puzzle, although there is no doubt that the clumsy double propeller shaft drive of the Type A must have prompted further and superior thoughts in this direction. The theoretical advantages of the Type B transmission are (a) a low seating position with the driver's seat set between the propeller shafts aft of the apex of the V, instead of on top of a single propeller shaft and (b) a light back axle due to the absence of a differential within it, and very short

Caracciola hill climbing in the Alps in 1932. The four external oil pipes seen running along the offside frame member were reduced to two from 1934 onwards. (Alfa Romeo)

half-shafts that were almost stubs and therefore very light in comparison with conventional half-shafts. It must be remembered that the P3 Alfa Romeo was one of the last Grand Prix designs before the general adoption of independent rear suspension, and perhaps this rear axle should have been the ultimate in non-independent design. Experiments were later made with a B Type fitted with swing axles and a transverse leaf spring at the rear, but it is thought that no car was actually raced in this form.

The writer recently discussed the P3 rear axle design with Peter Waller, an engineer by profession, who has regularly raced an E.R.A. in Vintage Sports-Car Club events since 1958, or for most of his adult life, as well as having had a very successful season in 1971 with the P3 belonging to Neil Corner, which he prepared for racing as well as driving it. First of all, although the seat pan is set between the two torque tubes, no attempt is really made to give the driver a lower seating position than in a single propellor shaft monoposto such as a Maserati, so (a) can be dismissed. With regard to (b), Peter Waller feels that, with the addition of the two bevel gears and propeller shafts, the reduction in weight of the rear axle is not really very significant in comparison with a conventional type. The one positive advantage he brings out, not mentioned above, is that the design allows for much greater facility in changing the final drive ratio than with the normal arrangement: always a useful factor in a

racing car running on different circuits and in different events (including international hill climbs in the case of the P3 in its heyday) during a busy season.

The scuttle on the P3 was made detachable to give easy access to the gearbox and interchangeable final drive ratio, and some drivers ran with the detachable part removed on slow circuits in very hot weather. The gearbox was between the driver's legs, with the clutch pedal to the left of it, the brake pedal to the right, and the accelerator pedal to the right of the brake. The central gear lever was cranked to the left at the top, for changing gear with the left hand.

The wooden-rimmed steering wheel had very little spring in it, spring steering wheels never being favoured by Italian drivers it seems, whilst on the dashboard the driver was faced by no less than two rev counters. These were said to be provided because it was easy to over-rev the very smooth engine, so insurance against rev counter failure was considered vital, and two rev-counters had also been fitted to the 'Monzas'.

1933—Almost a Sabbatical Year

Due to economic conditions, Alfa Romeo announced at the beginning of 1933 that they were withdrawing from Grand Prix racing, and that they would not even allow the Scuderia Ferrari to carry on racing the P3s for them as independents. Previously Enzo Ferrari had been responsible for organising the Alfa Romeo works racing, but the cars had carried the famous Alfa Romeo 'quadrifoglio' or four-leafed clover.

With the works withdrawal, Ferrari now had to fall back upon the older 'Monza' models for 1933, which were to carry his own Scuderia Ferrari badge in place of the 'quadrifoglio'. However, development work was done on the 'Monzas', which the Scuderia increased in capacity from 2.3 litres to 2.6 litres and, more important, the engines were fitted with Weber carburettors, Daini of Weber being responsible for their considerably better performance over the original cars rather than the capacity increase.

The Ferrari 'Monza' Alfa Romeos proved to be very competitive, particularly when Tazio Nuvolari was at the wheel, his talent being worth as much extra bhp as the increase in engine capacity or the re-working of the carburation. Perhaps it was the extra power available (178 bhp against the former 165 bhp) that caused a weakness in the back axle of the 'Monza' to show up, and this so aggravated Nuvolari, who had two victories snatched from his grasp as a result of it, that he left the Scuderia Ferrari and obtained a new 2.9-litre Maserati which he campaigned as an independent. After correcting an inherent weakness in the Maserati chassis design, the Maestro immediately showed that his monoposto Maserati was more than a match for the 2.6-litre 'Monzas', beating the Ferrari 'Monza' of Antonio Brivio (who was no mean driver) in the Coppa Ciano at Montenero by no less than eight minutes.

It was almost certainly this Maserati superiority which persuaded Alfa Romeo to release

Marcel Lehoux in a 2.9-litre car at Monaco in 1934. The flask behind the seat enabled the driver to take a drink through a rubber tube during a long race

Giuseppe Campari going to the start before his fatal accident in the 1933 Monza GP. His car carries the Ferrari shield on the scuttle.
(Alfa Romeo)

the Monopostos to Ferrari once again. Their first 1933 appearance was at Pescara in August, a single car being entered to be driven by Luigi Fagioli. The result was a victory for the Monoposto, but only by default, for Nuvolari's Maserati was delayed by a seized universal joint in the transmission when all set to win the race. At Comminges, in France, a week later Fagioli had a very easy victory, for no monoposto Maseratis were present, and at Miramas the P3s of Chiron and Fagioli finished first and

second, Nuvolari retiring his Maserati sixty miles from the end of the 300 mile race when he was almost certain of victory. Ironically, the reason for his retirement was back axle trouble.

In the Italian GP at Monza, Nuvolari on the Maserati was again all set for a win when he had to go to his pit to change a wheel only two laps from the end, giving victory to Fagioli, whose P3 put in a record lap on the old 10 km circuit of 115.82 mph. In the tragic Monza GP in the afternoon, in which Campari, Borzacchini

Luigi Fagioli at San Sebastian in 1933. The apertures in the bonnet side for the superchargers were a feature of the narrow-bodied 2.6-litre cars, but the very small rear brake drums used at San Sebastian were uncommon

A 2.9-litre engine of 1934/5. The apertures in the bonnet sides for the superchargers were done away with when the wider bodies were fitted. (Geoffrey Goddard)

The special streamlined P3 with which Guy Moll won the Avus GP in 1934 had a 3.2-litre engine and the very small rear brake drums as used on the 1933 Spanish GP cars.
(Alfa Romeo)

Guy Moll winning the Monaco GP in a 2.9-litre car in 1934. These 1934 Monaco cars were interim models having the wider cockpit but still retaining the low sides, whilst the apertures for the superchargers were still to be seen on the nearside

0 ft 1 2 3

The 1933 Spanish Grand Prix winner.

David Warner © *Profile Publications Limited*

and then Count Czaykowski were killed, it is of interest to record that for this track race the P3 in which Campari lost his life was running with the front brakes removed.

In the Spanish GP in September, Nuvolari once again led the P3s in his Maserati and made fastest lap, but after it began to rain he ran out of road, leaving Chiron to win in his P3 from the similar car of Fagioli.

There was some excitement amongst the leading amateur Grand Prix drivers in October, 1933, when Alfa Romeo let it be known that new P3s would be available to private owners for the 1934 season, and several of them sold their 'Monza' Alfa Romeos and Bugattis in anticipation. Before the end of the year, however, this offer was rescinded, and the net result was an increase in business for the Maserati brothers at Bologna.

1934—2.9 Litres

From 1934 new rules governed the Grand Prix Formula, under which there was no limit to the engine capacity but the weight of the car without driver, fuel, oil and tyres had to be less than 750 Kg (14.73 cwt) and the body width could not be under 33.5 inches. The pious intention behind all this was to prevent speeds escalating, yet it led to the introduction of the most powerful Grand Prix cars ever known, and thus a capacity limit was promptly imposed in the Formula which followed in 1938.

The new rules caused no particular problems to Alfa Romeo, or rather the Scuderia Ferrari, for the P3 cars were light in weight anyway, and the bodies of existing cars were widened by the introduction of gusset plates so that the sides of the cockpit bulged out, and big cutaways for the driver's arms were no longer necessary.

Although the road-holding of the 2.6-litre Monopostos had not been beyond criticism, for they did not handle so well as the heavier 'Monzas', the chassis design was not altered for 1934, but it was obvious that something would have to be done about the engine. At the 1933 Spanish GP Bugatti had introduced his straight-eight Type 59, then fitted with a 2.8-litre engine with the P3 stroke of 100 mm, and with the 2.9-litre Maserati also being in existence, together with the threat of even bigger-engined new cars coming from Mercedes-Benz and Auto Union, it was clear that a capacity of 2.6 litres would no longer suffice for the P3 Alfa Romeos.

Jano's answer to the problem was to increase the cylinder bore from 65 mm to 68 mm, so that the new 68 x 100 mm engine had a capacity of 2905 cc. Together with the increase in capacity went an increase in the compression ratio from 6.5 to 1 to 7 to 1, and a slight increase in blower pressure, so that the new engine gave 255 bhp at 5,400 rpm compared with the 215 bhp at 5,600 rpm of the 2.6 litre engine. On the debit side, the bodywork was now wider and heavier, so that the dry weight of the car had increased from 700 Kg to 720 Kg; in other words it had put on just over 44 lbs, or some 3 stone in human terms.

First-class drivers were engaged by the Scuderia Ferrari for 1934, including Achille

Varzi, Louis Chiron, the new star Guy Moll, Count Carlo Felice Trossi and Marcel Lehoux. Nuvolari remained faithful to Maserati, interspersed with the odd drive in a Type 59 for Bugatti.

At the beginning of the season the new 2.9-litre Monopostos proved to be more than a match for their rivals. At Monaco Guy Moll won from Chiron after the latter had made a last minute error of judgement and Trossi, the only P3 driver to retire, put up a record fastest lap. Dreyfus (Type 59 Bugatti) finished third in front of Lehoux's P3 with Nuvolari (Maserati) fifth and Varzi (P3) sixth.

Varzi won the final of the Bordino GP at Alessandria from Chiron, and an accident in this race to Nuvolari's Maserati proved a set-back to the Maestro's 1934 season, as he broke a leg.

At Tripoli P3s finished in the first three places: Varzi, Moll and Chiron, with the latter making fastest lap at 124.52 mph. Against negligible opposition Varzi won the Targa Florio on a lone 2.9 P3 in drenching rain. At Casablanca the opposition again was not serious and, surprisingly, the Scuderia Ferrari fielded a team of the old 2.6-litre P3s for Chiron, Lehoux and Comotti. Chiron won fairly easily from Etancelin's private 2.9 Maserati, with Lehoux third, Whitney Straight's Maserati fourth and Comotti fifth.

At the flat-out Avus circuit in May, the challenge of both the new Mercedes and Auto Unions was threatened, but the Mercedes team withdrew on the eve of the race, leaving the A type, 16-cylinder rear-engined, 4.36-litre Auto Unions of Hans Stuck, Prince zu Leiningen and August Momberger to face the smaller capacity P3s. However, although Varzi and Chiron drove normal Alfa Romeos, Moll had a special car with ugly and bulbous aerodynamic bodywork, including fairings behind the wheels and a streamlined headrest ending in a fin on the tail, plus an engine with the cylinders bored out from 68 mm to 71 mm, the 71 x 100 mm dimensions giving 3,165 cc and another 10 bhp at 5,400 rpm. Ing Pallavicino of Aeronautica Breda was responsible for the body design, which was used only at Avus in 1934 and 1935.

The effort proved worthwhile, for Moll won the 182 mile race at 127.57 mph after 1½ hours racing from his team mate Varzi, 1½ minutes behind, followed by Momberger's Auto Union. The other Auto Unions and Chiron's P3 retired.

A week later, in the Eifelrennen on the Nürburgring, the P3s had their worst thrashing to date, Chiron finishing the 213 mile race in third place 5 min 44 secs behind the winning 3.36-litre W25B Mercedes of von Brauchitsch and 4 min 24 secs behind the Auto Union of Hans Stuck in second place, even though the German cars had had to stop to refuel whereas the Alfas had not.

Nevertheless, the P3s continued their supremacy in races in which there were no Mercedes or Auto Unions, Trossi winning at Montreux and Varzi, Chiron and Lehoux were first, second and third at Penya Rhin in Spain after their main rival, Nuvolari (Maserati), dropped back because his leg was troubling him, and then he finally retired. In the Isle of Man, the Hon Brian Lewis won the Mannin

The Hon Brian Lewis winning the 1934 Mannin Moar race in the Isle of Man in a 2.6-litre Monoposto hired from the Scuderia Ferrari by Noel Rees.
(Autocar)

Varzi, whose P3 made fastest lap, leads Etancelin's 2.9-litre Maserati at the start of the 1934 GP de la Marne at Rheims in 1934

Count Trossi winning the Vichy GP, 1934

The Alfa Romeo T
the 1933 Spanish
(134.11 k.p.h.) for
The race was reviv
Sebastian after a la

David Warner © P

0 ft

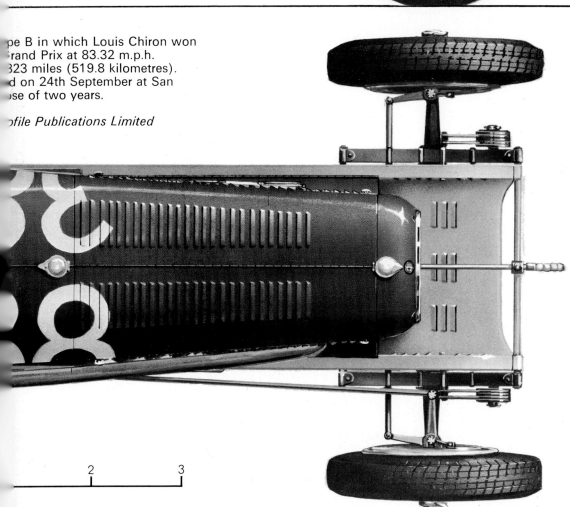

pe B in which Louis Chiron won
rand Prix at 83.32 m.p.h.
323 miles (519.8 kilometres).
d on 24th September at San
ose of two years.

ofile Publications Limited

2   3

Moar race in a 2.6-litre P3 which was actually hired from the Scuderia Ferrari by Noel Rees and tended by two Italian mechanics.

The French GP at Montlhéry in July was a remarkable race, as the 2.9 P3s of Varzi, Chiron and Trossi had to face three Mercedes, with engines increased to 3.8 litres capacity, two Auto Unions and three Type 59 Bugattis in the expert hands of Nuvolari, Benoist and Dreyfus. The Bugattis, too, had been increased in capacity and now had 3.3-litre engines.

The race began with Chiron going into the lead, and apart from a short spell when Stuck's Auto Union got past, he held it to the end, furthermore he made fastest lap, which was a record for the course. At the finish the three P3s were the only cars left in the race, Varzi being second and Moll, sharing with Trossi, being third, after Benoist's Bugatti had been flagged off.

With only Maseratis as serious opposition, P3s were triumphant in the GP de la Marne (Chiron) and the Vichy GP (Trossi), but in the German GP at the Nürburgring the best P3 performance was by Chiron who was third behind Stuck's Auto Union and Fagioli's Mercedes, though ahead of Nuvolari's Maserati, which finished fourth. The P3s also beat Nuvolari in the Coppa Ciano over the Montenero circuit, Varzi winning from Moll with Nuvolari third and Trossi fourth.

The Dieppe GP finished up as a momentous struggle between Lehoux's P3 and Etancelin's monoposto 2.9 Maserati, victory going to the latter after Lehoux stopped to change plugs.

In the Belgian GP at Spa, the Type 59 Bugattis were competitive with the P3s of Chiron and Varzi until they were delayed by the plug bothers that had afflicted them in the French GP. However, Chiron later crashed and then Varzi retired, so Dreyfus on a Type 59 not only won the race but Brivio's similar car, which finished second, broke the lap record.

Phi-Phi Etancelin in his privately-owned 2.9 Maserati again proved competitive against the Scuderia Ferrari professional organisation in the Nice GP round-the-houses race, for he finished in second place between the P3s of Varzi and Trossi.

The P3s performed well in the Coppa Acerbo at Pescara in which both Moll and Varzi held the lead at different times against full Mercedes, Auto Union, Bugatti and Maserati opposition, and even Pietro Ghersi, as a new boy to the P3 team, was third at one period. This was the race in which 24-year-old Guy Moll was killed whilst passing Henne's Auto Union on the Montesilvano straight at over 160 mph whilst gaining on Fagioli's leading Mercedes. The race ended in a win for Fagioli, with Nuvolari's Maserati second, Brivio's Type 59 Bugatti third and a P3 shared by Varzi and Ghersi was fourth.

The speeds recorded by the fastest cars of each make over the flying kilometre in this race are illuminating, Caracciola's Mercedes recording 179.6 mph, Sebastian's Auto Union 171.1 mph, Chiron's P3 168.7 mph, Brivio's Type 59 Bugatti 159.3 mph, Nuvolari's Maserati 155.2 mph and the Englishman Clifton Penn-Hughes's 'Monza' Alfa Romeo 141.3 mph.

It was now August in this long and arduous

The cockpit of Brian Lewis's 2.6-litre Mannin Moar car, with the twin rev counters prominent on the dashboard

Rear view of Moll's car after the fatal crash at Pescara, 1934, showing the displaced auxiliary fuel tank in the scuttle, whilst the main fuel tank forming the tail is missing completely

The Pau GP on 25th February, 1935, was a victory for Nuvolari driving the first P3 to be fitted with reversed ¼-elliptic rear springing

Over the tramlines and past the letter box goes Varzi in the 1934 Circuit of Biella race. The slotted valance over the frame seems to be characteristic of early cars converted to wider bodywork

Mechanics changing Lehoux's gearbox between a heat and the final at Dieppe in 1934, showing the higher cockpit side of the later cars and also the unique dual drive transmission

The near-side of Louis Chiron's 1933
Spanish Grand Prix-winning car, showing
the superchargers protruding through the
bonnet side and the refreshment flask
behind the driver's seat.

Left Radiator badge. *Right* Shield worn by
some Scuderia Ferrari cars in 1933 and
generally adopted for the 1934 and
1935 seasons.

David Warner
© *Profile Publications Limited*

The reversed quarter-elliptic rear
suspension first adopted at
Pau in 1935.

The famous *quadrifoglio,* or
four-leaf clover, badge carried by
many Alfa Romeo racing cars was
seldom, if ever, worn by P3s.

Detail of the new front axle with Dubonnet ifs introduced in time for the 1935 Monaco GP.
(Motor)

Monaco, 1935, showing the Mercedes opposition against four P3s, two fitted with ifs and two without.
(Daimler-Benz)

season for the P3 cars, and in the first Swiss GP over the new Bremgarten circuit at Berne they were never in the lead and had to give best not only to Auto Union, but also to Bugatti, the finishing order being Stuck (Auto Union), Momberger (Auto Union), Dreyfus (Type 59 Bugatti), Varzi (P3), Chiron (P3), Fagioli (Mercedes) and Ghersi (P3). Perhaps the only consolation was that Mercedes had an even worse day, due to weak brakes and fuel pump troubles.

Comotti saved the P3 fortunes at Comminges where there were no German cars, and Wimille's Type 59 Bugatti could do no better than fifth, whilst Trossi and Varzi dominated a similar state of affairs in the round-the-houses race at Biella.

The Italian GP was held over a very slow circuit full of chicanes at Monza, and the $4\frac{3}{4}$ hour race was very tiring and punishing for both cars and drivers, who shared the cars in many cases. Trossi in his P3 did manage to get into second place for a time when the German cars were being delayed by pit stops, and the final order was Caracciola/Fagioli (Mercedes), Stuck/Leiningen (Auto Union), Trossi/Comotti (P3), Chiron (P3), Nuvolari (6 cyl 3.3 Maserati), Comotti/Marinoni (P3), Momberger/Sebastian (Auto Union).

In the Spanish GP at San Sebastian, the P3s were simply too slow, and Varzi finished fifth to two Mercedes, a T59 Bugatti driven by Nuvolari and an Auto Union. Fifth was also the best Varzi could manage in the Czechoslovakian GP in which Nuvolari's new 6-cylinder Maserati was third to Stuck's Auto Union and Fagioli's Mercedes, whilst in the GP of Algiers Chiron's P3 finished second to Wimille's T59 Bugatti.

At the end of the season even victories in small Italian races were snatched from the P3s by Nuvolari's new 6-cylinder Maserati, this happening at Modena, where Nuvolari beat Varzi, and at Naples, where it was Brivio who came second in his first race for the Scuderia Ferrari since leaving the Bugatti team.

1935—The Ultimate P3

The outlook appeared to be bleak as regards the P3's chances of successes during the 1935 season. It would certainly need more power and better handling if it was to keep up with its rivals, but before even touching the car the Scuderia Ferrari went quite a long way towards solving its problems by signing up Tazio Nuvolari, who agreed to join them as Varzi was departing to Auto Union.

Nothing had been done to improve the chassis since its inception in 1932, and the car Nuvolari drove in the GP of Pau in February, 1935, was seen to be fitted with reversed quarter-elliptic springs at the rear. This was a hallmark of Bugatti design, and although the Type 59 may have been criticised for its lack of brakes and its poor acceleration during 1934, nobody seemed to fault its handling, and it is possible that the trio of erstwhile T59 drivers: Tazio Nuvolari, the Marquis 'Tonino' Brivio and Frenchman René Dreyfus, all Ferrari drivers in 1935, suggested this Bugatti feature might be beneficial if applied to the P3.

Certainly at Pau Nuvolari's car seemed to handle better than the unmodified car of Dreyfus, and it finished up as the winner of the race 16 seconds ahead of the Dreyfus car, which was second.

At the historic La Turbie hill climb, held near Nice on 18th April, Dreyfus appeared in a P3 with an additional major chassis improvement, the fitting of a tubular front axle with Dubonnet independent suspension, the design of engineer Chedru who was financed by André Dubonnet. At the Monaco GP four days later all the four Ferrari P3s entered had reversed quarter-elliptic rear springing with piston-type hydraulic shock absorbers. More changes were evident by the fact that, whilst Dreyfus and Brivio's cars had normal front suspension, those of Nuvolari and Chiron had the Dubonnet ifs with Ariston hydraulic braking; in addition Nuvolari and Dreyfus had cars with 265 bhp 71 x 100 mm, 3,165 cc engines.

In the race, Dreyfus, with his larger engine

R O Shuttleworth's P3 and C E C Martin's 3.3-litre Type 59 Bugatti in the 1935 Donington GP, which Shuttleworth won and normal front suspension came off best, for Nuvolari and Chiron were having trouble with irregularities in their hydraulic brakes. There were no Auto Unions entered and after the Mercedes of von Brauchitsch and Caracciola had retired, the similar car driven by Fagioli won at record speed with Dreyfus's P3 second half a lap behind and Brivio third another 400 yards in arrears. Etancelin (Maserati) was fourth, Chiron was fifth and Nuvolari retired.

Brivio had the satisfaction of winning the 5½ hour Targa Florio race in Sicily at record speed in a 2.9-litre P3 from his team mate Chiron. This was a week after Monaco, and another week later Varzi had his first victory for Auto Union at Tunis, where the P3s did not shine.

For very fast circuits like Tripoli and Avus the Scuderia Ferrari had produced the big *Bimotore* cars, which could have either a 2.9 or 3.2 litre engine both in front of, and behind, the driver in a lengthened Monoposto chassis, but they were prone to tyre bursting, and although outpacing their P3 progenitors in a straight line, they yet could not beat the German cars. Dreyfus drove the ex-Moll streamlined P3 at

Avus but, though third in his heat, he finished last in the final, and although he was the best P3 performer at Tripoli in a 3.2-litre Monoposto he could do no better than finish sixth behind two Mercedes, an Auto Union and the *Bimotore* cars of Nuvolari and Chiron.

That the latest P3 was still not yet a complete back number was shown in the Eifelrennen on the Nürburgring where Chiron on a 3.2-litre car finished third and beat all the German cars except Caracciola's winning Mercedes and runner-up Rosemeyer's Auto Union, earning the praise of his German rivals.

More power was desperately needed by the P3s, and this was forthcoming on June 23rd, 1935, where we have it on the authority of the official Alfa Romeo historian, Luigi Fusi, that the P3s entered for Nuvolari and Chiron to drive in the French GP at Montlhéry were fitted with 3,822 cc (78 x 100 mm) engines developing 330 bhp. Certain papers at this time reported that the cars were fitted with 3.5-litre engines, but since the publication of Signor Fusi's book *Le Vetture Alfa Romeo dal 1910*, the writer has become very doubtful if a 3.5-litre version of

The greatest victory — Tazio Nuvolari winning the 1935 German GP at the Nürburgring with the help of a 3.8-litre engine

After the war Shuttleworth's car was converted in England into a road equipped two seater after the style of Pintacuda's 1935 Mille Miglia winning car. Here it is photographed in the USA, where it belongs to Henry Wessells. (Simon Moore)

the engine ever existed, to the extent that in the results at the end of this Profile he has substituted 3.8 for 3.5 litres with reference to the capacities of race-winning P3s hitherto thought to have had 3.5-litre engines. Although some private owners raced cars with 3.2-litre blocks in 1935, there is no evidence that 3.8-litre Monopostos were ever passed on to private-owners, these bigger engines presumably being retained by Ferrari to go into the P3's replacement, the 8C-35, and 2.9 engines substituted in P3s before sale.

Thus, driving the most powerful-ever version of the P3, Nuvolari led on the first lap of the French Grand Prix and actually drew away from the German cars, led by Caracciola, whilst Chiron lay third. Alas, Chiron's car only lasted 8 laps before the transmission gave out, and then Nuvolari retired with similar trouble after 14 laps of the 40 lap race, when he had a 9 seconds lead over Caracciola. Both Alfas had been much faster than their rivals through the chicanes, and Caracciola said that he did not see

Monoposto, now the front line Scuderia Ferrari car, with the current chassis improvements of ifs and reversed rear quarter-elliptic springs and he was aided by a damp track and a burst tyre on Manfred von Brauchitsch's Mercedes on the last lap. He was also hindered by the breakdown of the refuelling pump in his pit, costing him an abnormally long refuelling stop of 2 min 14 secs compared with the 47 secs taken by his main rival von Brauchitsch. Nuvolari won the race by 1 min 44 secs from Stuck's Auto Union and Caracciola's Mercedes, and set the seal of everlasting fame on the name of Nuvolari and the P3 Monoposto Alfa Romeo. Oddly enough, the fact that Nuvolari's car had a 3.8-litre engine did not become common knowledge for many years.

In the Coppa Acerbo at Pescara there were no Mercedes and Nuvolari in his 3.8-litre Monoposto held second place to Varzi's winning Auto Union until retiring after ten laps. Brivio in his P3 finished third to the Auto Unions of Varzi and Berndt Rosemeyer. In the

A P3 with a spare wheel — Brivio winning the 1935 Targa Florio held a week after Monaco. (Alfa Romeo)

how Nuvolari could take such risks going through the chicanes and still hope to last the race. Nuvolari put up a record lap before he retired which was never beaten in subsequent laps. Only a week later Chiron scored the first win for the big-engined P3s in the Lorraine GP at Nancy, where Wimille's Type 59 Bugatti came second in front of Comotti's 3.8 litre P3. On the same day at Penya Rhin, Nuvolari and Brivio were third and fourth to two Mercedes.

Nuvolari did not drive in the Belgian GP at Spa, where Chiron and Dreyfus were entrusted to uphold the honours, and they finished third and fourth to the Mercedes of Caracciola and Fagioli. The extremely hot weather caused Chiron to collapse after the race, whilst Dreyfus had to hand his car over to Marinoni, the test driver, for the last few laps.

The P3's greatest hour was also one of the greatest hours in the history of motor racing, when Nuvolari won the 1935 German GP on the Nürburgring on July 28th against apparently impossible odds. His car was a 3.8-litre

Swiss GP at Bremgarten in the wet, Nuvolari finished fifth behind two Mercedes and two Auto Unions.

The replacement for the P3 appeared in the Italian GP at Monza in September for Nuvolari to drive. This was the all-independently sprung 8C-35, fitted with the familiar 3.8-litre P3 engine, but later destined to house the 12 cylinder unit for which it was designed. Although Nuvolari led at one time, and put up the record lap, he retired his car with a broken piston. Taking over Dreyfus's 3.8-litre Monoposto, he then finished second behind Stuck's Auto Union, though a broken valve caused the Monoposto to finish the race running on seven cylinders.

The season ended with Nuvolari in the 8C-35 and Chiron on a 3.8-litre Monoposto coming second and third to Rosemeyer's Auto Union in the Czechoslovakian GP at Brno.

As will be seen from the table that follows, several minor races held later in the season went to the P3s in 1935 where there was no opposition from the Mercedes and Auto

The Bimotore had a lengthened P3 chassis with either a 2.9- or a 3.2-litre engine fore and aft of the driver. This 5.8-litre example is seen at Brooklands in 1935 being driven by Austin Dobson, complete with the compulsory Brooklands silencing equipment.
(National Motor Museum)

The Multi-Union was a very special converted P3 driven by Chris Staniland which is seen here in its 1938 guise obviously modelled on Mercedes lines

Frank Ashby at Brooklands in August, 1939, in the car he converted with a special cast iron block and non-standard inlet and exhaust systems, the latter incorporating twin exhaust pipes.
(Louis Klemantaski)

Unions, the 1935 P3 generally being superior to its Maserati and Bugatti rivals.

One classic win in 1935 that has not been mentioned is the peculiar case of a P3 winning the Mille Miglia race for sports cars back in April. This was a special car prepared by the Scuderia Ferrari which had been converted into a narrow two-seater, complete with lights, mudguards and even a tiny hood. The latest reversed quarter-elliptic rear suspension was featured and the driver was Carlo Pintacuda who had the Marquis Della Stufa as his passenger. They won easily by 42 minutes from Mario Tadini's 2.6-litre 'Monza' Alfa Romeo.

The Rest of the Story

Luigi Fusi tells us in his book that six Monoposto Alfa Romeos were made in 1932, with enough spares to make up another three cars. In 1934 seven cars were built, with spares for another four, and in 1935 modifications were made to six of the 1934 cars to bring them to 1935 specification.

One modification not already mentioned which took place in the 1934/5 period was the strengthening of the gearbox, necessitating a reduction to three forward speeds instead of four. Fortunately the engine gave good torque at low revs; in fact when the Hon. Brian Lewis won the 1934 Mannin Moar race in a 2.6-litre Monoposto, third gear started slipping out after the first few laps and he used only second and top thereafter 'coasting round the corners in top gear like an American car' to use his own words.

The writer is indebted to Ken Stewart of Johannesburg and P3 owner John Clemetsen for supplying the following list of P3 chassis numbers together with their owners, where known, in 1972. Car Nos are given only where positively known. The writer's notes on each car help to carry the story on up to the present day when the Monoposto Alfa Romeo, with its handsome appearance and unmistakable deep exhaust note is looked upon as being one of the classic Grand Prix designs of all time.

Frank Ashby's car at the Dunlop Jubilee meeting at Brooklands in 1939, showing the narrow bodywork he fitted and the Dubonnet ifs with Ashby's own Lockheed brake conversion. (Louis Klemantaski)

Louis Tomei in Frank Griswold's ex-Count Villapadierna car in which Tomei finished 12th at Indianapolis in 1939. (Indianapolis Motor Speedway)

SPECIFICATIONS

ENGINE

Cylinders 8, in line, in two blocks of 4.

Cooling System Centrifugal pump. Capacity 2.3 gallons.

Bore 65 mm (1932/3), 68 mm (1934/5), 71 mm and 78 mm (1935).

Stroke 100 mm.

Capacity 2,654 cc (1932/3), 2,905 cc (1934/5), 3,165 cc and 3,822 cc (1935).

Bearings Plain throughout — white metal, crankshaft running in 10 main bearings.

Lubrication Dry sump, tank at rear, capacity 4.4 Imp gallons (20 litres).

Valve gear Twin ohc with central drive, two valves per cylinder in fixed head at 104 degrees.

Compression ratio 6.5 to 1 (1932/3), 7.0 to 1 (1934), 7.1 to 1 and 8.0 to 1 (1935).

Carburettors Two Memini or Weber.

Fuel pump Air pump driven off nearside camshaft.

Superchargers Two Alfa Romeo Roots-type, visible through apertures in bonnet sides on early cars. Boost approx 10 lbs.

Ignition One Marelli magneto, 18 mm plugs, one per cylinder.

Max power 215 bhp at 5,600 rpm (1932/3), 255 bhp at 5,400 rpm (1934) 265 bhp at 5,400 rpm and 330 bhp at 5,400 rpm (1935).

TRANSMISSION

Clutch Dry, multiple disc, steel and alloy plates.

Gearbox As fitted to 8C 2300 sports cars, 4 forward speeds on 1932/3 cars, altered by 1935 to 3 forward speeds and reverse by cutting out the old bottom gear and slightly lowering the old second gear, other ratios remaining the same.

Gear ratios Top 3.52 (3.3 optional)
Third 4.56
Second 6.54
First 11.8

Final drive Twin propeller shafts in torque tubes to separate bevels for each rear wheel, ratios 11/36, but first stage changeable final drive ratio housed between gearbox and differential.

CHASSIS AND BODY

5 ins deep side members, with tubular cross-members between extremities of dumb irons front and rear, plus two more between differential and back axle. Braced at front by 4-point mounted engine. Single-seater body, frame width of 26 ins 1932/3, widened outside frame width 1934/5. Colour — dark or cherry red, silver frame, black wheels in 1932/3; cherry red body and frame with black or silver wheels 1934/5.

SUSPENSION

Front Semi-elliptic springs with single friction dampers, or, in 1935, Dubonnet independent.

Rear Semi-elliptic springs outrigged from frame with double friction dampers, 1932/4. In 1935 reversed quarter-elliptic springs with double arm hydraulic dampers.

STEERING

Central, worm and sector. Wood-rimmed alloy-spoked steering wheel.

BRAKES

Rod operated as on 8C 2300 sports cars, 15¾″ dia drums 1932/4, Ariston hydraulic in 1935 with Dubonnet ifs, handbrake mechanical on the rear wheels only.

WHEELS

Wire, Rudge hubs, 6.00 x 19 tyres all round 1932/4, with rears only 6.50 x 18 in 1935.

FUEL TANK

In tail of car, capacity 30.8 Imp galls (140 litres).

DIMENSIONS

Wheelbase 8 ft 8 ins (Semi-elliptics), 8 ft 9¼ ins (Rear quarter-elliptics).

Track Front: 4 ft 7 ins (1932/4), 4 ft 8 ins (1935)
rear: 4 ft 5 ins
height to driver's head: 4 ft 8 ins.

Dry Weight 13 cwt 90 lbs (700 Kg) in 1932/3
14 cwt 22 lbs (720 Kg) in 1934
14 cwt 33 lbs (725 Kg) in 1935

Maximum Speed 140–170 mph

RACE WINS IN CHRONOLOGICAL ORDER

(2.6-litre in 1932/3, 2.9-litre in 1934 and onwards, except where known and otherwise stated)

1932
Italian GP (Nuvolari); French GP (Nuvolari); German GP (Caracciola); Coppa Ciano (Nuvolari); Coppa Acerbo (Nuvolari); Coppa Principe di Piemonte (Nuvolari); Monza GP (Caracciola).

1933
Coppa Acerbo (Fagioli); Comminges GP (Fagioli); Marseilles GP (Chiron); Italian GP (Fagioli); Spanish GP (Chiron).

1934
Monaco GP (Moll); Bordino GP (Varzi); Tripoli GP (Varzi); Targa Florio (Varzi); Casablanca GP (Chiron) 2.6 litre; Avus GP (Moll) 3.2 litre; Montreux GP (Trossi); Penya Rhin GP (Varzi); Mannin Moar (Hon. B E Lewis) 2.6 litre; French GP (Chiron); GP de la Marne (Chiron); Vichy GP (Trossi); Coppa Ciano (Varzi); Nice GP (Varzi); Comminges GP (Comotti); Circuit of Biella (Trossi).

1935
Pau GP (Nuvolari); Mille Miglia (Pintacuda); Targa Florio (Brivio); Lorraine GP (Chiron) 3.8 litre; German GP (Nuvolari) 3.8 litre; Circuit of Bergamo (Nuvolari); GP of Picardy (Sommer); GP de France (Sommer); Circuit of Biella (Nuvolari) 3.2 litre; GP de la Marne (Dreyfus) 3.8 litre; Circuit of Turin (Nuvolari) 3.8 litre; Dieppe GP (Dreyfus) 3.8 litre; Comminges GP (Sommer) 3.2 litre; Coppa Ciano (Nuvolari) 3.8 litre; Circuit of Lucca (Tadini); Donington GP (R O Shuttleworth).

P3 CHASSIS Nos WITH 1972 OWNERS WHERE KNOWN

Chassis No 5001. Car No 35.
Owner: Ernesto Dillon Buenos Aires Argentina
No details of this car are known.

Chassis No 5002. Car No 36.
Owner: Hon. Patrick Lindsay London England
Despite its early chassis number, this car has all the later modifications, including Dubonnet ifs. It went to Australia pre-war after its Ferrari days, owners including Snow, Saywell, Murray, Walmsley and Jarvis. Acquiring it engine-less in the late 'sixties, Patrick Lindsay has fitted it with the rear engine out of the ex-Austin Dobson 5.8-litre *Bimotore*, once driven by Chiron, but it has yet to show its true form in historic racing in England.

Chassis No 5003. Multi-Union
Owner: Hon. Patrick Lindsay London England
Chris Staniland raced this car in 1936 after acquiring it from Sommer, then it was extensively modified into the Multi-Union. The engine had special pistons and rods, modified manifolding and ports and maximum revs were 6,500 rpm. A special 4-speed gearbox was designed and made, Tecnauto ifs was fitted, and the rear axle was suspended by coil springs and located by a Panhard rod. GP Mercedes-like bodywork was fitted. In 1938 the car took the Class D 10 kilometre record at 139.6 mph won a 100 mile *Formule Libre* race at Phoenix Park, and in 1939 it lapped Brooklands at 142.30 mph running on only seven cylinders. The Fry cousins and G F Yates owned the car after the war, and it is now being developed for historic car racing by Patrick Lindsay.

Chassis No 5004.
Whereabouts unknown
This may have been the car in which Moll met his death at Pescara in 1934, or the special streamlined car he drove at Avus. The latter car is rumoured still to be in existence in France.

Chassis No 5005
Owner: Alfa Romeo Milano Italy
This car, in original 1932 form with narrow bodywork, is exhibited in the Alfa Romeo Museum and looked after by Luigi Fusi.

Chassis No 5006
Owner: Neil Corner Durham England
Georges Raph raced this car on the Continent. It has the 2.9-litre engine with Weber carburettors, a 3-speed gearbox and semi-elliptics all round. After the war it was raced by A. Powys-Lybbe, who won the 1953 Frank O'Boyle Trophy at The Curragh in Eire, remarking on how the car liked the long straights. John Vessey drove it to second place to a 2.9 Maserati in the 1955 VSCC Seaman Trophy race at Silverstone, and in the 1966 Coupe de l'Age d'Or race on the fast Rouen-Les Essarts circuit W H (Bill) Summers built up an enormous lead before retiring with overheating. Summers and Neil Corner had minor successes with the car, but 1971 was its best season when Corner handed it over to Peter Waller who raced it extensively, cured the overheating, and came third in the Seaman Trophy at Oulton Park to a W125 Mercedes and the 2-litre ERA R11B. Waller remarks that 5006 is quite a large motor car to handle in comparison with an ERA, even if the P3s were referred to as the 'little Monopostos' when they first appeared.

Chassis No 50001
Owner: John Willock Connecticut USA
The extra '0' in the chassis number evidently denotes new cars made in 1934, as distinct from earlier cars brought up to date. 50001 has quarter-elliptics at the rear and was bought from Ferrari by the English driver Luis Fontes in 1936, but it was not raced, its engine seeing service in a boat, and it was imported into the USA by George Weaver in 1955. The car is now in good shape, whilst keeping its originality.

Chassis No 50002 Car No 42
Owner: Dave Uihlein Wisconsin USA
The Spaniard, Count de Villapadierna, raced this car in 3.2-litre form, painted yellow, in 1936. In 1939 it was acquired by the American Frank Griswold, who entered Louis Tomei to drive it in the 1939 Indianapolis '500'. It qualified at 118.425 mph and finished 12th in the race. It still bore the same racing number, 58, at the 1940 Indianapolis race, but there was a new fairing for the radiator and a streamlined headrest on the tail. Al Miller qualified the 2.9-litre car at 120.228 mph, but it retired on lap 41. In October, Griswold drove the car to win the New York World's Fair road race at Flushing, Long Island. As the Don Lee Spl the car retired in the 1946 and 1947 Indianapolis races driven by Hal Cole and Ken Fowler respectively, highest qualifying speed being 123.423 mph in 1947. Today the car is unrestored without engine or transmission, and it has a non-original rear axle.

Chassis No 50003 Car No 43
Owner: Robert Cooper Wiltshire England
CEC (Charlie) Martin bought this car in 1936 and is said to have had the quarter-elliptics conversion done on it. He came 2nd to a V8 Maserati at Pau, 2nd to a T59 Bugatti at Deauville and 2nd to the Seaman/Ruesch 8C-35 Alfa Romeo in the Donington GP, Martin using a 3.2-litre block on this occasion. At some time the car was fitted with its present Ashby block (see No 50006 below) but with standard manifolding. It went to Australia post-war where it was raced by Lex Davison and Steve Ames, and then was extensively restored by Laurence G. Rofe, who sold it to D H Jarvis. Sir Ralph Millais, Patrick Wicks, Gary Woodhead and Robert Cooper all drove the car in English historic races in the late 'sixties and early 'seventies, when it had yet to find its old form.

Chassis No 50004 Car No 44
Owner: John Clemetsen Illinois USA
Another ex-Sommer car which stayed in the USA after being bought by Joel Thorne who drove it to 5th place in the 1937 Vanderbilt Cup. Other owners were Lee, Weaver, De Belle and Holman, the car at one time having a Ford and then a Jaguar engine. Clemetsen is a great Alfa enthusiast who has managed to find the correct engine for the car from an 8C 2900B sports car, whilst the missing gearbox has been replaced by that from an 8C 2300 Alfa Romeo.

Chassis No 50005 Car No 45
Owner: William Clark Christchurch New Zealand
This is the famous 1935 German GP winning car, now a 2.9 litre. It still has Dubonnet ifs and was raced in England pre-war by Austin Dobson and Kenneth Evans, the latter also finishing 9th in the 1937 German GP. Post-war Roy Salvadori, then a novice, bought it, and had some successes, though he drove it with tyre pressures too high and shock absorbers badly adjusted, so at anywhere near maximum speed it would weave all over the road and terrify him. It then went to New Zealand where Ron Roycroft drove it to win the 1953 Lady Wigram Trophy race, and for some years it has been in the excellent hands of Bill Clark.

Chassis No 50006 Car No 46
Owner: Leon Witte Lyttleton New Zealand
Another Dubonnet-suspended car, the engine was extensively modified pre-war by English owner Frank Ashby, who designed a cast-iron block for it, and altered the inlet manifolding so that one blower fed the central four cylinders and the other the four outside ones, instead of one blower to each separate block as standard. This particular car was given twin outside exhausts. Ken Hutchison used the car for sprints post-war, and the next owner, J H Goodhew, sold the car to Australasia, where John McMillan successfully raced it. It is now painstakingly restored by Leon Witte. Capacity is 2992 cc.

Chassis No 50007
Owner: Henry Wessells Pa. USA
Englishman Richard Shuttleworth is thought to have been the original owner of this car, which had quarter-elliptic rear springs and Memini carburettors. Shuttleworth won the Donington GP with the car in 1935, also the short Mountain Championship race at Brooklands and made ftd at Brighton Speed Trials. He did not race the car again after a crash in the South African GP in January, 1936. Post-war the car was made into a two-seater for road use in England for Geoffrey Barnard, and then it went to Henry Wessells, the American Alfa enthusiast. The body is now being altered into a replica of Pintacuda's 1935 Mille Miglia winning 2-seater P3.

Chassis No 50008
It is not known if this car still exists.

Chassis No 50009 Car No 49
Owner: Ernesto Dillon Buenos Aires Argentina
Nothing is known of this car, except that it is being preserved by Ernesto Dillon.

Jack Bartlett at Brooklands, Whitsun 1939, driving a P3 fitted with de Ram front shock absorbers.
(Louis Klemantaski)

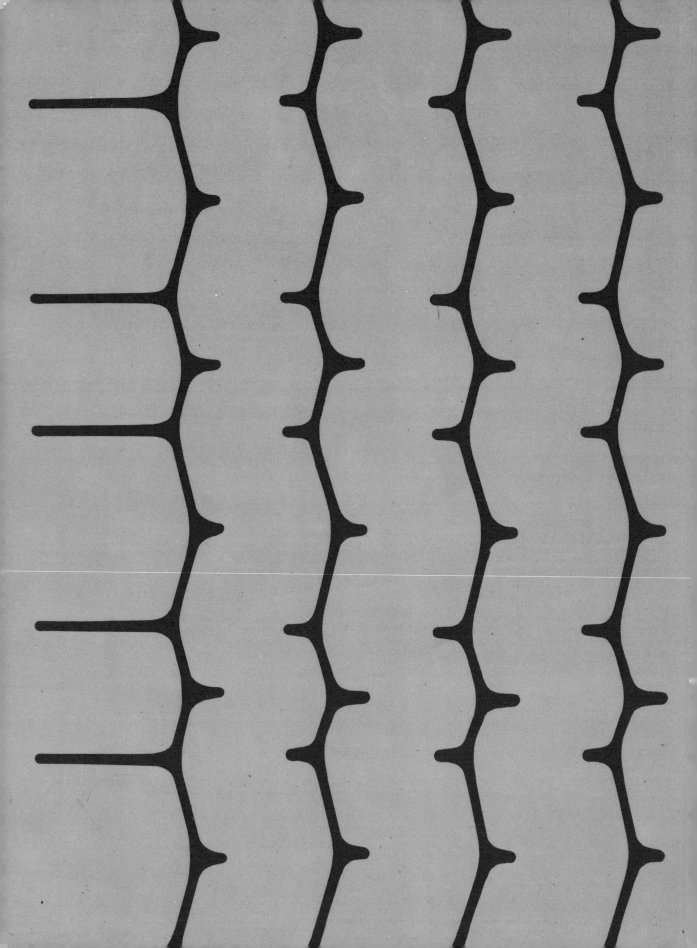